Changing University Teaching

Open and Distance Learning Series

Series Editor: Fred Lockwood

OPEN AND DISTANCE LEARNING SERIES

Changing University Teaching

Reflections on Creating Educational Technologies

TERRY EVANS AND DARYL NATION

**KOGAN
PAGE**

Dedication

This book is dedicated to our friend and colleague, the late Dr Alistair Morgan. His commitment to research, critique and improving students' learning continues to inspire our work.

First published 2000

Apart from any fair dealing for the purposes of research or private study, or criticism or review, as permitted under the Copyright, Designs and Patents Act 1988, this publication may only be reproduced, stored or transmitted, in any form or by any means, with the prior permission in writing of the publishers, or in the case of reprographic reproduction in accordance with the terms and licences issued by the CLA. Enquiries concerning reproduction outside these terms should be sent to the publishers at the undermentioned addresses:

Kogan Page Limited
120 Pentonville Road
London
N1 9JN
UK

Stylus Publishing Inc.
22883 Quicksilver Drive
Sterling
VA 20166-2012
USA

© Terry Evans and Daryl Nation, 2000

The right of Terry Evans and Daryl Nation to be identified as the authors of this work has been asserted by them in accordance with the Copyright, Designs and Patents Act 1988.

British Library Cataloguing in Publication Data

A CIP record for this book is available from the British Library.

ISBN 0 7494 3064 8

Typeset by Kogan Page Limited
Printed and bound by Creative Print and Design (Wales)

Contents

Contributors

Terry Evans and Daryl Nation

Terry Evans and Daryl Nation have worked together on many research projects in open and distance education. Their most recent joint project is funded by a three-year Large Grant from the Australian Research Council. They have authored many internationally published articles and chapters. Books they have jointly edited include: *Critical Reflections on Distance Education* (1989), *Reforming Open and Distance Education* (1993), and *Opening Education: Policies and practices from open and distance education* (1996). Terry Evans has also written *Understanding Learners in Open and Distance Education* (1994). Professor Evans is Director of Research in the Faculty of Education at Deakin University, Australia. Associate Professor Nation is Deputy Director of the Centre for Learning and Teaching Support at Monash University, Australia.

Shirley Alexander

Shirley Alexander is Director of the Institute for Interactive Multimedia, and an Associate Professor at the University of Technology, Sydney. She has over 10 years' experience in the design, development, evaluation and implementation of interactive multimedia in education. Shirley Alexander is also a member of the National Committee for University Teaching and Staff Development (CUTSD) where she is Director of Technology Projects. Her research interests include: the application of current learning theories to the design of interactive multimedia learning materials; the evaluation of interactive multimedia materials; and the use of communication and information technologies in the globalization and internationalization of education. She has recently completed a Department of Employment, Education, Training and Youth Award (DEETYA). This was a commissioned study to evaluate the contribution of information technologies to university learning. This study reviewed 104 IT-based projects in Australia and will shortly be published as a report with videotaped case studies.

Terry Anderson

Terry Anderson is a Professor in the Faculty of Extension, and the Director of Academic Technologies for Learning (ATL) at the University of Alberta. The ATL programmes are designed to assist faculty members in developing quality, accessible and cost effective learning and teaching technologies within the context of a major research university. Dr Anderson's current research interests lie in evaluating WWW learning environments to support both distance and class room delivery, and in the use of electronic communication tools to support 'virtual' professional development activities. He is the co-author of a 1998 text entitled *Networked Learning: Pedagogy of the Internet* published by Cheneliere/McGraw-Hill. Previous to his appointment at the University of Alberta, he was the Director of Contact North, a distance education delivery network in Northern Ontario, Canada.

Chere Campbell-Gibson

Dr Chere Campbell-Gibson is an Associate Professor and Chair of the graduate programmes in Continuing and Vocational Education at the University of Wisconsin-Madison. She teaches courses relating to the adult independent learner, instructional design for distance learning and issues in distance education. Print as well as audio-, video- and computer-conferencing are routinely incorporated as part of these learning experiences. An unsuccessful distance learner in her early life, Dr Campbell-Gibson's research foci now includes the learner at a distance, with a specific emphasis on persistence and learner support as well as cognition and group dynamics in computer-mediated conferencing.

Robert Fox

Robert Fox is a Senior Lecturer in the Centre for Educational Advancement, at Curtin University, Perth, Western Australia. He has more than 20 years' experience in further and higher education in open, distance and flexible learning, and in the area of professional development in Australia, Hong Kong and Europe. He has presented at major national and international conferences, and contributed articles to journals and chapters in books. He has also undertaken consultancies in the field. Robert Fox's research interests concern technological change and practice in higher education.

Randy Garrison

Dr Randy Garrison is a Professor and Dean of the Faculty of Extension at the University of Alberta. He previously held the position of Associate Dean (Research and Development), in the Faculty of Continuing Education, at the University of Calgary. He began his academic career at the University of Calgary as Director of Distance Education. There he developed a successful Master's degree specializing in workplace learning that was accessible to working professionals through computer mediated communication. Dr Garrison's areas of research are related to the teaching and learning transaction in the context of adult, distance, and higher education. He has published extensively in these areas.

Samuel Haihuie

Samuel Haihuie is the Co-ordinator of Social Sciences courses with the Institute of Distance and Continuing Education at the University of Papua New Guinea. He is involved in encouraging the development and implementation of new approaches to distance education within the University's regional centres.

Neil Hanley

Neil Hanley is a Senior Lecturer in Mass Communications and Writing at Monash University and Co-ordinator of Communications Studies at Monash's Sunway campus in Kuala Lumpur. He has worked with colleagues to develop a range of degrees involving Communications/Mass Communications. His research interests include: online learning, virtual classrooms, flexible learning, and the impact of communications technologies on the South-East Asia region.

David Harris

David Harris is especially interested in the ways in which social theory can be developed in and across media studies, cultural studies and distance education. These themes have been pursued in three books – *Openness and Closure in Distance Education* (1987), *From Class Struggle to the Politics of Pleasure* (1992) and *A Society of Signs?* (1996). He is currently working on a more deliberately pedagogical piece *Teaching Yourself Social Theory*.

Allan Herrmann

Allan Herrmann is a Senior Lecturer in the Centre for Educational Advancement, at Curtin University, Perth, Western Australia. He has been involved in higher education for more than 20 years, in open, distance and flexible learning, and in the area of professional development in Australia. He has presented at major national and international conferences, contributed articles to journals and chapters in books, acted as editorial reviewer, and has also undertaken consultancies in the field. Allan Herrmann's current interests are in staff development in open and distance learning, and research and development in alternative learning experiences for distance and open learners.

Olugbemiro Jegede

Olugbemiro Jegede is Professor and foundation Director in the Centre for Research in Distance and Adult Learning at the Open University of Hong Kong. Prior to this, he was foundation Head of the Research and Evaluation Unit of the Distance Education Centre at the University of Southern Queensland, Australia, and Professor and foundation Dean in the Faculty of Education at the University of Abuja, Nigeria, West Africa. His areas of interest include: applied cognitive science,

science education, computer-mediated communications, instructional design, foundational issues in open and distance and adult education research and cultural studies in education. Professor Jegede has over 150 publications including: six books, several chapter contributions to books, refereed journal articles, and refereed conference proceedings. He is Editor in Chief of the *Electronic Journal of Instructional Science and Technology,* and is also a member of the Editorial Board of several international journals that include: *Distance Education: An International Journal,* the *Journal of Computers in Science and Mathematics Teaching,* the *Journal of Research in Science Teaching,* and the *Journal of the Science Teachers Association of Nigeria.* He has twice served as guest editor of the FID News Bulletin of the International Federation for Information Documentation, for the two issues on 'Africa in the Cyberspace' (1995), and 'Distance Education' (1999). Furthermore, he is the co-ordinator of the Special Interest Group on cultural studies in science and technology education of the International Organization for Science and Technology Education (IOSTE).

Stewart Marshall

Stewart Marshall is Professor and foundation Executive Dean of the Faculty of Informatics and Communication at Central Queensland University in Australia. Previously, he was the foundation Professor of Communication Studies in the Faculty of Arts at Monash University. He has worked in the higher education sector for 26 years in England, Papua New Guinea, Australia and Southern Africa. His experience in distance education goes back to 1974 when he tutored for the Open University in the UK. More recently, during 1996 to 1998, he was seconded from Monash to the newly formed Institute of Distance Education in Swaziland, Southern Africa where he was the Foundation Co-ordinator of Academic Studies. His research interests are in the roles of communication and distance education in developing countries.

Ron Oliver

Ron Oliver is an Associate Professor in the School of Computer, Information and Mathematical Sciences at Edith Cowan University. He has been involved in the field of computer education, multimedia and instructional technologies for more than 20 years. He currently lectures in multimedia programmes at ECU and supervises postgraduate students. He has had extensive experience in both the design and development of multimedia and computer-based learning materials including developments for CD ROM, networked and WWW-based learning and telecommunications supported learning environments. He has a comprehensive research background in multimedia and educational computing, and currently leads a major research team at ECU in this field. He has published in excess of 150 papers and monographs, and has contributions in most of the major international journals in this field. He is currently the Editor of the *Australian Journal of Educational Technology,* Associate Editor of the *Journal of Interactive Learning Research* and the *Australian Educational Computing.* Furthermore, he is on the editorial boards of *Distance Education* and the *British Journal of Educational Technology.* He is also a successful and effective teacher, having won several awards for excellence in teaching, including the inaugural Australian Award for University Teaching for the use of Multimedia in Teaching, in 1997.

Otto Peters

Otto Peters is Professor Emeritus at the Fern Universität in Hagen, Germany. He was born in 1926 in Berlin. He studied Education, Psychology and Philosophy at the Humboldt Universität and the Free University in Berlin, and earned his doctorate at the University of Tübingen. Since 1965, he has been active in describing and interpreting distance education for purely academic reasons. First at the Educational Centre in Berlin, then at the German Institute for Distance Education Research and later as Professor of Didactics in Berlin. In 1975 he became the Founding Rector of the Fern Universität in Hagen, and served in this function for nearly 10 years. After this he devoted his time exclusively to distance education research. Since 1991, he has been dealing mainly with pedagogical and didactic problems of distance education. He has visited many distance-teaching institutions on all continents and written many articles and books. His latest book is *Learning and Teaching in Distance Education* (1998). Dr Peters has received three honorary doctor's degrees (The Open University, United Kingdom, Deakin University, Australia and Empire State College, New York). For eight years he served as vice-president of the International Council for Distance Education.

Michelle Selinger

Michelle Selinger is a Senior Lecturer in ICT Education and Director of the Centre for New Technologies Research in Education, at the Institute of Education at the University of Warwick, UK. In 1994, she introduced computer-conferencing into the Open University's distance taught course for graduate teacher training. She joined Warwick University in January 1997 to develop a course to train secondary IT teachers and to enhance the computer education provision in the Institute. She recently led the evaluation for one of the UK government's funded projects on the use of the Internet in schools. She has published widely in the field of telematics in education, and is currently implementing a number of telematics pilot projects across Warwick University.

Richard Wah

Since 1991, Richard Wah has been the Head of Distance Education and Deputy Director of University Extension at the University of the South Pacific in Suva, Fiji. He is a Fijian. Besides being interested in the systems administration of distance education, Richard Wah is also interested on what he calls the 'secondary effects' of distance education. He has written a number of papers on these issues, and is currently completing a PhD thesis, which looks at them in more detail. His other interests include technology education and postcolonial theory.

Sandra Wills

Sandra Wills is Director of the Centre for Educational Development and Interactive Resources (CEDIR), and an Associate Professor at the University of Wollongong. She has over 25 years' international experience in the fields of education and technology from primary through to university education, including teacher training, curriculum development and software development. In addition to her academic career, she has held a number of positions and consultancies in marketing and industry development, as well as being active on the international lecture circuit. She was elected a Fellow of the Australian Computer Society in 1991. Awards include Australian Computer Society Lecturer of the Year, and the International Federation for Information Processing (IFIP) Silver Core Award for services to computers in education through her role as Chair of several national and international conferences, boards and committees. She is currently on the boards of Impart Corporation, Propagate and two DEETYA-seeded ventures fostering Australia's multimedia industry.

Series editor's foreword

Those of us involved in teaching and training are aware that our world is changing – and changing quickly. The increasing use of Communication and Information Technologies (C&IT) is resulting in a radical change to learning communities, as traditional forms of teaching and learning, are converted to online and virtual environments. It has been argued that the change we are now experiencing is as fundamental as the one that was marked by the production of the first printed texts. Furthermore, it has been suggested that the availability of C&IT offers a unique opportunity to change the nature of our teaching, and to reconsider the process of learning. For many C&IT is seen as a panacea that has the power to solve the problems of reduced educational funding, increase student numbers and provide increased access and equality. For others it creates more problems than it solves and illustrates the gulf between the infrastructures of developed and developing countries, as well as the cultural preferences for modes of study. As such, it is timely, that this book offers us a chance to pause, to reflect, and consider the implications for teaching and learning in higher education in the next millennium.

In this edited collection of chapters, *Changing University Teaching: Reflections on creating educational technologies*, Terry Evans and Daryl Nation have assembled a rich resource that reveals an awareness of the broad economic, social, cultural and political contexts in which we are working, and the new technologies that are being employed. The collection of chapters are drawn from managers and practitioners, teachers and researchers, course developers and policy makers. What they all have in common is a commitment to providing a high quality learning experience, and an awareness that we need to reflect on the process of teaching and learning, if we are to understand changing perceptions and attitudes – and exploit the new technologies. They all have in common the ability to reflect on their own practice and to point to implications for the future of these new educational technologies. This is achieved by a combination of case studies and illustrations, as well as consideration of previous research and new findings, models, frameworks and personal testimony.

The combination of open and distance learning methodologies and C&IT represents a powerful mix. This, coupled with an acceptance that pedagogy is more important than technology, means that we can be involved in changing university teaching. Terry Evans and Daryl Nation and , together with their contributors, have given us this opportunity. It is up to us to grasp it.

Fred Lockwood
January 2000

Introduction

Terry Evans and Daryl Nation

Changing University Teaching is a collection of reflections on policy and practice by contributors from a variety of different backgrounds and contexts. Their particular tasks were to deal with the matter of changing university teaching in ways that both related directly to their work, and also allowed them to air their views and ideas on this important topic. Therefore, within this brief the contributors have sufficient scope to ensure that a diversity of ideas, opinions and experiences are provided on changing university teaching.

It seems inescapable that every educational organization has to address the imperative for change. Arguably, this is especially the case in universities where the teaching and research nexus is a fundamental and distinguishing feature. Research is particularly concerned with discovering new knowledge and constructing new ideas. Not only are universities expected to engage in research, but also to train people to do research, in particular through doctoral programmes. This places universities in a position where their new knowledge contributes substantially to change and innovation in most, if not all, the areas of human and scientific endeavour outside of the university. The curriculum of their courses may also change as a result, so in this sense, universities have a fundamental connection with change in society.

However, as organizations, they have often been characterized as conservative and reluctant to change. The circumstances of the past decade or more have been that new computer and communications technologies, together with a mélange of social, demographic and economic changes, have torn at the fabric of the traditional university. Nowadays, universities are seen to be stitching together various activities and approaches in order to cope with, or maybe to be seen to be coping with, the challenges of the times.

Despite their often awesome and intimidating physical structures, universities are not walled machines geared to the political, social and economic engines. They are typically large collections of people who are structurally related to one another through employment and pedagogical relationships. Arguably, more than any other organizations, universities rely on the intellectual activities and capacities of their members in order to be what they are: universities; that is, teaching and research organizations. Thus, changing university teaching is fundamentally about people changing. In this sense, *Changing University Teaching* can be understood as a collection of reflections by university people about their own engagements with change. However, the contributors also paint a wide canvas in that they typically draw broader implications, and some have even been involved as agents of change on an institutional, or even national or international scale. We illustrate this point ourselves in our own careers and, indeed, as editors of this collection, this book also becomes an artefact of it.

It is worth dwelling on our own experiences briefly to explain the point above, and to explain the purpose of *Changing University Teaching*. For about 25 years we have earned our living teaching in universities and colleges in Australia. We have also travelled to several other countries in the course of our work, and spent time at various universities and other educational institutions. If we merged our career histories it would show that our own teaching has been an important element, but not the majority, of our work. Also, at various stages, we have worked to help others to develop their teaching, thus further increasing the profile of teaching in our careers. However, throughout this period, we have always had a strong involvement in research and scholarship. We have also worked increasingly in management and administration, such that now we both have managerial work as our principal activity.

We use the terms 'work', 'teaching' and 'earn our living' above quite deliberately. Although we did work together for about four years in the same sociology department, most of our work together has been as 'colleagues at a distance'. Occasionally this has been directly related to our respective teaching activities – we have written and recorded course materials for each other's courses – but usually it has been about our research and writing. *Changing University Teaching* is the latest of four books we have co-edited together, and this chapter is the most recent of many items we have co-authored. Our work together has also involved research projects, and this collection is partly inspired by our most recently completed Australian Research Council Large Grant project, which investigated the development of new educational technologies in universities. In the final chapter we draw explicitly on the ideas and findings from this project.

We would like to make it clear that, although teaching has been an important part of our lives, this teaching has only partly been about the sort of teaching one does in front of a class, with 'chalk in hand'. Indeed, our sort of teaching has been far more to do with writing and developing course materials, communicating by phone and computer, and recording audio and video programmes. Over the past few years we have witnessed many teachers setting aside the chalk for the computer; using it to prepare materials for print, CD ROM, the Internet or the World Wide Web. Whereas, at one time we saw ourselves as undertaking a marginal activity by teaching at a distance, nowadays we bear witness to many university teachers undertaking some of these tasks as part of their mainstream activities. Teaching at a distance has 'come in from the cold' and is insinuating itself into university life.

It is arguable that, as university teaching is seen to embrace such tasks, the nature of the work of university teachers *and* other staff also changes. Teaching becomes less of a solitary activity with a teacher in a classroom, and becomes more of a team or collaborative activity between academics and specialist general staff together forming an integral part of the teaching system. So, although teaching is the core business of the contemporary university, it does not mean that to keep universities teaching, one only needs teachers and 'teaching' to be undertaken. It is perhaps ironic, that as the focus has become more on mass education in the world's universities, often the proportion of teachers has declined and the number of support staff has increased. There are other changes as well, of course, some of which we shall address in the final chapter. However, it is important to make it clear that *Changing University Teaching* is not narrowly concerned with improving teaching through the use of new educational technologies. Rather, it is broadly concerned with the way that the university enterprise is changing and the ways in which university staff structures, roles and responsibilities are also changing.

This book is *for* people who think about and construct new ways of teaching in universities. It is also *by* people who have thought about and constructed new ways of teaching in universities. Our experience in forms of open and distance education, and our concern for some, if not all, the values and practices of flexible learning and lifelong learning, have encouraged us to invite the contributors to this book to share their experiences. Later in this chapter we shall return to this theme in terms of the notion of the reflective practitioner.

Why change?

Experienced staff within universities are becoming increasingly frustrated, annoyed and angry about the demands for change that are being put upon them. In many nations, if not all, class sizes have risen inexorably over the past decade, making the act of teaching more onerous, even if the work remained the same. However, in addition, there have been extra demands for research and publication, accountability and monitoring – often as part of quality improvement and quality assurance approaches – and for providing new 'economically relevant' curricula. The resistance to these changes is understandable. Few people wish to take on more work, and many staff entered careers in university teaching in the 1970s, seeing before them a pleasant and comfortable career that was both intellectually stimulating and challenging. For the most part their work was paid for by the state and 'market forces' did no more than affect the price of food and housing. By the 1990s, two decades of interrelated political and economic changes had produced a diminution in state provision and funding for many social, educational, health and welfare services. Yet demographic changes played their parts to increases the demand for these services.

Together, these forces have produced an intense pressure on the workers in each of these services, education included. The solutions were to be found, so it was believed, in the new political and economic dogmas of the times.

The rise of market capitalism and 'new right' ideologies, fostered these new dogmas in a climate where the bastion of state capitalism, the Soviet Union, was crumbling. There was a congruent fall in the broadly socialist ideologies that undermined the potential for different solutions to arise from those of the 'new right'. Indeed, as Giddens's (1994, 1998) work attests, forms of opposition have fragmented considerably during this period. New political parties and groups have mushroomed around particular community interests or ideological (including religious) positions, using the new communications and mass media to prosecute their positions, and have occasionally formed expedient, if fragile, alliances to achieve particular political ends. The trade unions have not been immune to the new circumstances and have found that their power and influence has generally been substantially eroded as a result, and occasionally, they have been under vigorous attack and sustained serious damage, from 'new right' governments.

It is in this immediate historical context that the changes to higher education can be viewed. It is arguable that the 'new right' ideologies are past their peak and that there is a slight resurgence of authority (through government and elsewhere) for those parties and groups who value social, environmental and community ends over economic ones. However, this resurgence cannot be seen as a return to the socialist dogmas and solutions of the immediate past, but it represents a 'new realist' position edging aside the (hard-line) 'new right'. The 'new realists' tend to be formed from the 'old left' parties and carry with them some of their previous socialist agendas, reframed within a valuing of economic (and often environmental) sustainability. The tensions can be enormous, of course. The simplistic solutions to poverty and inequity, for example, are ones that involve (the redistribution of) wealth. But, in the new conditions, the creation of wealth is respected as a key economic *and* social driver, so that redistributing wealth from those who 'create' it to those in need is seen as weakening a main driver of these new societies. The *trick* for the 'new realist' governments is to try to strike a balance, or at least to have sufficient voters believe that they have done so.

For education, these political shifts are crucial to understanding and reconstructing its future. Education itself is dominated by the school sector. Government policies and interests still remain predominantly focused on schools. Ironically, schools contain very few voters, whereas, with the reductions in the age of majority in most democratic nations over the past two decades, universities contain substantial numbers. Of course, it is parents who vote partly on their children's schooling interests, although one would still expect that with the increase in university participation, including mature age students, the voting power of the university sector had increased considerably. In this sense, one might expect that the political power of the university sector would have increased.

It is arguable, however, that the political power of the universities has been weakened in two significant respects. One is that the previous political power of the few 'establishment' universities was not sustained through votes, but through their influence over, and patronage from, the university-educated élite in government and the senior echelons of the bureaucracy. With the rise of mass higher education, universities in most developed nations now represent a much larger group of institutions. Some are new institutions created in the 1960s and 1970s; but some have their roots in working class institutes and colleges of the first half of the 20th century, rather than in the ruling class, ivy-clad, sandstone, Gothic colleges of the first half of the 19th century. The competing interests and tensions that prevail can be quite profound. In Australia, for example, we have seen the wealthiest seven or eight universities jostling to corral themselves into an élite group for the purposes of increasing their wealth and influence. The diversity in the contemporary university sector and the tensions it leads to, appear to have contributed to weakening its influence, at least until a new form of collective set of interests emerges.

The second respect in which it may be argued that universities have been weakened is in relation to the (trade) unions. Whereas, the unions were often quite strong in some of the working class colleges, this was not necessarily the case in the universities. The advent of mass higher education could have been the foundation for stronger union organizations, but it seems that the university attitude to unionism prevailed which contributed to a relative decline in the unions. In addition, the 'new right' governments were ideologically opposed to trade unions and in this context the university staff unions were drawn, simultaneous with their own need to recreate themselves a new mass-higher education union(s), into the bigger battles over the rights and status of unions more generally.

It is arguable, that if the universities and their unions had been more collectively focused, they may have been better able to prevent some of the privations that have been experienced over the past decade or more. Although, there is no doubt that both the conditions and circumstances of universities were going to change anyway, and the unions would need to adapt in order to deal with them. What is undeniable is that the conditions and circumstances of universities have changed markedly and that they are not going to return to those of previous decades.

However, we would argue that the aforementioned weakening of universities' political power and authority over the past few years is countered by an increase in the size and substance of their position in society. Universities are no longer (just) the 'finishing schools' for the élite, or the training grounds for the intelligentsia. In the developed world, and increasingly so in the developing world, they now provide a 'tertiary layer' of education for the mass of young people and for a rapidly expanding proportion of mid-career people. Tertiary education is commonly justified in terms of the economic benefits to a nation. We submit that more fundamentally, university education in particular is providing intellectual texture to the fabric of contemporary democracies. The debates, policies and practices engendered by governments, oppositions, minor parties, interest groups and non-government agencies are fuelled substantially by the knowledge, values and skills acquired through university education. They are also received, understood, interpreted and criticized by a populace that draws on university experiences, either directly, or vicariously through the mass media and personal networks.

Changing University Teaching takes, as its starting point, the position that the social, economic and political conditions in which university teaching occurs have changed irrevocably and significantly over the past two decades. In addition, the technological conditions within which universities operate have also changed in very significant ways. In particular, the technologies that have been developed which exploit telecommunications and computing, have altered the ways in which the world communicates, does business, and entertains and informs itself. This new electronic and digital world has been partly developed and encouraged by universities – for example, universities were at the forefront of the Internet and electronic mail development and use. However, universities are also surrounded by technological conditions not of their making, and to which they have to conform or adjust – the World Wide Web (the 'Web'). These new conditions represent threats and opportunities for universities. For example, the Web provides enhanced opportunities for universities to extend their marketing and teaching, but likewise it also threatens the universities' privileged positions as the 'gate-keepers' of knowledge and its dissemination.

Perspectives on *Changing University Teaching*

We have invited contributors to *Changing University Teaching* who adopt different positions in relation to the changes that surround universities today. One view is that 'paradigmatic' changes of a technological kind are occurring in universities in the 'developed world' and that the challenge is to help/develop staff so that then everyone is able to participate effectively. Another view is that universities are operating in anachronistic and outdated ways and, if they do not 'open' themselves to new ways of teaching and organizing their activities, they will be required to close or be taken over by other universities that have made the change. A further view is that the 'developing world' universities are facing a formidable crisis where the costs of keeping up with 'developed world' universities are so huge that they cannot be contemplated by their governments. Yet without a viable university system, a developing nation is unable to sustain its own economic, social and cultural development. There is also the view that new political circumstances surrounding universities are leading to a range of 'quality control' surveillance measures that, amongst other things, risk the adoption of restrictive instructional approaches.

Although there are other views and positions made by the contributors to *Changing University Teaching,* there is, however, a common thread that concerns the circumstances and processes of change in universities. The significance of the development of the new educational technologies is part of this thread, as is the inevitability of change and the need for universities, as organizations of people, to adapt critically to the ideas and consequences of change. In essence, our intention is that this book makes a contribution to the capacity for people involved with, and concerned for, universities to reflect critically on changing university teaching.

Changing University Teaching is the fourth collection we have assembled and edited. Each has been produced on the basis that the process of constructing the book itself should reflect a process of critical reflection. For both of the first two collections we used a process in which drafts were circulated to all contributors and then these were discussed in contributors' seminars . The drafts were usually received on disc and were printed and distributed by mail to the group. Communications were by fax and e-mail, with a shift towards the latter for the second collection. For the third collection, which was assembled for rather different reasons, and without a deliberate critical reflection process built in, chapters were received by electronic attachment or disc, and communications were by e-mail. For *Changing University Teaching* we decided to use electronic mail to mediate a critical reflection process between sub-groups of contributors, and e-mail attachment for the receipt and transmission of drafts and notes for contributors. It seemed that the changes to the use of electronic communications were sufficiently well spread that we should be able to use them for the book.

It was certainly the case that we were able to use electronic mail with all the contributors who were spread around the globe. Electronically attached drafts to e-mail messages generally worked well, although we did experience some difficulties of formatting losses etc. Technically what we had established did prove feasible, however, practically the process fell down mainly because some contributors were unable to meet the deadlines for draft documents to be submitted to sub-groups. In our first two books, which were assembled approximately eleven and eight years ago, we had the (much tougher?) requirement of attendance at a contributors' seminar, and yet we achieved a high level of participation. Indeed, for the second, which had a range of international contributors, a contributor from each chapter attended one or both of the contributors' seminars held in Melbourne and Cambridge (to coincide with other conferences).

The transition to 'virtual' contributors' seminars seemed an obvious step to make and one that would make it easier for contributors to participate. No doubt we could have had difficulties holding contributors' seminars anyway, but there is the question of whether our contributors would have seen a 'real' seminar as in some way more significant, and worked towards completing their drafts in time and attending? On reflection, it seems that some of our contributors were 'victims' of the sorts of changes to university life outlined above. That is, the intensification of their work and the increasingly disparate demands make drafting a chapter for a collaborative scholarly activity, such as a virtual contributors' seminar, a relatively lower priority than might have been the case a few years before. Initially, we wondered if it was because we had a more senior group of contributors than previously. However, for each of the collections we try to have a good mixture of people with different levels of experience. For some, being a contributor has been their first experience of writing for a book. For others, they have written many chapters, and often books as well. *Changing University Teaching* has a similar mix as before, with a deliberately international range that specifically includes contributors from developing nations. Likewise, in terms of seniority, *Changing University Teaching* has a range from people in relatively junior positions through to those with senior management responsibilities, as did the previous collections.

It is unwise to draw conclusions about the changing nature of university teaching on the basis of our experience in producing this book, however, we can state that the shift from the real to the virtual, while technically feasible, has proved to be practically flawed. This reinforces a point we have made in other contexts about educational technology. That is, 'technology' is not a synonym for 'tool', although many people do use it that way, including some of our contributors to *Changing University Teaching*. Rather, technology is the art, craft and science of how to use or deploy a particular tool for particular purposes. Therefore, educational technology is the broad understanding of how to use a particular tool for educational purposes. One may see that e-mail is a tool that can be adapted knowledgeably and skilfully in the hands of an educator to construct, for the educator, an extension to their repertoire of educational technology. In the instance we gave above, we chose to adapt this same tool for the purposes of encouraging collective critical reflection in writing for our book. However, as it was broadly unsuccessful, our repertoire of 'critical reflection' technology has still been extended, to the extent that we are more knowledgeable of using (or not using) e-mail as a tool for our purposes.

The e-mail experience for *Changing University Teaching* is also illustrative of other aspects of the processes and circumstances of changing university teaching. As several of the contributors argue, there is a pressing need for a critical engagement with the new computer and communications tools, and the technologies which inform them, if these are to be constructed into worthwhile educational technologies. However, there is often an implicit assumption that the adoption of such new tools is necessary and worthwhile. It is important to realize that such new tools do come, quite literally, at a heavy price and, therefore, in these times of increasing financial pressures on universities, they can only be adopted if commensurate income increases and/or cost savings can be made. In this respect, 'investment in new technology' is not just an investment in the equipment, but also in the necessary staff development. For the 'investment' to produce a return, a university must be able to know where this return is to be found. Hence, to expand an institution's repertoire of educational technology must include understanding how the benefits can, at the least, be cost neutral. Failure to do so will damage the viability of the university and maybe threaten its existence.

As was noted previously, *Changing University Teaching* is partly about recognizing the significance on the social, economic and political changes that have occurred over the past decade or more, and the concomitant imperatives for change in universities that result. The advent of new computer and communications media means of teaching, learning and managing universities is not a panacea. Indeed, we would argue, that to deploy uncritically these approaches could mean ruin for those universities already operating close to their financial limits, or a bruising encounter for those with strong reserves. However, to remain static in the changed and changing higher education circumstances is also to court disaster or, at least, gradual decay. We suggest that what is required is a critical engagement with the new computer and communications media and, on that basis, to construct sustainable educational technologies for the universities of the future.

We hope that *Changing University Teaching* assists in this task. The chapters have been ordered in a way that seems best for most readers, but some may well find it useful to take their own pathway through the book. In the final chapter we return to the themes we have raised here and take them further within a more theoretical and critical framework. We place these matters on a broader canvas on which the contemporary issues of globalization and lifelong learning are mapped. However, all these matters are partial and fluid. At any point in time, and depending on the reader's perspective, they may or may not mean a great deal!

Chapter 1

The transformation of the university into an institution of independent learning

Otto Peters

In most countries, universities are faced by unprecedented challenges:

- rapid technological and societal changes;
- changes to educational paradigms;
- volatile increases in the significance of distance education and open learning;
- the beginnings of digitization of learning and teaching;
- chronic financial difficulties;
- the quest for quality and steadily increasing industrialization, commercialization and globalization.

In German universities, teaching continues to have a lower priority than research. Lectures, classes, seminars and periods of practical training are usually overcrowded. There is a general lack of support services for students. The jungle of courses, degrees and examination requirements means that students, above all in their first few semesters, are faced with almost insurmountable problems. The consequences of the above are excessive periods before students can actually sit their degree examinations, frequent changes of courses and high dropout levels (Ehrhard, 1997). These are all factors that quite naturally have a considerable negative effect on studying. Mittelstrass diagnosed (1994: 7) that the 'non-updated university' finds itself 'in a serious structural crisis' and for other important reasons as well, for example in its 'inability to reform itself'. Furthermore, Glotz warns us in his critique that it is now '5 minutes to 12' in the university. He gave his polemic the harsh title 'Rotten to the core?' (Glotz, 1996: 1).

The situation described here is aggravated even further because university graduates in the emerging information society will have to have qualifications and competencies that are different, or differently weighted, from those in the industrial society with which we are familiar (Heid, 1995; Klauder, 1992; Conference Board of Canada, 1991). 'Today's production methods, communication technologies, perceptions of problems and problem solving strategies can be overdue and obsolete tomorrow' (Bardmann and Franzpötter, 1990: 424). In the future, there will be greater emphasis placed on the ability to:

- learn and to continue to learn independently and autonomously;
- communicate to others deliberately and on a differentiated basis;
- collaborate with others in a group;
- show social sensitivities;
- accept social responsibility;
- be ready and willing to be flexible, and to have experience of flexibility.

According to Höhler (1989), in the future the search will be for creative, self-confident, convivial, committed, communicative and socially competent employees.

In view of the many difficulties referred to here and the deficiencies that I have also indicated, and in addition to that the digitization processes that are already altering learning and teaching, perhaps now is the time to consider whether universities in their present form, with their classical self-image and their traditional methods of teaching and learning, are actually in a position to impart these ideals. If this question is answered negatively, we are faced with the task of imagining how much the university must change to cope with new tasks and challenges. What is particularly interesting here is how learning and teaching at university in the first decades of the next century will have to be conceived and organized. Our attention is therefore mainly directed to the required pedagogical processes.

Will this type of change have to be a radical change? University teachers who, in spite of all obvious difficulties, continue to insist that the university is 'basically healthy', will answer 'No' here, and will tend to speak in favour of a gradual adaptation of traditional forms of studying to new situations. Futurologists, who have analysed the problems we are likely to face in the information society, are of a different opinion. They believe that the university will have to take on a completely different shape in the next century. For example, Drucker has even prophesied, in view of the digital revolution, that '30 years from now big university campuses will be relics' (Drucker and Holden, 1997: 1745). Casper, the President of Stanford University, takes it even further and asks, with some presentiment, if in fact we will have in future a 'world without universities' (Casper, 1996: 1). The present situation of the university is therefore serious. There is no doubt that it is an acute 'modernization crisis'. In fact, the only treatment available is a bold wave of modernization such as never before in the 'history of the academic instruction universities' (Paulsen, 1965: 1).

In order to make clear the structural change that has become necessary, I will show how learning and teaching at the university could develop, if it were to recognize the challenges of the present and the future, accept them and react to them in a committed manner. A primary concern here is to define and to describe the functions of digital information and communications technology (Bacsish, 1998), because they quite obviously, not only suggest a structural change, but in part further it or even force its implementation. Furthermore, this type of sketch can supply criteria in which, experiences from abroad in this field can be analysed, and evaluated under the aspect of what they can contribute to planning the future of university teaching. In addition, we should examine whether they inspire and encourage us to take new paths.

New changes

The educational and policy aims and requirements for universities suggest the following changes for university teaching:

- Teaching must not continue to be peripheral, carried on by the incidental interests and activities of some members of the middle hierarchy (Woll, 1988). It must be made into an essential task of the university that is taken up in the first place by all university teachers.
- Because academic education and further education stretch over complete adult life, universities must admit and look after adults of all ages.
- Universities must be 'open universities' in several respects.
- Because of the extension of university activities, the number of students will increase considerably. It may not be possible to look after them with the traditional systems and approaches of teaching on-campus. For this reason, a different – and cheaper – teaching and learning system is necessary, which will enable many more people to obtain undergraduate and postgraduate education.
- In order to achieve the highest degree of flexibility and to be able to cope more easily with the different life situations of students, most of whom will be older and in employment, learning must be separated from prescribed locations and times.
- One of the aims of universities should be preparing students for the information society. They must be able to work in virtual companies, organizations, working groups and project teams in the emerging 'virtual economy' (Baron and Hanisch, 1997). This presupposes a considerable degree of 'media competence' (Lange and Hillebrandt, 1996).
- The curriculum must no longer be made uniform and fixed for long periods by means of degree course regulations, but be variable and adaptable to current needs, for example, in professional life. It must be related not only to individual learning requirements, but also take account of the challenges and demands of practitioners and anticipate future trends.
- It must be possible to impart to students not only cognitive, but also methodical and social action skills (Arnold, 1995). 'Autonomy and integration' (Gottwald and Sprinkart, 1998: 55) must be the preferred aims of academic education.

- In general, there must be a 'conversion from a teaching to a learning culture' (Arnold, 1995: 300).

To sum up, learning and teaching at university must be oriented to a much greater extent than before to the principles of continuing education and lifelong learning (Dohmen, 1996). It must have an egalitarian character and be open as well as student-, practice- and future-oriented. It will have to proceed with flexible teaching and learning programmes which impart not only cognitive, but also communicative and collaborative, competence. Along with classical expository teaching and receptive learning, autonomous and self-controlled learning should be cultivated (Candy, 1988; Dohmen, 1997; Friedrich and Mandl, 1997; Lehner, 1991; Paul, 1990; Weingartz, 1991). This should be oriented towards the research process. In addition to this, students must also be prepared to prove themselves in the 'virtual world'.

A new structure for university education

It is obvious that the above changes cannot be met readily within the framework of traditional degree courses and classical forms of teaching, such as lectures, seminars, classes and teaching in laboratory courses. Hence, new approaches will have to be sought based on the following three basic forms of academic learning:

Guided self-study and self-study

These are forms of learning that developed from correspondence education and distance education over the past 150 years. They provide the following specific learning activities:

- working independently through self-instructing study programmes;
- working independently through learning packages in different media (eg tapes and videos);
- reading recommended and additional specialist literature independently;
- discussions (face-to-face or through communications media) with tutors and counsellors that students initiate themselves, the course of which is also determined by the students;
- optional participation in tutorials in small groups in study centres;
- self-initiated and organized discussions with fellow students locally (self-help groups);
- solving training and examination problems relatively frequently for the purposes of controlling the student's own progress;
- corresponding with the persons responsible for correcting written assignments;
- voluntary or obligatory participation in seminars.

Studying in a digital learning environment

The following learning activities are currently in use:

- using networks for the purposes of scientific information, communications and collaboration;
- targeted individual searching and selecting, evaluating and contextually applying information: transforming information into knowledge;
- making individual efforts to obtain advice, help and additional motivation through professional tutors, course counsellors, moderators and experts on a subject;
- establishing individual social contacts on several levels;
- joint learning in small and larger working groups, whereby problems that students themselves have thought up are solved, for example in project work, or new areas of knowledge are opened up for all those taking part, such as knowledge building communities (Scardamalia and Bereiter, 1992);
- individual interactive work with CD ROMs, a medium that offers a great number of new educational opportunities (Hoyer, 1998);
- individual participation in virtual courses of lectures, virtual seminars, virtual teaching in a college class, virtual examinations;
- studying 'at virtual universities'.

Taking part in teaching events at traditional universities

However, this does not imply delivering traditional lectures, but above all provides the opportunity for direct communications, in particular taking part in live scientific discourses and in 'social intercourse' (Casper, 1996: 26). The following experiences from this field might be absorbed and developed further through:

- advisory talks with a teacher (at set times);
- counselling by tutors and study guidance, either singly or in groups;
- discussions in colloquia, seminars, classes and practical courses with the aim of active participation in the scientific process;
- free academic discourse;
- preparation for and participation in oral examinations;
- informal talks with other students and with other members of the university.

Two possibilities for combining the learning activities of these three basic forms of academic learning spring to mind here, an additive and an integrative method. In the additive version, the university enables students to develop those learning activities that are possible on the basis of their private circumstances and employment obligations. The priority here is to reach those persons as well as those who have been prevented from studying because of the traditional organization of university education (egalitarian function). But what is of special interest is the integrative version, because here students can put together their own personal 'menu' of learning activities from these three areas (pedagogical function) depending on their own interests, preferences and practical requirements. When doing this students construct particularly effective combinations in which, among other things, the deficiencies of one form of studying can be compensated by the strengths of other forms. The interplay of learning activities from distance teaching, studying in a digital learning environment and traditional face-to-face teaching, which is planned from a pedagogical viewpoint, could generate such optimum study conditions that cannot be found in any one of the participating forms of study by itself. We would then refer to a mixed-mode university.

On the whole, the university of the future will have to be the result of a fundamental process of transformation in which it changes into a university that mainly enables self-studying in all its forms oriented towards the research process. The university supports this and in the end makes it into the foundation of its curricula and teaching. A strict orientation towards research must in fact be presupposed for all three forms of learning. *Learner empowerment* (Baron and Hanisch, 1997: 1) is the decisive overriding and comprehensive educational category.

The educational structure that results from the combination and integration of the three basic forms of academic learning constitutes a fundamental change in university study. We should not recoil from this, in particular as two of the planned basic forms have already proved their value.

Focus points: Self-learning, tele-learning and 'social intercourse'

If we attempt to imagine a university that is able to do justice to the new demands referred to above, and in which studying takes place in the framework of the three basic forms of academic learning outlined here, we can be quite certain that we are not imagining a traditional university. In the information and communications society it is possible to take part anywhere in teaching programmes, even when travelling. Professors and lecturers can teach, advise, discuss and examine from any location. Even more: 'The global network of students will follow on the global network of scientists' (Casper, 1996: 21). This means that the localization of university teaching is practically obsolete. 'Distance is dead!' announced Nicholas Negroponte, Director of the Media Lab at the Massachusetts Institute of Technology and a distinguished thinker on the digital future (Negroponte, 1997).

In fact, space and time have become negligible parameters for data transmission. Even now they cross over borders. It is inevitable that our university of the future must see this, accept it and use it for its own purposes. It must draw consequences from the overwhelming progress made by information and communications technologies that are changing not only our ways of learning, but of working as well, and in fact, are even changing our lives. If it does this, then the traditional model of university teaching will lose its previous binding character, and university teaching that is independent of prescribed space, time and personnel will be on the march. Those who have always interpreted all learning and teaching as an exchange of information, will understand the changes that have taken place and will tend to accept them. The final reservations will be broken down when people see that adult higher education and the required system of lifelong learning cannot be made possible in any other way.

Self-learning

The ubiquity of learning that is achieved thanks to distance teaching and studying in a digital environment is the decisive innovation that we have to get to grips with regarding the development and consolidation of self-study. Distance teaching detaches and isolates the students as the focal point of learning is displaced from the university to the home, the workplace or a learning centre. Simply from pure necessity, and not even because of the educational ideal of autonomous learning, they are required to determine the location, time, sequence and arrangements for learning themselves, and even to test the success of their own learning. Distance students are even forced to take over a number of important functions which, in traditional systems, the universities or their teachers carry out. They learn under their own aegis, and thus have more responsibility, achieve a greater level of self-determination and in this way achieve a certain degree of learning autonomy.

Tele-learning

The extent of independence that is conceded can become even greater with self-learning in the ubiquitous digital learning environment. Where the autonomy of students studying self-instructing courses in distance education is related above to the external, organizational sequence of studying, it can also be supplemented here through *curricular* autonomy. It is true that the digital learning environment is also used to take students by the hand and guide them in small steps through heavily structured programmes, and to subject them to a rigorously heteronomous learning system, but at the same time, it offers autonomous learning new and greater chances that were previously not thought possible. Here students can in fact set their own targets and select the content, apply their own methods of learning, establish criteria for evaluating and in fact use them to evaluate what they have achieved. This new form of studying, therefore, enables an incomparably high degree of autonomy and self-guidance, which is manifested in many forms. For example, the Empire State College of the state of New York has carried out pioneering work in this field through the development of 'contract learning' (Peters, 1997).

We are dealing here with a change of educational paradigms, namely from a dominant theory of expository teaching and reception learning to a dominant system of learning by working out. New dimensions of self-learning are being developed for students through the integration of the distance teaching tradition with the extraordinarily diverse educational opportunities of the digital learning environment that are being opened.

'Social intercourse'

The third basic form of study in the university of the future will finally and neces-sarily provide traditional university teaching as well. This will not be presentational, but interactive and communicative forms of teaching, because, from the aspect of educational philosophy, the latter forms involve personal encounters. Here, free ac-ademic discourses in seminars, classes or laboratories will be aimed for and devel-oped further.

Where persons come together to learn or discuss, when they are 'eyeball to eye-ball' (Wedemeyer, 1971: 135) with their discussion partners, a specific atmosphere is created in each case characterized by their individuality, which can only be repro-duced in part, and indeed in a reduced form, by mediated means. A dialogue in the same room has more elements than in an abstracting tele-conference, even where this is not merely the asynchronous exchange of messages, but is in fact a video-conference. Those taking part experience an original and authentic dialogue. They absorb non-verbal signals and unconscious behavioural reactions. With all their senses they become part of a multi-dimensional encounter that can be ana-lysed with psychological and sociological criteria; for example, 'Geselligkeit' (social intercourse), which Goethe in 1791 understood to be 'active intercourse with edu-cated persons' (Goethe, 1994: 406).

Casper (1996) asks whether the university will survive in the age of communica-tions technology, and comes to the conclusion that this will only happen if it is 'irre-placeable'. He concludes that such irreplaceability is probably 'only the link between research and teaching in laboratories and seminars' under the precondition that universities create 'those working conditions for professors and students' (which) 'presuppose and really enable social intercourse' (Casper, 1996: 25).

Is it old-fashioned to presume that this direct participation in university dis-course has an 'educational' effect in the true meaning of the term? The contribution that it can provide, for example, to the development and differentiation of the stu-dent's own scientific thought processes through conscious or unconscious imita-tion, through following the teacher's train of thoughts or arguments or through spontaneous contradiction, is incomparable. What it can achieve during the acquisi-tion of (spoken) academic language, and above all in the process of academic social-ization and the development of habits of mind, is of great educational value. Bates says: 'There are many things that are valuable in education, as in life, which technol-ogy cannot do, and we need to recognize that' (1997a: 95). Klafki, the distinguished German educationalist, when asked by a journalist about the chances for learning in a virtual university replied succinctly, 'It is clear that a university will fail if it disre-gards direct communications between persons. We should not even try this out' (Seyfferth, 1998: 75).

These arguments should be used to respond to those technology enthusiasts who believe that, on the one hand, face-to-face teaching, as practised in traditional universities, can be replaced and, on the other, the lack of direct communication in distance teaching can be effectively and cheaply compensated for by means of e-mails and tele-conferencing. Without wishing to diminish the educational oppor-tunities that the digital learning environment can have in combination for 'learning together apart' (Kaye, 1992: 1) and for 'teaching face-to-face at a distance' (Keegan, 1995: 108), the self-deception that is found here must be pointed out. A technically imparted discourse is reduced and altered in important points in a virtual seminar (Fabro and Garrison, 1998; Hesse and Giovis, 1997; Kiesler, 1992). The protagonists of electronic communications assume that with the help of technical communications media, learning in distance education and learning in a digital learning environment, will emulate the learning forms that are obtained in traditional teaching (see the criticism by Beaudion, 1998: 98). According to them, its standing in the scientific community will increase (Garrison, 1993: 20). What a fatal error for university education!

Forms of traditional academic teaching, in particular if they are based on address and rejoinder and personal dealings, will be indispensable in the university of the future. In these forms, the autonomy of tele-students that is acquired in independent learning in distance teaching and in the digital learning environment can prove itself, be consolidated and develop further. We are dealing here with a constitutive component of learning in the university of the future.

Organizational preconditions

In order to provide these three basic forms of academic learning with opportunities for development, combination and integration, the university of the future must be reorganized, restructured and rebuilt. The following matters will need to be addressed in this regard.

Instead of having lots of lecture halls and organizing mass teaching events on the campus, the university of the future will have a communications system that enables links to networks (Internet, the Web), television and radio. It will have to maintain laboratories for developing audio, video and multimedia teaching and study programmes (including hypertext and hypermedia) at the state of the art. The university library will be converted to a great extent to online operations, once the catalogues have been digitalized and, for example, electronic journals, world literature and documents about current scientific developments have been made available. To achieve all this, a technical platform will have to be developed consisting of servers, author environments and tools for university administration and library access (Unger, 1997).

At the same time, the structure of the university's workforce will have to be altered by means of a previously unheard-of number of educational designers, graphic artists, media experts, Internet experts, project managers and the respective technicians. However, the structure of appropriate development institutions can only be justified financially with high numbers of students, such as those which, up until now, have generally been achieved by a few distance-teaching universities. Equipping traditional universities of average size with technology that is required for distance studying and for studying in digital learning environments only increases their costs in these times of chronic financial difficulty, instead of reducing them. The only reduction in costs with increasing student numbers at present is taking place in the distance teaching 'mega-universities' (Daniel, 1996).

The integration of the elements of the three main forms of learning and teaching provides the university, whose traditional ways of working have solidified and quite often become ritualized, with a flexibility and variability that it has never before experienced. In this way, it is now able to deal with the special private situation and occupational requirements of older students as well, and to take sufficient account of them. For this reason, it will no longer prescribe fixed and binding locations and times for learning and personnel for teaching. Studying may be started, interrupted and restarted at any time, and may be carried out either full time or part time, whereby students may also switch between the two forms. Where this is necessary and possible, the curricula can also be oriented more closely to students' private and vocational experience, as studying will become extremely individualized and student-centred, and mainly based on self-learning. Students may decide on one of the three basic forms of studying that have been referred to here, but at the same time evolve learning activities from the other two basic forms and combine them with one another in parallel and consecutively. It will even be possible to take up courses offered by several universities simultaneously, for example those of a 'real' university and those of a 'virtual' university.

As a counterweight to the great emphasis on self-learning and tele-learning, the university requires a professional student guidance system that is technically competent and very well organized. This system will no longer be on the periphery, but will be of central importance. Great emphasis will be placed on personal counselling from tutors, which will advance to become an important component of academic teaching.

Sceptics may ask whether this type of university of the future can in fact reduce the problems and deficiencies of present-day university education that were referred to at the outset. Of course, no one can see into the future, in particular as it may also be determined by factors that are unknown today. We can, however, see the following already:

- Due to the fact that the learning locations are being moved to students' homes, workplaces or local learning centres, there will be no more overcrowded lecture halls and seminars in the future.
- Other unacceptable aspects of mass universities today (long journeys to university, badly scheduled lectures, classes, etc) will no longer apply, because self-learning and group learning is becoming decentralized and individualized in real rooms, and in some cases takes place everywhere in virtual rooms.
- As a result of the upgrading of guidance and counselling as legitimate components of university teaching, students will be additionally motivated and better oriented with regard to their personal needs.
- As lifelong continuing education becomes more established, and students can no longer 'stockpile' what they have learnt, it will be possible simply to reduce the duration of basic degree courses, and this will reduce loads.
- Links to occupational and private practical situations are provided, or easy to establish, through the experience of (mostly older) students and of many tutors.

- Teaching will not be neglected at the costs of research, but will tend to be stressed as multimedia courses will be carefully planned and professionally developed. Also the educational skills of teachers at university will no longer consist of presenting content, but of enabling, facilitating and supporting research-related learning, preferably by 'discovering'.
- Autonomous learning in self-study develops and strengthens students' abilities to make autonomous and independent decisions for their own lives, and also to accept responsibility for these.
- The problem of studying for overlong periods disappears if, on the one hand, the basic degree course is reduced and, on the other hand, continuing academic education (lifelong and recurrent) is spread over a lifetime.
- Changing courses frequently will no longer be frowned on if studying has to be flexible and variable and is constantly adapted to meet new societal, technical, and employment market requirements.
- The increased interactivity in virtual and real rooms gives studying a structure in which students will be able to gain skills in acquiring knowledge and become used to working in teams. Those methodological and social skills that are already in demand in the workplace (communication, collaboration, understanding) can be developed and trained during and in the framework of higher education.
- The special skills required in the information society can be acquired more easily when studying takes place continuously in a largely digitized and networked information system, and not in the forms of classical academic teaching, which are, in fact, pre-industrial forms.
- The circle of students can be increased enormously, and this meets the demand of employers for university graduates. In many countries, for example, it is practically impossible to obtain a career without a bachelor's degree.

For many people, the new educational structure of academic studies justifies a new fundamental humanitarian aspect. The reason for this is that it enables those capable of academic studies to start, continue and conclude their studies at any time, where this is desirable for private or professional reasons. This can be done relatively independently of the residential location, the student's age, social background, social position or vocational and private obligations, or of any disadvantages the student has experienced in the past.

The transformation of the traditional university into an institution of self-study and distance teaching has, therefore, wide-ranging structural consequences. If the university wishes to prepare itself for the tasks facing it in the future, it is not sufficient for it to regard the new technologies merely as additional media units, and to misunderstand them as an extension and extrapolation of the previous familiar teaching operation. It must not use these technologies in the same way as it used the audio-visual media in the past. What the university of the future needs are fundamental new educational concepts. Self-learning, tele-learning and 'active intercourse with educated people' (Goethe, 1994: 405) are the most important. They form the basis of a culture of self-study that, by the way, should be aimed for generally.

Conclusions

The scenario shown here for learning in a university of the future points to an institution that looks completely different to a traditional university. It will be the result of delimiting and destructuring processes, such as those Kade has described (1989) for adult education, and Arnold (1996) described for the dual mode university. Also traditional universities are subject to processes of extension that are becoming even more intensive. Their traditional structures are becoming brittle. Gradually, a 'deprivation of power' (Kade, 1989: 801) is taking place in this once monopolistic institution of research and teaching.

This is certainly not a unique feature but a general process, which is at present changing our society as a whole. Giddens argues that we are dealing here mainly with the separation of time and space, the creation of embedding mechanisms and the reflexive acquisition of knowledge (1995: 72). He speaks of a space-time 'increase in distances' that is typical for today. Through the 'detachment from the constraints of local habits and practices... various possibilities for change' are opened up (Giddens, 1995: 32). At the same time, social systems are 'disembedded'. Social relationships are lifted out of local interaction contexts and restructured so that they overlap with the help of unlimited space-time margins. These findings, which are related to society as a whole, apply in a particularly concise manner to the university of the future that has been sketched here. This would then have to be interpreted not only as the result, but also as a component of the processes of change within society in the sense of its modernization.

In fact, the close connection between space and time in traditional teaching becomes obsolete here. There are now 'increases in distance' of any size between teachers and students. The acts of teaching and learning are removed ('disembedded') from the traditional context and dislocated. The decoupling in terms of time is expressed in the asynchronicity of most acts of teaching and learning and of academic discourse. In concrete terms: we are witnessing the change from traditional on-campus teaching to that of a university without walls; from a university that remains closed to many, to an open university; from an exclusive system of teaching and learning to an inclusive system. Here we can only mention the great importance that the reflexive acquisition of knowledge has for self-learning, self-studying and even more for the formation of the identity of students who are autonomous, self-regulating and who work individually.

As a consequence of the delimiting and destructuring processes, the university of the future will have to:

- extend its objectives;
- admit and counsel new groups;
- use new methods and media;
- evolve new functions for its teachers;
- organize studies as a whole in a completely new manner with regard to time and space.

Research will naturally continue to be the starting point, objective and means of teaching. However, even research is not exempt from the typical processes of de-limiting and destructuring, and is subject to them even now to a great extent. An important feature of the crisis facing universities is in fact the 'emigration of research to other areas' (Mittelstrass, 1994: 7).

Will the teaching and learning of the future adopt professional planning with well-thought-out strategies? Or will the more casual activities of individual, re-form-friendly university teachers encourage others and lead to this type of university almost by accident? These might be the teachers who are full of enthusiasm for technical progress, and who are at present experimenting with CD ROMs and tele-conferencing. It may be the teachers who, convinced of the necessity of lifelong learning, are committed to the concept of continuing education, or teachers who are inspired by new concepts of university education and experiment with forms of open learning and test single mode or dual mode distance teaching. These could be three starting points for the development of a university of the future that would have to be brought together, combined and integrated, with traditional teaching and learning patterns. Even though this development appears obvious, and in fact corresponds to previous efforts at reform, it is not really desirable, because internal and intra-institutional collaboration necessitate a strategic approach. In this context it is naturally helpful if educational policy planners attempt to work out the financial, le-gal, structural and institutional consequences of a possible university of the future.

The situation becomes more complicated if the obstacles and difficulties are in-cluded in the calculation. Will the majority of university teachers leave their cher-ished forms of teaching without complaint? Will they accept the deterioration of the traditional model of the scholar which might result in a transformation of the very nature of scientific knowledge and lead to closing our minds instead of opening them (Campion, 1996: 147)? Will educational policy necessities, such as opening universities, turning to new groups of students and supporting the concept of au-tonomous learning, not be bogged down by traditional structures? Do university teachers, in fact, possess the skills that are required in a university of the future? Will they be prepared to see the most important part of their activities in counselling self-learning students, and not in lectures? Will they be prepared to develop their re-search results in the form of hypertexts and complicated multimedia presentations in collaboration with experts? Will they be prepared to answer questions from their students via e-mail?

In this type of situation universities will have to reflect and proceed strategically. According to Bates it will be necessary for them to develop clear perceptions of the following:

- what learning and teaching in universities will look like in the information age;
- which new learning models are favoured or rejected;
- how this completely different system of teaching and learning can be financed;
- how those university teachers who are still sceptical and hesitant can be convinced to co-operate;
- what kind of technical platform must be in place;
- how university teachers will be prepared systematically for their new tasks, and

given continuing training subsequently;
- how important professional project management is;
- whether and how the organizational structure of the university will have to be adapted to the new requirements;
- whether the university of the future can perhaps only be created on the foundation of collaboration of many, or even all, universities in a country in the form of a consortium (Bates, 1997b: 7–19).

If these strategies can be successfully applied, the university of the future will be realized. What it will look like cannot be prophesied today. Hoyer, who as an engineer and expert for control engineering is averse to all educational speculation, has characterized this new university as follows: 'It will be more like a distance-teaching university than a traditional university' (Hoyer, 1997).

Chapter 2

Transforming and enhancing university teaching: stronger and weaker technological influences

Randy Garrison and Terry Anderson

Traditional universities are by their nature collegial, research focused and zealous defenders of their culture and traditions. As a result, they have been very resistant to change. This is particularly evident with regard to instructional practices that have long been hidden behind closed classroom doors. The lecture format with its historical roots in public reading of rare texts has evolved as the primary means of university teaching. Despite inherent resistance to change, budget reductions and increasing numbers of students have forced universities to become more efficient. A first and common response to these pressures is to increase class size and to continue, or even expand, the use of the lecture format. This is troublesome because lecture presentations to large numbers of students reduce opportunities for interaction and critical discourse. This in turn reduces opportunity for facilitation of higher-order cognitive abilities – the defining characteristic of a university education.

There is much discussion and speculation with regard to the emergence of powerful and inexpensive communications and information processing technologies to mitigate the move to larger lectures. Will the ubiquitous and varied forms of synchronous and asynchronous communications technology fundamentally change university teaching and move away from the dominance of the lecture? Will these new technologies force universities to rethink their approach to teaching and learning?

The premise of this chapter is that these new and emerging technologies will be disruptive to current approaches to university teaching. Along with the opportunities and demands from new market sectors, these technologies have the potential to precipitate a rethinking of what it means to teach and learn in higher education; however, the impact of these learning technologies will not be uniform nor immediate.

We argue that learning technologies will have both a stronger and a weaker influence on the quality of university teaching and learning outcomes. The weaker, and more immediate, influence is to enhance current teaching practices by providing increased access to information, improved presentation quality to lecture presentations and, perhaps, increasing opportunities for interaction. In this application, the technology is an 'add-on' and reinforces existing delivery methods and outcomes. While the rhetoric of universities is to support critical discourse and produce critical thinkers, the reality may be quite different. Too often, the emphasis is on disseminating, assimilating and reproducing information. The focus is on acquiring information, not thinking. The development of critical thinkers can be largely fortuitous.

The stronger influence of technology on teaching would fundamentally change our outcome expectations, and thereby, how we approach the teaching and learning transaction. In this regard, new markets such as continuing professional development are increasing the pressure on traditional universities to be more relevant and accessible. Here the focus is on the quality of learning outcomes (ie developing critical thinkers) and adopting approaches to teaching and learning that are congruent with such outcomes. If the goal of higher education is to translate theory to practice and produce critical and continuous learners, then opportunities for critical discourse and meaningful knowledge construction must be facilitated. Ironically, the stronger, transformational influence of technology is an opportunity to remain aligned with the traditional values and goals of the university – including the facilitation of critical reflection and discourse.

We begin by describing the nature of the teaching and learning transaction in higher education. Employing the concept of sustaining and disruptive technologies, a discussion of stronger and weaker technological influences on teaching and learning, is provided. Concurrently, examples from our experience within a faculty that functions as a 'change agent' will be used to illustrate these technological influences on university teaching and learning.

University teaching and learning

To understand the capacity for technology to change university teaching, it is useful to understand the current state of teaching in higher education. This will provide a baseline to assess the nature of desired change in university teaching associated with technology. More specifically, it should reveal the characteristics of teaching in higher education that are in need of change and the reasons for that change.

The complexity of the teaching and learning transaction does not lend itself to a clear consensus of what constitutes excellence in teaching. What we do know is that until relatively recently, effective teaching focused largely upon presentational teaching characteristics. Of course, this reflects the dominance of the lecture method in university courses. Congruent with a presentational focus, the consistent finding is that effective teaching places high importance on preparation, organization, clarity, and enthusiasm (Feldman, 1988; Sherman *et al*, 1987).

In the last two decades, however, increasing attention has been directed towards the quality of learning outcomes (Entwistle and Ramsden, 1983; Marton and Saljo, 1976). The central finding is that there are two fundamentally different ways in which university students approach their learning. They tend to use one or other of two levels of information processing: deep/meaningful or surface/reproducing. A deep approach is directed towards comprehending the significance of the content and its relationship to existing knowledge frameworks, while a surface approach represents an unreflective, rote learning strategy. As we shall see subsequently, there are important distinctions related to these approaches when considering the influence of technology on university teaching and learning outcomes. Only when we understand the nature of intended learning outcomes can we hope to design effective teaching–learning processes and use technologies appropriately to enhance these processes.

Effective teaching should be judged according to the quality of learning outcomes achieved. Teaching that relies heavily on presentation and reproduction of large amounts of information will, by necessity, encourage a surface approach to learning (Ramsden, 1992). Effective teaching for the purpose of deep and meaningful learning is more than presenting content clearly and enthusiastically. It emphasizes facilitation of understanding through critical reflection and discourse. Through collaboration, students are encouraged to take responsibility for the construction of meaning and confirmation of understanding. Facilitation of deep learning uses reflective and collaborative teaching strategies to externalize meaning, provide alternative explanations, diagnose misconceptions, and confirm meaning within a context that provides choice and respect.

In contrast to presentational teaching, facilitative teaching encourages students to take a deep approach to learning and the development of higher order abilities such as critical thinking and learning how to learn. A facilitative approach to teaching and learning is a collaborative approach and requires sustained two-way communication. A collaborative approach facilitates critical discourse and deep, meaningful learning outcomes. A facilitative and collaborative approach to teaching includes various forms of interaction amongst teacher, learners and content. All six possible combinations of interaction among these primary components of the educational transaction are relevant to a facilitative approach to teaching. As such, 'interaction between and among learners, teachers and content promises to increase opportunities for, and experience of, deep and meaningful learning' (Anderson and Garrison, 1998: 110).

A facilitative approach to teaching is very different to a presentational approach. It is the difference between sharing meaning and sharing information. As Schrage (1995: 5) suggests:

> Creating a shared understanding is simply a different task than exchanging information. It is the difference between being deeply involved in a conversa-

tion and lecturing to a group. The words are different, the attitude is different, and the tools are different.

This contrast dramatizes the difference in process between facilitative and presentational approaches to teaching and learning and reflects a fundamental shift in expected learning outcomes. Moreover, it suggests that the use of tools or technology will also be different, depending on desired outcome and approach.

While discussing the influence of technology on presentational and facilitative approaches to university teaching, we need to keep in mind the general belief that the primary goal of higher education is the development of higher-order learning such as critical thinking. For this reason, we argue in the next section that technology can influence university teaching in two ways. It can enhance the presentational, prescriptive approach to university teaching and the dominance of the lecture; or it can fundamentally alter the teaching and learning transaction by providing the opportunity and means to approach teaching in a facilitative and collaborative manner. The latter, stronger influence of technology, will inherently alter approaches to learning towards the development of deep and meaningful learning outcomes.

Stronger and weaker technological influences

From the perspective of university teaching, technology can be used to enhance and sustain dominant practices such as lecturing, or it can transform and disrupt these practices. A useful insight into the influence of technology in changing university teaching is the concept of sustaining and disruptive technologies. According to Christensen (1997), organizations are at risk when they do not recognize the distinction between sustaining and disruptive technologies. Sustaining technologies improve the performance of established products and services, while disruptive technologies can have an adverse effect on established products and services. Disruptive technologies 'are typically cheaper, simpler, smaller, and, frequently, more convenient to use' (1997: xv), and target less profitable customer groups. Initially, disruptive technologies are not as efficient as sustaining technologies and, therefore, are often ignored by established organizations.

Christensen developed his concept of sustaining and disruptive technologies in a business context. There is a place for both sustaining and disruptive technologies, just as there is a place for traditional and innovative practices. While universities are not business organizations, there are some parallels and lessons from the distinction between sustaining and disruptive technologies with regard to changing established practices in any organization. In this sense, we argue that learning technologies can have either a weaker or stronger influence on changing university teaching.

The weaker influence on changing university teaching uses technology to marginally enhance dominant practices and learning outcomes while serving existing students. This generally represents a significant additional cost with marginal increases in the quality of learning outcomes. While it is more likely that technologies that enhance dominant practices will be adopted, their lasting effect will also be minimal and likely short-lived.

The stronger influence uses technology to do things differently and produce new learning outcomes intended to serve existing and new markets. With new powerful and inexpensive communications technologies, there are opportunities to significantly increase the quality of learning outcomes with modest investment. This, however, demands a rethinking of our desired educational outcomes and the means of achieving these learning goals. At the same time, it should be noted that stronger and weaker technological influences are not mutually exclusive. Universities can work on enhancing sustaining technologies while using disruptive technologies to transform other transactions such as professional development programmes.

There are advantages to using technology to change university teaching in both the weak and strong sense. Universities should continue to develop sustaining technologies that enhance current practices so that students and professors can become comfortable with new technologies and their instructional applications. Through direct experience anxieties are reduced, opportunities are presented to understand how technology can be used effectively, and new approaches to teaching can be envisioned. While there are gains in providing student access to the Internet and for professors to organize their lectures using presentation tools such as PowerPoint©, it must be realized that these technologies will continue to produce the same outcomes as before – only in a marginally more efficient or effective manner.

The risk of this approach is that the true potential of learning technologies may not be realized. As Brown and Duguid (1996: 19) argue, universities are highly conventional institutions and 'without more thought to students and their practical needs, we fear that not only will these technologies be under-exploited, but they may well reinforce the current limitations of our higher education system'. That is, there needs to be a rethink of university teaching if technology is to have a stronger influence on learning outcomes.

On the other hand, technologies can strongly influence conventional university teaching. There are technologies such as computer-mediated communications, particularly computer conferencing, that have the potential to transform university teaching (Harasim *et al*, 1995). These technologies are especially powerful when used to target a new market segment, such as professional development, that are less tradition bound, more receptive to collaborative and social learning outcomes and place higher value on independence of time and distance during the educational process.

Educational activities that exploit the power of interpersonal communications for adult learning such as co-operative learning (Johnson, Johnson and Smith, 1998) provide the pedagogical basis for the effective utilization of these tools. Computer conferencing technology is a dominant choice because it is a cost-effective way to deliver graduate and professional development courses at a distance without extensive development and packaging of independent study course materials.

However, more importantly, computer-conferencing can provide the capability to develop communities of inquiry and the shared application of new knowledge within authentic contexts – usually the learner's workplace. The challenge for instructors, in such programmes, is to use the technology to achieve relevant and practical learning outcomes. This requires that they create and manage discussion groups in which the students interpret and translate current theory to relevant practice. This cannot be done using traditional lectures or prescriptive course packages. The technology and client groups are demanding that conventional teaching practice change.

Other examples of the stronger applications of technologies include the problem based learning programmes developed at the University of Alberta for professional development of practising pharmacists. In this programme audio, text and visual data was delivered via the World Wide Web (WWW) to students working in distributed groups. Through computerconferencing based discussion, as well as 'interviews' with the patient (simulated by an instructor pseudonym), students construct and then post for peer review a pharmacy treatment plan for the patient. In each of these examples, technology is used extensively to promote in-depth conversation between active learners engaged in solving meaningful problems – the conditions ideal for the development of critical thinking skills.

Christensen (1997) underscores the difficulty of adopting disruptive technologies within the mainstream operation of an organization – even if these technologies will eventually be adopted throughout the organization. To have a stronger influence in changing university teaching, disruptive communication and learning technologies must be adopted. However, to reduce the risk to the 'present market' and traditional values, new specialized markets such as professional programmes should be developed to introduce disruptive technologies. By demonstrating the effectiveness of these technologies in a smaller market with few risks, there is an opportunity to strongly influence university teaching in the traditional core programmes. This may well be the best strategy for technology to significantly change outcome expectations and reshape the educational process.

The impact of innovation with information and communications technology does not proceed uniformly through the ranks, but rather follows a bell curve pattern that differentiates 'early adopters', from mainstream faculty and 'laggards' (Geoghegan, 1994; Moore, 1991; Rogers, 1995). Geoghegan (1994) identifies four factors that exacerbate the effort to traverse the 'chasm' that separates the early adopters from mainstream faculty. Firstly, there is an ignorance of the gap between faculty and an assumption by administrators and change agents within the University that faculty are a homogenous group. Secondly, Geoghegan describes a technological alliance between hardware and software manufacturers and early adopters that tends to create an élite hierarchy of 'techies', who maintain control, over application of instructional technologies. Thirdly, he identifies profound alienation of many faculty members from technologies that they conceive as dehumanizing and incompatible with the model of campus and classroom based learning to which they have become acclimatized. Finally, Geoghegan identifies the lack of a compelling reason to change that is based upon lack of exposure, relative advantage, inability to trial and lack of incentives as classic inhibitors to technology adoption by many earlier writers.

Empirical evidence for this gap and each of the four conditions noted by Geoghegan was extracted from analysis of surveys of faculty undertaken at the University of Alberta in 1996 and 1997 (Anderson, Varnhegan and Campbell, 1998). From these studies we realized that no amount of support and encouragement of early adopters – often institutionalized in the form of 'New Media Centres' on North American campuses – would allow us to leap the chasm separating early adopters from main stream faculty (see http://www.newmediacenter.org/). Through annual faculty surveys we document the use of barriers perceived and attitudes towards instructional technology on-campus, thus helping decrease the ignorance of the gap of awareness between early adopters and the majority of teaching staff.

There is a large and ongoing need for professional development and support mechanisms that help faculty first learn to use and gain confidence in the use of instructional technologies; and also, how to develop learning activities that utilize the tools without creating unsustainable increases in faculty workloads. Our survey data indicates that no single training format best meets the diverse needs of faculty. Early adopters value most time and access to the tools and prefer to learn by themselves. Mainstream faculty prefer a variety of presentations, hands-on laboratory sessions, peer support and time for independent practice.

To meet these needs we have developed a whole range of training programmes. Each day during the university term, we offer a different presentation format inservice session, where both technical experts and peers demonstrate application of instructional activities. We hold annual workshops for new faculty and extensive week-long 'immersion' sessions. Finally, we employ trained undergraduate students to provide personal assistance to faculty in tasks such as Web design, data entry or presentation creation. Our Web site (http://www.atl.ualberta.ca) becomes the distribution and information session for ongoing support activities and a repository of tips, training sessions and presentations – allowing for asynchronous training activities delivered 'just in time' when and where most needed by our teaching staff.

Moreover, we have increased efforts to provide exposure and visibility of successful innovation through provision of showcases, in print and WWW publications celebrating innovation. We have purchased development systems and provide comprehensive, but easy to use, synchronous and asynchronous development and delivery tools such as WebCT (http://www.webct.com). We also support 'standards bodies' that allow materials to be easily shared amongst developers and adopters (Apple's Education Object Economy – http://trp.research.apple.com and EduCause's IMS project – http://www.imsproject.org/). Finally, we stress the need to develop department based task forces charged with leading by example and developing technology integration plans at the department or faculty level (Szabo, 1996).

Change within the university environment requires continuous communication across all ranks (Clark, 1998). One of the most cost-effective tools to inform and build a community of innovation on-campus has been a simple mail list. ATLNet is distributed to over 500 academics and teaching graduate students. It serves firstly as an announcement vehicle for campus activities. Secondly, it serves as a means of distributing and reacting to information items that are gleaned and filtered by our staff from the research journals and online forums and information resources. The list is not moderated in the sense that any member may post new, or react to, items posted by other members. This openness results in occasional wrong postings and inappropriate messages not intended for all 500 members. However, the openness also carries on a tradition of the university to provide mechanisms for the comments, suggestions and ideas of all members of the community.

Each of these initiatives is developed within a series of incentive programmes that support innovation by individual faculty members, graduate assistant and support staff. It is clear that technology can be used as a tool to reform higher education practice. However, the adoption of these technologies is not a simple process and requires the asking of difficult questions and the re-prioritizing of many of our budgetary assumptions – activities that neither faculty, nor administrators, relish.

Institutional constraints and caveats

Universities are 'highly conventional' and we need to examine the teaching-learning transaction if learning technologies are to have a stronger influence on shifting intended outcomes and practices. The ideal of the university as a community of learners is a traditional value worth maintaining. From an institutional perspective, how we use technology to change university teaching needs to be examined closely.

Using technology to create a communications infrastructure is not the most serious constraint to changing university teaching. The real challenge will be to induce teaching staff and students to examine the core values (eg 'the community of learners') and intended outcomes (eg 'critical thinking') of the teaching-learning process. From the perspective of faculty members, the time necessary for the acquisition of new skills, plus the time needed to develop new teaching materials, represents an 'opportunity cost' that takes valuable time from more highly rewarded activities – notably discipline based research. This time cost could be substantially reduced by the extensive use of materials and content created by others; however, a craft tradition of instructor-created lecture notes and assignments combined with a 'not invented here' mentality places limitations on this more effective mode of sharing learning materials. Fortunately, the distributive and collaborative culture of networks such as the Internet tends to mitigate this provincial attitude – especially amongst active network users.

Another barrier to change is a culture that emphasizes individual accomplishments and independence. Competitive faculty evaluation schemes often fail to recognize collaborative teaching or research even when this type of activity represents more efficient use of faculty time and energy. A final barrier is a reliance on input measures (eg class hours, size of syllabus, etc) and unstandardized evaluation criteria (instructor created and evaluated examinations) to measure teaching impact. Until we make the difficult effort to define and evaluate higher order thinking skills, it is unlikely that we will be able to use technology effectively to enhance their acquisition.

Students, too, face challenges when using technologies to support higher order thinking. Many students begin their university experience with a history of success through effective surface and instrumental learning strategies. They are unskilled and often unwilling to make the efforts to use tools and techniques that require them to think deeply and to collaborate extensively with peers. It is ironic that the communication tools that we believe to have great potential for increasing deep and meaningful learning also facilitate plagiarism, paper and project purchasing, and other unethical behaviour. Finally, rising tuition and debt loads created by government policies requiring students to pay a higher percentage of the costs of their education, make it increasingly difficult for students to afford the capital and operational costs of personal computers and communication devices.

A final challenge to the university infrastructure is the demands for professional development and lifelong learning. Universities are finding it difficult to maintain their services at a high level of quality for traditional students who are able to attend classes on-campus. Asking traditional universities to divert resources towards students at home or workplace is a difficult challenge. Often these non-traditional students are expected to pay extra for services such as library delivery and communication costs that are traditionally available free to on-campus students.

These and other challenges can be met by a clear focus on mission and values that are operationalized in policy and practice. Universities cannot meet the needs of all students, faculty and taxpayers. But they must insure that they are clearly focussed on research, teaching and service that meet a clearly defined subset of these needs. They then must use tools and technologies that most effectively and efficiently support attainment of these goals.

Conclusion

New and emerging technologies provide opportunities to reduce the reliance of universities on presentational and broadcast approaches to teaching and learning. However, in the short and medium term, technology will only have a weaker influence on the traditional undergraduate client base. The reasons for this are the financial constraints that universities face as well as the limited expectations of students themselves. The immediate financial pressures on universities will focus attention on doing things more cost efficiently, which will not enhance the quality of learning outcomes appreciably. The real challenge to those seeking stronger influences of technology is to envision new and better ways of achieving significant qualitative advancements in learning outcomes.

Technology will have its strongest influence when learners demand high quality teaching–learning transactions and outcomes and competitors emerge to meet these demands. For traditional universities, the real threat of competition comes not from newly emerging 'virtual universities', but from other credible, established universities that have learned to use technologies to meet student/client needs for meaningful learning opportunities. There is such a client group, in the continuing professional development sector that demands accessible, relevant programmes of learning. This client group is becoming increasingly important to universities and an ideal incubator for disruptive technologies. This is where the stronger influence of technology will be felt in the short term. This customer group has the resources to pay for innovative programmes and there are credible institutions that are willing to meet their demands. To serve this growing client group successfully, approaches to teaching need to be fundamentally rethought. Universities must understand that it is possible to meet traditional high-quality learning goals in an affordable and personalized manner and that effective use of communications technology is a key to meeting these goals.

The question is will technologies be used, in the stronger sense, to create quality learning environments and outcomes, or will they be used simply to enhance presentation quality and to access more fragmented and potentially meaningless information? There is little doubt that technology will influence university teaching; the important task is to use it to enable fundamental changes to our approach to teaching and learning. That is, to facilitate a teaching and learning transaction, that is collaborative and develops students who think critically and construct knowledge meaningfully. We believe that new and emerging communications technology will influence society and students to demand more from their professors and change approaches to university teaching – for the better. With the increasing influence of new, affordable technologies and the demands for relevant learning outcomes, even in the largest and most conservative universities, traditional presentational teaching practices and structures can no longer continue to dominate.

Chapter 3

Knowledge and networks

David Harris

Introduction

To begin, a brief description of some salient features of contemporary higher education in the UK is necessary. The newly proposed Institute of Learning and Teaching (ILT) heralds a new phase into the development of higher education (although uncertainty and simmering resistance prevail). The ILT is expected, in effect, to license and credentialize lecturers, within an emphasis on a new version of 'learning-centred teaching'. This kind of approach has long been advocated, of course, largely as a voluntary response to the move towards a 'mass' system of higher education. The UK Committee of Vice-Chancellors and Principals have produced extensive materials to promote their version(s) of 'active learning' (for example, Eastcott and Farmer, 1992). There is also a network of voluntary schemes of accreditation of lecturers, under the aegis of a body called the Staff Education and Development Association (SEDA) (see their Web site – SEDA, 1998).

The SEDA schemes feature a strong emphasis on a version of 'student-centred' learning. Here lecturers have to demonstrate the attainment of objectives and a commitment to 'underpinning principles', such as, being aware of individual differences among students in terms of how they learn, as well as in terms of their right to equal opportunities. SEDA schemes also exhibit an expected commitment to reflective practice that foregrounds methods (or technologies) and expects experimentation with alternatives (especially student-centred ones).

These initiatives are likely to gain a considerable amount of clout from recently perceived Government pressures via the Dearing Report (1997) for institutions to opt for a core status, as either a research institution or a teaching institution. It is now becoming clear that opting for the latter would substantially boost the market for formal accreditation of staff, from SEDA or via membership of the ILT, in anticipation of some kind of future request for quantifiable evidence of commitment.

There is another significant development in that the UK Open University (UKOU) has established a new course that will tie together SEDA accreditation and ILT membership via a new Post-Graduate Certificate in Teaching and Learning in Higher Education. History looks like repeating itself as the UKOU finds itself able to supply a substantial market for teachers seeking credentials, this time in higher education rather than school teaching, as was the case in 1970. The SEDA values and principles lie at the heart of this new course as well.

To add one final layer of possible influence, the Higher Education Funding Council for England (HEFCE), the main funding body for non-specialist higher education, is also sponsoring some projects to develop and then widely disseminate teaching and learning materials in social sciences (see the Web site – SSP2000, 1999). These projects are co-ordinated by a national team, based at the Centre for Higher Education Practice at the UKOU that virtually overlaps with the course team for the new UKOU Postgraduate Certificate. Developments like these have undoubtedly propelled this version of student-centred learning into a strong position of influence.

There may be, of course, certain contradictions here. As a student on one of the UKOU modules, I have found a tension, as the instrumental need to amass a suitable portfolio for assessment bumps up against the more fleeting, unplanned, unpredictable and intangible moments of student activity that it is not common to record. As might be apparent, the materials themselves can also offer a double emphasis, still focusing on conventional teacher-led course and lesson production and design, while advocating student reception as the overall test of effectiveness. The materials seem poised at present between these two poles, offering a rather cautious form of student activity, perhaps, still within an overall teacher-centred pedagogy. There are also many implications to follow, as these new commitments filter into university practice and meet the inevitable constraints arising from the equally apparent reductionist turn in university management that appears not to prioritize skilled teaching at all.

Here, in particular, I intend to pursue one set of implications via a discussion of the concept of 'knowledge as a net', which is also prominent, if less explicitly modelled, in the SEDA values and commitments.

Knowledge as a net

It could be argued that it is this concept that really permits a more genuinely student-centred learning. As Bernstein pointed out, curricula embody certain 'frames' that 'refer to the strength of the boundary between what may be transmitted and what may not be transmitted in the pedagogical relationship' (1970: 50). Frames both organize concepts and the social relations between teacher and taught. Tightly framed curricula leave new learners powerless, with nothing to contribute, in effect, since they have no expertise inside the boundary of the subject matter. 'Student activity' here means that they have only to learn pre-defined material until they have become master practitioners in turn. There may be different routes to mastery, of course, as we shall see below – but the network of concepts has a definite limit or boundary as between, say, 'astronomy' and 'astrology'. In weakly framed (but strengthening?) subject areas such as 'Cultural Studies' – which I shall discuss in more detail below – there may be currently a much wider network of possible concepts:

- crossing conventional subject boundaries;
- crossing between academic work and journalism;
- engaging the actual 'practical concepts' of the students as participants, insiders or even as connoisseurs.

Pask and 'knowledge structures'

The metaphor of knowledge as a net was used to develop a teaching technology at the UKOU, in the 1970s, with the work of Pask and his associates. I have discussed this work in more detail elsewhere (Harris, 1987). However, it is still relevant today in showing the power of the metaphor, in fairly strongly framed subject matters like probability theory, or in particular discrete applications (like learning artificial taxonomies in the laboratory, or modelling expert systems). Pask was content simply to let the relevant authorities set the boundaries to the topics (including the 'numinous course team' at the UKOU, but within those boundaries he argued strongly for maximum flexibility. Concepts, themselves, should be thought of as nodes in a well-connected net. There might be a need for some hierarchy, based on logical entailment or on some effective sequence of command, but this would still leave a good deal of flexibility in terms of learning styles. Indeed, the project was premised on there being such styles – for Pask, 'serial', 'holistic' or mixed information-processing preferences (Pask, 1976). Depicting knowledge as a net, rather than as a mere list-structure, as the 'planning by objectives' model did (and still does), permits students to work their own way through the connections, and thus to reconstruct the net (or their preferred portion of it) for themselves. Moreover, the structure of the net even permits critical interrogations on the part of the students and a more creative use of the concepts once mastered (as new additions to the net can be conceived, if only by analogy).

My objections to the project were based on what might be seen as the unacknowledged limits of what seemed then like a liberating proposal (and it still does, especially compared to the now almost ubiquitous use of objectives in course design). I argued Pask's work was abstract and formalist, and thus seemed far more universalistic than it really was. Indeed, it seemed based on some general philosophical commitment to a version of Russell's set theory as a universal metalanguage (Harris, 1987). More concretely, it would encounter difficulties if transposed to different and untheorized contexts (from the laboratory to a distance teaching system based on 'telling'), and given different contexts (from strongly framed artificial taxonomies to far more weakly framed social theory). In those contexts, new priorities would structure the net and its uses – particular routes, would be privileged by forming the basis of student assessment, for example, or by reflecting the unstated preferences of course teams. I felt that, at least, Pask's net structures should be accompanied by some kind of meta-argument about those privileging and preferring activities: my fear was that this would be submerged and neglected by the drive to design a net on purely logical grounds. Pask's emphasis on the universal logic of his scheme worried me – he seemed to see this logic as offering some privileged discourse 'behind' or 'beneath' all academic discourse and he used provocative terms like 'sanitization' to describe the process of translating actual academic argument into the logical structure.

At that time, I had not heard of postmodernism, but I was already 'sceptical towards metanarratives' and their 'emancipatory intents' (to borrow Lyotard's famous phrases (1986)). This came about mainly from reading 'critical theory'. In order to claim universality, all metanarratives have to do violence to concrete narratives (well-intentioned though this might be), and all emancipatory intentions are accompanied by moments of subjection or domination. Most educators are aware at some level of these paradoxes, of course, as when we gloss the issue of the problematic 'applications' of educational theory to actual classrooms, perhaps, or when we compel students to attend our lectures in order to liberate them from their unclear thoughts.

Electronic text

However, I suspect that a major factor in the failure of Pask's project to become more widely adopted at the UKOU, turned on matters of cost, rather than postmodernist scepticism. It would have been simply far too expensive to produce multiple versions of printed correspondence units and TV broadcasts, which were the dominant forms, in the 1970s. The advent of electronic communication has drastically weakened those constraints, although, of course, there are additional difficulties for the pedagogue too. However, had the Internet been established in 1970, things might have been very different.

The pros and cons of using electronic text are well known, and summarized in the context of teaching literature (McGann, 1995). At the production end, it is possible to offer a net-like structure, instead of a mere list of key concepts and allow much more choice in sequencing, using hyperlinks to join sections within a document, and to add other documents located elsewhere. Kaplan (1995) is a good example of a paper written in this style. Electronic communications also permit the closer integration of text, graphics, video and sound, although not without adding some cost and requiring some skilled labour, at least, when working with Hypertext Markup Language (HTML) (Siegel, 1996). Excellent examples of other educational applications (such as computer supported collaborative learning) are found in Dede's 1996 survey.

However, the real changes from conventional media depend on the uses made of electronic text at the reception end. Readers of paper documents have always been able to interpret and amend them – to make marginal notes, to summarize and edit and so on – but an electronic form makes these interventions and restructurings possible on a new scale (assuming minimal keyboard skills). As my own 'electronic tutorial' suggests (Harris, 1998), students can:

- cut and paste sections of text in accordance with their preferred sequences of 'theory' and examples (or 'deep' and 'surface' elements);
- highlight key principles and paste them in each page;
- add their own comments;
- combine my views with those of others in a kind of 'assemble-edit'.

Again, 'post'-critics of various kinds, usually better known to those working in areas like Media Studies, have argued that texts are so radically interpreted by readers that the distinction between reading and writing has been overcome. At last, the manipulations available to users of electronic text seem to bear this out. When students manipulate texts, as I have suggested, they are 'writing' them in an important sense. It could be argued:

- they are deciding what are the 'deep' or 'surface' elements;
- they are distinguishing between general principles and specific examples;
- they are constructing their own educational narratives.

There is a further analogy too – those same critics have emphasized the essential intertextuality of modern texts, the constant references to other texts, called variously, for example, quotation, citation, 'homage', parody, inversion, critique or tribute. Once more, such intertextuality takes place at both the production and reception phases, as writers add hyperlinks, and as readers also recall and refer to other texts they have read.

   For committed critics of this kind, there is no alternative, of course – there is no individuality 'outside' of texts, and with electronic text this is apparent to all. Thus, in the rhetoric of one exponent (Barthes, 1977), individual readers, writers, and indeed, individual works 'disappear'. I think this notion of 'disappearance' lies at the base of many of the anxieties about the impact of the Internet, as I shall argue below, since it threatens many established university conventions. However, the notion opens the possibility of a new critical study, a 'new semiology' for Barthes – the examination of ways, in which this endless flow of textuality becomes fixed, frozen or reified into distinct discourses. Barthes never develops this insight very far himself, but others have made some useful suggestions, especially 'critical theorists', and more fashionably, Foucault (Dreyfus and Rabinow, 1982) – power and its deployment sets the shape, of course, not just pedagogical intent.

Teaching Cultural Studies

I have shown elsewhere how British Cultural Studies (BCS) has developed as an academic discipline in a university context, which includes struggling for autonomy and respectability, and has thus become, partly as a consequence, a strongly framed discourse (Harris, 1992). This account is at odds with most of the others, which see

BCS as an open-ended, non-dogmatic and emancipatory discourse. For me, however, there was a number of constraining factors in BCS, which gradually forced it towards closure. These included certain academic commitments to a research programme based on the work of a 'founding father', the Italian Marxist hero Antonio Gramsci. As is common with Marxist theories, there were also political commitments. In this case, a kind of cultural politics, a peculiar kind of UK university-based cultural activism suitable for a group without connections to trade unions or to a strong Communist Party.

The foundational concepts of what I have called 'gramscianism' include terms like 'hegemony', 'articulation' or processes of 'settlement and crisis'. A great deal of work was undertaken to make these fit a wide range of cultural activities, from youth cultures to the history of recreation, to television sit-coms and Bond movies. The work included theoretical struggles to ensure the supremacy of gramscianism against a number of rivals, including 'bourgeois subjects' like sociology or history and various other marxisms. This kind of academic struggle, to explain and subordinate rival concepts in the terms of your own preferred discourse, was given a strong institutional support, when the leading exponents of gramscianism were finally able to construct an academic course on popular culture at the UKOU (Open University, 1982). Here, I would like to suggest that the closing and managing tendencies of UKOU notions of good pedagogy (including the development of strong organizing academic narratives that privilege certain general frameworks) heightened the existing tendencies.

As with all such ventures, this sort of development energized a lot of subsequent work, much as 'paradigms' do in natural science. The UKOU course became a kind of template for subsequent courses in other institutions, attracting adherents for its well-organized pedagogic structure as well as for its other commitments. Institutional links via validating bodies or external examiner networks, and a formidable published output assisted the diffusion of gramscian work. Much of the work penetrated into other social science curricula (particularly sociology and media studies). As a result, a fairly strong orthodoxy has developed in BCS, especially in the new generation of analysts, underpinned by a powerful combination of theoretical, political and pedagogic commitments.

Criticising such work in a manner suggested by Barthes or by critical theory has not been easy. Although, it is a straightforward and obvious matter to argue that BCS must be every bit as constructed a discourse as Port Royal economics, psychiatric medicine, jurisprudence or any of the other examples discussed by Foucault (Dreyfus and Rabinow, 1982). I have tried to deconstruct the apparent unproblematic evolution of BCS offered in sympathetic accounts, and to try to 'lay bare the devices of the assemblage' of the key works themselves. It is a project that can be unattractive to academic colleagues and students, who are often grateful for the apparent ability of a concept like hegemony to 'explain everything' (as one put it).

There are other traditions to which students can be referred, which raise possibilities that cannot be managed easily by the organizing concepts of BCS, and other cultural practices or objects. The Internet, or the Web, is the most useful device here as a source of 'wild' objects and practices with materials organized in very different ways. One can almost guarantee a lack of fit between the BCS orthodoxies on, say, punk rock, and the material offered on more than 41,000 Web sites devoted to that topic. It is easy to expose the parochialism of BCS by searching for sites on, say, Japanese or Australian popular culture (Iwamura, 1994). Comparative work, in particular, is astonishingly convenient to do on the Web, although in a limited fashion. The universalistic BCS claims (sometimes made implicitly) to be able to make sense of these 'wild' objects, can be tested by students: such tests can be arranged with ease using this medium, and they offer a genuine chance for students to contribute, to blur the boundary between 'student' and 'researcher'.

This kind of exposure to the huge variety of sites on the Web may not be applicable at all to the specifics of teaching in other subject areas. Even when there may be a strong need to open things up like this, there are risks. These range from exposing students to pornographic sites to inducing an excessive openness. Excessive openness leads to a hopelessly confusing relativism, especially one which makes browsers open to the 'prime knowledge' of those offering easy answers at the end of all the confusion, whether this be the avuncular pedagogue, the Webevangelist, or the commercial company. Even with my limited project on teaching about BCS, some students may wish to cling to their hard-won certainties, while others may not stay 'on task' once they are hooked up. As usual, there is just no one way to teach, and the Web itself offers no easy technical fix.

My own Web site (Harris, 1998) offers another compromise – a very limited attempt to organize knowledge in an open manner, and one designed so that students can experience some of the developments highlighted by some postmodern critics in particular. I have worked privately and with only my own materials, but even so it has been possible to try to limit (if not abandon altogether) BCS-type organizing metanarratives by including the files in alphabetical order. This threw up some nice (possibly surreal) accidents, such as, having the 'baking a cake' file next to the Bourdieu file (both involve the concept of 'taste', naturally!). Possibly, I could have represented these materials as nodes in some kind of logically connected (if rather idiosyncratic) network of my own, but I am more interested in what sort of structure students might impose.

I have tried to demonstrate the points about the 'collapse of internal differentiation' by colliding together handouts and conference papers, pieces on distance education and pieces on media theory. I believe that the conventional distinctions between these areas and 'levels' can be arbitrary and unhelpful, and now students can try this out for themselves. My electronic tutorial encourages them to pursue their own priorities with my works; while my external links page offers connections to locations, as various as a site on workplace bullying and one on student cheating, as well as to databases and archives. Incidentally, the now widespread ability to publish material on a personal Web site breaks another old distinction, which I have found slightly limiting – between writer and publisher.

I should add that I have no idea, as yet, how students actually do use my own Web site. I am working at present on some evaluation. If I get funded, I hope to establish whether students approach electronic materials in any of the ways in which they seem to approach conventional materials – for example, in terms of 'deep', 'surface' or 'strategic' orientations. I am interested in researching whether the structure of hyperlinks in my Web materials and in others really do encourage a kind of 'three-dimensional' exploration of my materials, or whether the possibilities are domesticated at the reception end. Work on the media audience seems promising as a parallel.

Implications for university teaching

Private experiments of the kind I have been developing and limited exercises on my specific courses may not be generalizable. There is a good deal of anxiety with the full, unmediated use of the Web on the part of university academics and administrators, and it is worth briefly examining some of the well-known reservations.

Universities are not designed exclusively to teach effectively, and there are other important dimensions to their activities (what Habermas (1987) might call the 'system imperatives' – the need to organize finance and to marshal sufficient power to act relatively autonomously). In particular, they are required to certificate students and increasingly, to guarantee the quality of the knowledge base of their courses. The development of new Web-based pedagogies might lead to conflicts with these institutional constraints, since the conditions of production of knowledge are no longer under control. It is worth adding that the conditions of publication are no longer regularized either, and thus there is a widespread anxiety that electronic publications might not count in the UK Government's periodic surveys of research output (on which substantial funding depends).

There are also worries about student plagiarism from the Web, and it is true that the flexibility of electronic text makes plagiarism very easy and almost undetectable. What you do is download a number of pieces from databases or archives, then assemble-edit, cut and paste, change spellings from US to English variants if necessary, use the online thesaurus to change some words, and finally, print out an assignment. I am fairly sure that some of my students have actually done this. They carefully negotiated a change in essay title, ostensibly to follow a burning interest in a particular film director, but probably because they could more easily locate material on that director and not on the ones I had specified.

A determined plagiarist could do all this before, with conventional print, of course. In my view, plagiarism is a cultural matter, the visible tip of a much more widespread instrumentalism, and it is hard to see why it should be the subject of such anxiety (and, often, of punitive over-reactions). Academic culture is actually rather ambiguous about instrumentalism and plagiarism, as we know from the occasional scandal involving faculty, let alone students. The concept is increasingly hard to define anyway, it might be argued, as the old conception of the author as an isolated bourgeois individual owning his (sic), intellectual property fades in the light of collective, collaborative and deliberately intertextual academic work. Sometimes the rage I have witnessed directed against student plagiarists seems to be a rage that plagiarism is now somehow 'too easy' thanks to electronic text, or an anger that an old technology has been displaced by a less skilful one.

UK universities have been forced to try hard to maintain the quality of their courses, and this too is threatened by the relativism of the Web. Many sites on the Web are commercially sponsored, or structured by strong commitments of their own, or offer strong preferences or prejudices. However, contrasting universities with these rival organizations is not quite as easy as it once was, perhaps, since universities themselves became suffused by commercialism or political commitments, especially during the recent attempts in the UK to 'simulate a market in higher education'. Against the genuine ambitions to 'maintain quality', many institutions had to become used to offering 'what the market will bear', or to seeing students as 'units of resource' and staff as mere fungibles. There might even be a case for arguing that some UK universities have come to represent some of the worst aspects of managerialism – McDonaldization in the terms of Ritzer (1994) – creating a climate in which 'quality' is now a low priority in reality, despite the need to survive the occasional inspection or TQA visit. In this sort of context, the freedom (including the freedom to write, to explore or to transgress) offered by the Web could be far more attractive.

Materials on the Web also vary, as we all know, and it is not too difficult to find some of equal or even superior 'quality' to our own. A random search probably will not find them – but do many users actually employ random searches? There has emerged some sort of fairly relaxed system of gathering Web sites into databases that promise to test for quality – the UK-based Social Science Information Gateway (SOSIG) (1999) is one such, which, I am pleased to say, recently included my own Web site. Nor are these problems exclusive to electronic text again – printed materials also vary considerably from the pornographic to the limp and dull and to critical masterpieces, and we have long relied on students being able to tell the difference in their browsing of print.

I think it is the authority of the university in the eyes of another audience that is in question, and the way in which that authority has traditionally been based on some conventions like the individual ownership of intellectual property. The quality issue arises especially acutely since universities have agreed a particular way of assuring politicians of the quality by reference to the regulation of the production processes of their courses, and by sampling the quality of outputs usually via some overview of student results. This version of the 'logic of confidence' (Meyer and Rowan, 1988) may be untenable given that the Web offers knowledge produced in unknown circumstances, outside of university walls (but often by university-trained personnel, perhaps).

For some postmodern thinkers, as a result, the end of the university is at hand. Universities can no longer monopolize (quality) knowledge at the production end, nor guarantee the reliability of measures of student attainment at the other end, given the impossibility of preventing plagiarism or, for that matter, syllabus independence (where a student chooses to find their own sources of knowledge outside what the course might offer). Increasing uses of distance education leads to a kind of independence from institutions and their cultures. It could be argued that students 'normalize' university syllabi by subordinating them to their lifestyles rather than the other way around. For faculty members too, the Web can offer some sort of experience of an 'invisible college'. A virtual department with none of the banalities or parochialism of their actual concrete ones, and there is a utopian promise of academics being able to liberate themselves from a specific institution with a specific managerial system. In these circumstances, funding an expensive purpose-built institution based on outdated assumptions about knowledge will seem increasingly unattractive to politicians and taxpayers. This might not be a bad thing, of course.

However, I intend not to succumb to such pessimism (rather uncharacteristically). There may well be a role for the university, although a different one, as many people have argued. This role will consist, not of providing knowledge in the form of undergraduate courses, but perhaps, as in working at the cultural level to help regulate the knowledge provided by others. In other words, universities could find a role as practitioners of the 'new semiology' discussed above, offering a set of tools (key skills if we must call them that) to deconstruct discourses found elsewhere, to explore their universalistic claims, and root around for the actual mechanisms that produce apparent coherence. This sort of effort would apply to material 'fixed' by commercial or any other purposes.

In the process, the university might devote itself to re-considering the issue of 'quality', to turn away from the positivist concern with processes and organizational structures of production, and to turn towards something more like an applied aesthetics. My own preference for such cultural resources would lead, ironically perhaps, to works in social theory as the most relevant. As well as, for example, Bourdieu (1988), Barthes and Foucault as above, we might want to consider Habermas (1976) on counterposing 'distorted communication' to 'the ideal speech act', or even to those debates in the philosophy and sociology of science, which illuminate the mechanisms of 'rational theory choice'.

Whatever the resources, though, the task of the university would be to oppose any fixity, universalism and reification of discourses. Not to lead to a deep relativist despair, but to point to what some might call 'the sublime' (in Lyotard's sense – roughly that ultimate value, which can only be alluded to but never directly represented) (Docherty, 1993). The insight that all concrete representational discourses are limited, and that this limiting is both 'good' and 'bad', enabling and disabling. Just as cinema delivered this insight, according to Deleuze (1992), with its capacity to widen human perceptions, so might the experience of immersion in the Web – although I have doubts whether this too does not involve some dubious universalistic claim. I suspect that specific competencies, as yet unresearched, will influence students' experiences here as well.

Concluding thoughts

I am aware that some colleagues will not find this vision of the future at all attractive, especially those teaching BCS, perhaps. Some regard it as their duty to be committed and to share that commitment with students. Such commitments, whether to a political position, an academic tradition or a perceived professional or vocational requirement will serve to close off the outer reaches of the knowledge net. There may be additional pedagogic reasons too, in that you have to explore a net from somewhere and beginners might get vertigo if they see that net stretch off into infinity.

Yet these positions can also lead to discomfort, perhaps of an increasing intensity. Closing off sections of the knowledge net seems to require increasing amounts of power, for example – student use of the Web would have to be regulated (via electronic surveillance?). More difficult still, the authoritative concepts in the canon would still have to be defended zealously (and here, even gramscianism can become exhausted in the end). This kind of pedagogy might have worked in the mediaeval monastery or in the old elite universities, but it would seem to be a labour very much against the trends in modern mass universities. Only crude tokenist constraints seem available now for such a project – an insistence on attendance, for example, or a reliance on forms of assessment, which make forbidden forms of plagiarism more difficult (such as formal examinations again). The university would run the risk of becoming irrationally authoritarian or irrelevant and elitist – and that sort of future seems unattractive to politicians and taxpayers.

At present, the concept of knowledge as a net seems rather a congenial and controllable metaphor – a mere technique to assist in the 'new' pedagogy. Perhaps it will remain as a mere ideology, glossing more authoritarian realities. However, ever-present, and just a click or two away, is a much more extensive network, and one with much more challenging implications.

Chapter 4

The wedlock between technology and open and distance education

Olugbemiro Jegede

Although the history of open and distance education is never complete without reference to the practical alliance between technology and teaching, indications are that the long honeymoon may soon be over. Several developments in areas such as applied cognitive psychology, philosophy, instructional design, computer and communications technology within the current ferment in the emerging post-structuralist and post-modernist global community necessitate that a second look be taken at how technology is deployed to meet the needs of distance higher education. Technology is hereby examined from a range of perspectives including the design of instruction, the development and use of software and hardware, and the use of information and communications technologies in delivering instruction. Technology in its broad definition, therefore, includes the art and science of instructional design and the soft and hardware gadgets used in facilitating communications or interaction between individuals or groups. Although there are several uses of technology in open and distance education, it is its use as information and communications technology that this chapter focuses upon.

Since the marriage of open and distance education and ICT (information and communications technology) several things have changed. These include new pedagogical goals for instruction, new taxonomies of learning applicable to interactive learning environments, a more organic and iterative approach to instructional systems design, and the need to empower the learner to own the process of the construction of knowledge. However, contemporary developments in education indicate that the more things change the more they remain the same. Educational practitioners and organizations are still not proactive in the development and use of ICT. Indeed, ICT companies rarely consult those within education while they develop equipment that could be used for teaching and learning, and educational practitioners wait to adopt and adapt technology to their teaching rather than dictate what should be developed for a particular instructional event, environment or task. The learners' views are hardly considered, and neither are their motivations to learn, or their socio-cultural environments, which may mediate or inhibit learning. Within these interacting cultural milieu (technology, learner's environment, etc), borders must be crossed for learning to occur.

This chapter examines the use of ICT in distance higher education, the shifting terrain of education within a changing global society and the explosion of knowledge. The argument here is based on critical reflections on my practice, including my research and development experiences, with the implementation of technology in non-contiguous forms of higher education, especially in forms of open and distance education.

This chapter provides a cognitive explanation of the ways that students cope with learning, resulting from what may be called 'border crossing'. The thesis is that the days of uncharted, 'off-the-cuff', 'emotional' uses of technology in education are fast coming to a close. Consequently, it signifies the need to allow reason to rise above emotions in the all important mission of preparing for the next millennium, a society whose citizens can use knowledge in new situations and react and function in a multi-faceted manner. It concludes with a glimpse of the future, particularly drawing attention to issues to be addressed by universities within technology, teaching and learning, and research.

Enter technology...

What can now be termed as a wedlock between open and distance education and technology began with a long courtship, when in the 16th and 17th century, people experimented with the idea of using print technology to teach the subject of 'short hand' by post. Beginning, therefore, with print purposely for correspondence education, this delivery of education to remote students has since gone through the use of radio, television, and now the computer (Holmberg, 1989: 7–11). Several people in open and distance education, notably Bates (1995), Grabe and Grabe (1998) and Taylor (1995), have traced the entry of technology into the instructional delivery environment in university open and distance education. Taylor (1995), for example, has drawn on the notion of the four generations of technology in distance education comprising: print and correspondence, tele-learning, mixed media, and ICT-based interactive multimedia.

A number of societal, technological, economic, and educational factors have converged to influence the use of technology in universities. The discussion of the full impact of these issues is not the focus here, but mention should be made of one or two issues concerning the entry of technology into distance education. First, the rapid and significant developments in the fields of computers and telecommunications have meant the continual availability of ever better versions of a range of technologies, at increasingly affordable prices in the consideration of 'posting' instructions to students. Second, the ever-expanding provision of education independent of time, pace of learning, and location to a variety of students, in different award and non-award programmes, and of different environmental, physical or social circumstances have necessitated the use of technology in some form.

The changing nature of the use of technology in education, of whatever generation, forces the marriage between technology and open and distance education. Those responsible for developing and producing the technological hardware, together with the policy makers, managers and teachers in open and distance education have consciously or unconsciously 'officiated' in this wedding by facilitating the use of the various generations of technology. A major attraction which led to the wedlock was the need to 'take the distance out of education' and to enhance its interactivity (Bates, 1995). The economic journalist Frances Cairncross writes of the 'death of distance' due to the influence of ICT (1995). She argues that this occurs as a consequence of the rapidly decreasing relative costs of ICT that will probably amount to the most important economic force in the next half century. In universities it will further unleash changes in the practice and conception of education. For instance, it is conceivable that the divide between open and distance education institutions and traditional face-to-face higher institutions will be abolished as the use of information and communications technology becomes more pervasive. Teaching may become more collaborative and technologically facilitated, and more responsive to the needs of an emerging population requiring flexible, interactive and lifelong learning.

The changes to both open and distance education and university teaching can be construed as the honeymoon period between open and distance education and technology. This honeymoon has got several features. The first feature is a romantic, ever seductive starry-eyed view of new technology. For those many technological 'boosters' in universities, any new technology has immediate application to teaching regardless of its cost, effectiveness, appropriateness, or acceptance by university teachers as effective.

Since the beginning of distance education by correspondence, the range of communication technologies available for education and their use in various instructional environments is quite impressive. They include:

- audio (AM/FM radio, audiotape, packet radio, compact disc, two-way SW/UHF radio, telephone, answering machine, voice mail, audio-conference);
- audio visual/video (slides/still video, videotape, television, teletext, 'talkback' TV, videodisc, videoconference, audiographic);
- data & computing (file transfer/storage, personal computing, electronic mail, computer assisted learning, computer managed instruction, CD ROM, Web, computer-conference);
- image (electronic whiteboard, facsimile), text/print/communications cable, satellite).

Of all the new technologies the versatility enabled by the computer amazes even the computer enthusiasts. Digital technologies made possible with the use of computers are creating new media and leading to the convergence of entertainment, telecommunications, publishing, and news media. Computers make possible the creation of new products that combine digitized audio, video, image, animation, etc. The new digital communications systems, such as Cellular Digital Packet Data, create the potential for anyone anywhere to be able to use e-mail or connect to other Internet based services. The romantic and seductive appeal of new technologies continues for educators.

Universities could be said to be entering a new era fostered by several converging social and pedagogical changes. University teaching is changing to meet these changing needs of learners, teachers and the use of information and communications technology. Some of the changes, driving the honeymoon as mentioned earlier, include the experiences that learners now demand in preparation for lifelong learning. The second factor is the emerging view of knowledge and learning as being context-dependent, situational, constructed and socially mediated. The third driving force is the array of opportunities and facilities being provided for teaching and learning through new information and communications technologies.

Another characteristic of the honeymoon between open and distance learning and information and communications technologies is the notion of arranged and 'shotgun' marriages. In Australia, such 'arrangements' have been engendered by the Committee on University Teaching and Staff Development (formerly the Committee for the Advancement of University Teaching), which encourages research and development activities, on the use of emerging technologies in university teaching. Previous governments have also used the tactic of making across the board cuts to university funding, then using the funds to establish a 'priority reserve fund', against which universities can bid for defined projects in new technology, in particular.

Lessons from wedlock

Although new developments in technology can be exciting and seductive, their effective, efficient, and educationally sound usage in open and distance education depends on educators themselves, devoting time to take stock and reflect critically on what lessons are to be learnt from history regarding the emergence of technologies and their uses in education.

Given current changes in open and distance education and university teaching, it would appear that the honeymoon between information and communications technology and non-contiguous education is definitely over. The business of integrating technology and instruction has just begun and there is a huge mountain of work for distance and open education practitioners to overcome. It is clear that the marriage between technology and open and distance education goes beyond mere usage. Many universities acquire extremely costly technology to the detriment of other equally important areas, which require more funding. In others, the use of equipment rarely goes beyond a few months of its acquisition. The 'shotgun' marriage collapses and the students are left estranged. Presently, almost every institution wants to rush into Web-based teaching, with very little consideration of its pedagogical implications and value.

The use of information and communications technology in university teaching must meet a specific purpose, chart a definite path to realise a specific goal, and must use a cognitively sound justification within a defined context. The issue is not just that of hardware and software.It also encompasses appropriateness, values to be added to learning, competent technical and instructional development staff, cost effectiveness, readiness to be familiar with and use the new learning environment, and consideration about the social and cultural milieu in which the technology is put to work. Some of the lessons from history indicate the following:

- Technology will not by itself bring to bear any appreciable change in the educational system unless certain conditions are fulfilled. According to Frost (1937), although radio was expected to revolutionize education and schooling when it emerged, educators did not spend adequate time to develop effective programmes for the medium.

- Related to the above point is the need for educators to take the lead and be proactive in the design, development and use of technology in higher education. Hardly any of the technologies emerging today were developed with educational issues at the heart of the design and development. The result is that educators use communications technology without sufficient reason, or they attempt to make the best of a tool or medium not directly useful for teaching (Laurillard, 1993; Moore, 1997).

- In the current world of megatechnology and multinational corporate control (Mills, 1997), few educators, evaluators, and researchers have, according to Ehrmann (1995), paid much attention to educational strategies for using technologies. The focus should be on the effective use of technology to convey specific content to any learner, no matter the location or goal of study.

- The increase in the use of information and communications technologies in open and distance education has been accompanied by investigations comparing different technologies and their use in different modes of delivery, for example, face-to-face and distance education. Several studies have shown that students learn as well through the use of communications technologies as they do in face-to-face teaching (Clark, 1983; Russell, 1995; Schlosser and Anderson, 1994).

- Bates (1995) concludes that the potential effectiveness of technology-based open learning is not at issue; rather the issue is how to design and develop effective educational technologies (Knight, 1996). I accept Moore and Kearley's (1996) assertion that what makes a course good or bad is its design, delivery and implementation, not whether it is contiguous or non-contiguous.

Innovations

My experience of more than two decades in higher education includes management, teaching, instructional design, evaluation and research. In recent previous experience at the University of Southern Queensland (USQ), I have researched and trialled innovations involving the use of technology for peer tutoring, audiographics, and the use of the Smart 2000 audiographics software with desktop video conferencing. In the peer tutoring project, a model called OPTEN (On- campus-Off-campus Peer Tutoring Electronic Network) was developed and tested for employing computer mediated communication to support constructivist learning. For one semester on a Law course, dyadic groups were trialled consisting of one on-campus student with one off-campus student and their roles as tutor and tutee being alternated weekly. Using several evaluation procedures, it was found that the OPTEN model, as an electronic peer tutoring prototype, effectively integrated distance and on-campus tutoring using a CMC medium in which the learning environment for peer engagement promotes equality and mutuality.

The second project at USQ used an interactive teaching and learning model involving desktop video conferencing and other audiographic facilities. This model was trialled at with a group of distance education students, having weekly two-hour sessions, for their second level mathematics unit. It was demonstrated that it was feasible to integrate the systems used, together with applications software, to enable the representation of algebraic, geometric, and numeric concepts, all of which are essential for learning higher level mathematics. These two projects (marriages!) were funded (arranged) under the auspices of the Committee for the Advancement of University Teaching.

The third project was a longitudinal study in Queensland on the use of audiographics conferencing to deliver education and training programmes to geographically dispersed locations. Issues such as time/flexibility, interactivity, difficulty, learning environment and educational/cognitive demands were investigated. The sponsor was the Queensland Open Learning Network, an agency charged with the responsibility of providing education and training to community, business, industry and government organizations. It uses 42 Open Learning Centres scattered throughout the State in its effort to provide Queenslanders, especially those in the remote and distant regions, with efficient and effective open and distance education. As described by Oliver and McLoughlin (1997), in an audiographics environment, teaching and learning are undertaken through telecommunications links between computers and an audio-conferencing medium through which telephone lines link students with their teachers using two-way audio and graphic combinations. A typical setting, as was the case in Queensland, was having a teacher connected to several remote sites with a simulation of a face-to-face environment through the audiographic technology.

It needs to be emphasized that although the case studies described above relate mainly to computer mediated communications, computers have a very central role behind many educational processes (James and Beattie, 1995). For instance, in many parts of the world, all administrative and management roles are integrated through computers. The wedlock between technology and open and distance education extends beyond just the delivery of instruction. Computer technology is used in several other aspects, which include graphic design, print production, audio and video editing and production. The greater use of computers/digitization, which appears to be a sign of things to come in the near future, also extends the integration between the various technologies.

The experiences, skills and knowledge I gained from these projects, as well as others, have taught me some important lessons and confirmed matters which others have also found. They include the following:

- Communication technologies can be used in different ways for different goals. Students can use technology as tools in attaining certain instructional goals. For example, a Web browser can be used by learners to gather information or to organize the myriad of information available at any one time in a course.
- The use of communications technologies responds to the various learning styles of the different students in a course.
- Communications technologies are not used specifically to enhance achievement over and above any other mode, especially the face-to-face mode.
- More than anything else the use of communications technologies, especially in distance and open education, is most useful in engendering social interactions in learning. Experience has shown that the usage of communication technologies, which mirror real life social interactions, are most preferred and indeed most successful.
- The introduction of communication technologies in higher education imposes an additional demand on staff and students. These demands may not have been provided for by the institution and are often regarded by teachers as extra to their normal work. For example, there is a need to shift from the old paradigm of the teacher being the centre of teaching to one of being at the periphery as a facilitator or manager of student learning.
- Institutions need to plan strategically regarding the use of communication technologies. It is often more manageable and taken more seriously if there is an institution-wide policy, and interest in the introduction and use of technology in instruction.
- Above all, the use of technology in education must assume a cognitive perspective aligned closely with the need to understand how learners think and understand concepts.

The ultimate and significant goal of instruction in higher education at a distance is to transform teaching and learning through the systematic innovative application of technology to:

- the way instruction is designed and developed;
- the way and style students learn;
- the way instruction is delivered;
- and the way instruction and learning are assessed.

All this must be done within the contexts of the prevailing environment of the learner. In education, new technological means should be applied functionally and practically to achieve the goal of instruction. The simple rule is: if you do not need it, or if it is not going to make any positive difference: *do not use it*!

The experience from many parts of the world suggests that with minimal capital outlay, simple, appropriate and affordable technology can be used to bring education to distance learners. In 1950s Australia, for example, correspondence schools and Schools of the Air brought schooling and education to isolated and remote families. Outback children received a lot of their schooling in this manner. A number of Australian universities with distance education facilities are addressing the needs of those in special circumstances such as prisons, offshore oil rigs, or Antarctica.

The issue, therefore, is to recognize that pedagogy is more important than technology. Technology, although important, is one of the last things to consider, while pedagogy is among the essential important issues to be examined initially. In this regard and with special consideration to the way and manner students learn, it is necessary that consideration be given in distance higher education to the various cultural borders, which learners must cross, in order to make learning meaningful within their immediate environment. Learners need to cross several cultural borders to make sense of all that distance education brings to their door-steps.

Cultural border crossing and collateral learning

Currently, the use of technology in education is rarely undertaken with a consideration of the learner's views, his or her motivation to learn, or the specific socio-cultural environment that might mediate or inhibit learning. The current push for globalization and the use of communication technologies to extend or erase boundaries has led many universities to participate in global higher education through the exportation of courses they made originally for their local students. In such a situation several cultures intersect to further throw the learner into confusion. There is the culture of the content being learnt and the cultural framework through which it is being presented. Then there is the native culture or the culture of the immediate environment of the learner. Finally, there is the culture of the use of technology and of the particular communications technology chosen to convey instruction to the learner at a distance. In places, such as North America where distributed learning is the preferred type of distance learning in higher education, the students would need to cross other borders still.

Within these interacting cultures, borders must be crossed for learning to occur. I would argue that the incorporation of the learner's ownership of knowledge and the learner's voice is essential for them to construct knowledge. This is to aid in the production of active, reflective and ampliative learners, who not only generate mental models of what they learn, but also control their internal strategies of learning for meaningful learning to occur. There is a need for further research on the mediating influence of cultures and how they affect learning. This paradigm should be examined carefully with a view to applying it to the use of technology in distance and open learning.

Due to the limited success of the conceptual change movement, according to McTaggart (1991), cognitive explanations of the way students cope with learning resulting from border crossing are being sought (Aikenhead and Jegede, 1999;

Jegede, 1995). All learning is mediated by culture and takes place in a social context. The role of the social context is to scaffold the learner, and provide hints and help that foster co-construction of knowledge, while interacting with other members of the society (Linn and Burbules, 1993). Contemporary literature has shown that recognizing the social context of learning as well as the effect of the learner's socio-cultural background on teaching, and learning, is of primary importance; that is, if a strong basic foundation is to be established for successful achievement and affect outcomes (Driver, 1979; Jegede, 1995; Ogawa, 1995; Solomon, 1987). Indeed, the call appears now to be for culture-sensitive education, which probes what actually occurs in the minds and hearts of learners, when they are being taught (Hewson, 1988; Hodson, 1993). The wedlock between open and distance education and technology presents a new and 'strange' culture whose borders must be crossed by students if their learning is to be effective. The learner becomes suspended in a web of interacting culture which must be 'disentangled' for meaningful learning to occur. This is of particular relevance in the present circumstance of changes in learning and teaching strategies that the use of technology brings, and the current growing swell for global higher education economy (Taylor, 1998).

From the viewpoint of cultural anthropology, to learn any subject via the distance education mode and communications technologies is to acquire the culture of that subject (Maddock, 1981) and that of the technology used. To acquire the culture of the subject, learners must travel from their everyday life-world to the world of that subject transmitted through another culture, of the technology medium. Different cultural processes are, therefore, involved in the acquisition of concepts through distance education. The culture being learnt can either be generally in harmony or at odds with a learner's life-world culture. The latter situation forces the need to cross borders because these cultural clashes between learners' life-worlds and the world of distance learning can create hazards for many learners which they must deal with to learn meaningfully. The ideas of cultural border crossing and collateral learning can inform this important mode of education, which is gaining globally acceptance, by offering new insights into the resolution of distance teaching and learning using technology.

Using the idea of cultural border crossing of Giroux (1992), Aikenhead (1997) explains the various scenarios of cultural border crossing. Briefly, border crossing is:

1. smooth when the cultures of learner and the new culture are congruent;
2. manageable when the two are congruent but different;
3. hazardous when the cultures are diverse;
4. and almost impossible when the are highly discordant.

A concept that describes the high risk of failure during cultural border crossing is 'cultural violence', the explicit version of Bourdieu's (1992) tacit 'symbolic violence'. Any of these can result when a distance learner attempts to learn a new culture (content) through an unfamiliar culture (technology). If smooth border crossing does not occur, then all the efforts to employ technology comes to naught.

The cognitive experience of border crossing is captured by the theory of collateral learning (Jegede, 1995). Collateral learning theory explains why many learners experienced culturally related cognitive dissonance in their studies (Jegede, 1995). Collateral learning generally involves two or more conflicting schemata held simultaneously in long-term memory as, for example, the understanding of the use of technology and the learning of a subject matter through the use of the technology. In some of my previous work (Jegede, 1995, 1996, 1997) I discussed variations in the degree to which the conflicting ideas interact with each other, and the degree to which conflicts are resolved. Collateral learning theory postulates a spectrum of cognitive experiences (parallel, simultaneous, dependent, and secured collateral learning) to explain cultural border crossings. These four types of collateral learning are not separate categories, but rather points along a continuum depicting degrees of interaction/resolution. At one extreme, the conflicting schemata do not interact at all, as for example, if the technology being used in distance teaching is inappropriate or incompatible with the student's learning style of personal disposition to the learning event. This is parallel collateral learning, the compartmentalization technique. Learners will access one schema or the other depending upon the context. At the opposite extreme of collateral learning, conflicting schemata consciously interact and the conflict is resolved in some manner. This is secured collateral learning. The person will have developed a satisfactory reason for holding on to both schemata even though the schemata may appear to conflict, or else the person will have achieved a convergence towards commonality by one schema reinforcing the other, resulting in a new conception in long-term memory.

Between these two extremes of parallel and secured collateral learning we find varying degrees and types of interaction between conflicting schemata, and we detect various forms of conflict resolution. In this context it will be convenient to designate points in between the two extremes, one of which is called dependent collateral learning. It occurs when a schema from one worldview or domain of knowledge challenges another schema from a different worldview or domain of knowledge, to an extent that permits the student to modify an existing schema without radically restructuring the existing worldview or domain of knowledge. A characteristic of dependent collateral learning is that students are not usually conscious of the conflicting domains of knowledge, and consequently students are not aware that they move from one domain to another (unlike students who have achieved secured collateral learning).

The other type of collateral learning is simultaneous collateral learning. A unique situation in which learning a concept in one domain of knowledge or culture facilitates the learning of a similar or related concept in another milieu. It does not happen often, but when it does, it is usually co-incidental. For many learners, learning a subject in order to imbibe its culture meaningfully often involves cognitive conflicts of some kind. This involves learning it through the medium of technology. Think of the initial problems people have with getting into the culture of using electronic mail. Now imagine what it will be like for a distance learner using the medium of desk top video in an environment previously dominated by print and correspondence. The learner's culture may also have some characteristics at odds with the use of such a technological medium. Therefore, meaningful learning often results in parallel, dependent, or secured collateral learning. Learners who need to move into the culture of the subject or technology require an effective use of collateral learning, with a heavy reliance on successful cultural border crossings.

The argument and focus in this chapter is for practitioners and learners alike to appreciate that the days of uncharted, off-the-cuff, 'emotional' use of technology in education are fast coming to a close. This signifies the need to allow reason to rise above emotions in the all-important mission of providing for the world, a society whose citizens can use knowledge in new situations. The citizens should also be able to react and function in multi-faceted dimensions, and with a capacity to demonstrate multi-level multi-mediated advanced skills necessary for effective living in the next millennium. The choice of technology and, indeed, the decision to use technology is no more as simple as using it because it is available or the need to be fashionable. It has to have a cognitive and pedagogical base to be of any consequence.

Chapter 5

Managing the introduction of technology in teaching and learning

Sandra Wills and Shirley Alexander

Introduction

Current economic and political climates, together with the need to provide more flexible learning opportunities for students, have placed unprecedented pressure on education to use information and communications technologies (CIT) as an effective means of coping, without decreasing the quality of offerings.

This chapter reviews the introduction of technology in teaching and learning in higher education from the theoretical perspective of the MIT 90s framework developed in Yetton *et al* (1997). It will draw upon case studies of the introduction of technology in teaching and learning in two institutions, and a study of the outcomes of a national initiative to improve the quality of teaching and learning in Australia.

The analytical framework for the chapter is drawn from a collaborative study conducted in 1996/97 by the Universities of Wollongong (New South Wales) and Melbourne. Their research on 20 Australian universities (ie half of the national system) records a substantial shift in the importance of CIT in teaching and administration, and, particularly, in how universities, therefore, position themselves strategically in the market. The consequent report to the Australian Government, *Managing the Introduction of Technology in the Delivery and Administration of Higher Education* (Yetton *et al*, 1997) has been very influential in policy making.

The report highlights five factors in which organizations must exhibit a 'tight fit', for the introduction of technology to be successful: strategy, structure, management processes, roles and skills, and the nature of technology itself. This chapter refers to each of these factors, but places an emphasis on new roles and skills. Considerable emphasis is given to developments within two case studies: the University of Wollongong and the University of Technology, Sydney (UTS).

In a separate study, funded by the Committee for the Advancement of University Teaching (CAUT), a project team reviewed the processes and outcomes of 104 information technology (IT) projects for university learning in 33 universities across Australia (Alexander and McKenzie, 1998). The major finding of this study was that the use of information technology, of itself, does not improve learning. Rather, a range of issues were identified which contribute to the success or otherwise of learning and teaching with technology. Each of these issues is discussed within the framework identified above.

Strategy

Strategies were defined by Wills and Yetton (1997: 20) as 'how one university competes or co-operates with another in order to improve its performance relative to other universities in the higher education sector'.

The interviews with the senior management of the 20 universities in the study revealed five main imperatives for reviewing universities' CIT strategies as a basis for competition through differentiation in the 'market-place':

- the need to improve the quality of teaching;
- the need to reduce costs;
- the need to service new but small multiple campuses;
- the competition for students; and
- the changing profile of the student base.

In their study, Alexander and McKenzie (1998: 34) asked the project leaders of the 104 IT projects surveyed about the outcomes they had intended for students, staff, departments and institutions at the start of the project. Each of the imperatives listed above was also reflected in the responses. Case percentages may total more than 100 per cent, because respondents have given more than one answer to a question.

In both studies, improved quality of learning was highlighted as a reason for using ITs. The intention to increase productivity, efficiency and access to learning noted in Alexander and McKenzie is referred to in Yetton *et al* as cost reduction, servicing small campuses and changing profile of the student base. The increased departmental and institutional recognition noted by Alexander and McKenzie is recognized by Yetton *et al* as competition for students.

Clearly, the rationale for the use of information technologies in education has changed. Five years ago, CIT was viewed by university management as experimental seeding, on the edge of mainstream teaching, and as an expensive, if necessary, administrative resource. Now, the vice-chancellors speak of 'mainstreaming the digital revolution'. For CIT to become mainstream, however, universities will need to put significant resources into staff development to equip staff to undertake the new roles required. The next section discusses this development.

Table 5.1   *Summary of intended outcomes of the project*

Intended outcome for	Students	Staff % of cases	Department % of cases	Institution % of cases
Improved quality of learning/teaching	87.0	34.4	21.3	29.1
Increased productivity/ efficiency and access	39.0	39.8	38.6	30.4
Improve attitudes to learning/motivation	16.0	–	–	–
Professional/staff develeopment	–	29.0	17.8	24.1
Increased profile/ recognition	–	2.2	13.9	31.6

Developing new roles and skills

It is incumbent on those institutions in the 'mainstream' of education increasingly relying on ITs to recognize the need for new roles for both academic and non-academic staff, and to provide staff development opportunities for those staff who will maximize their investment in CIT.

The majority of universities appear to be lagging behind in this area according to Alexander and McKenzie (1998). They noted a range of issues which have prevented staff involved in an IT project from completing a project, or which prevented the project from being as successful as it otherwise may have been.

Analysis of the experiences of academics and students in the Alexander and McKenzie study indicates that the most important qualities of academics who develop information technology projects are no different to those of good teachers more generally. The qualities listed below, from Ramsden *et al* (1995: 24), are qualities that researchers 'generally agree are essential to good teaching at all levels'. They provide the critically important underpinnings in developing CIT projects. These qualities are:

- Good teachers display enthusiasm for their subject, and a desire to share it with their students.
- Good teachers encourage deep learning approaches, rather than surface approaches, and are concerned with developing their students' critical thinking skills, problem-solving skills, and problem-approach behaviours.

- Good teachers recognize the importance of context, and adapt their teaching accordingly; they know how to modify their teaching strategies according to the particular students, subject matter, and learning environment.
- Good teachers demonstrate an ability to transform and extend knowledge, rather than merely transmit it; they draw on their knowledge of their subject, their knowledge of their learners, and their general pedagogical knowledge to transform the concepts of the discipline into terms that are understandable to their students.
- Good teachers are also good learners; for example, they learn through their own reading, by participating in a variety of professional development activities, by listening to their students, by sharing ideas with their colleagues, and by reflecting on classroom interactions and students' achievements.
- Good teachers set clear goals, use valid and appropriate assessment methods, and provide high quality feedback to their students.
- Good teachers show respect for their students; they are interested in both their professional and their personal growth, encourage their independence, and sustain high expectations of them.

In recognition of the critical importance of good teaching practice when using CITs for teaching, Alexander and McKenzie (1998: 257) recommend that 'staff development opportunities be provided in good practice in teaching'.

The second issue relates to projects that require significant software development, and the skills required for successful completion of these. Perusal of the papers from numerous CIT and education conferences indicate the extent to which academics sometimes see their role in development projects as also encompassing graphic designer/ programmer and/or media developer. However, as Alexander and McKenzie's report notes, very few projects which required significant software development were successfully carried through by the lone academic assuming a range of roles from educator, to graphic designer, to programmer, to media producer. The vast majority of such projects, despite being carried out with the best of intentions and enthusiasm, commonly failed because the particular academic simply did not have the time, or the expertise to carry out every role.

Where the introduction of CIT in teaching includes a significant software development, a further set of qualities, in addition to those noted above, is required:

- recognition of new roles (project manager, technical director, teacher);
- understanding of individual roles within a team and team dynamics;
- skills in software development.

Many of the issues/problems highlighted above could have been avoided with adequate project management of software development projects by a skilled project manager. This person would not only ensure that adequate planning and scoping of the project occurred, but would also keep the team working together as a group, while steering it through the planning, development, evaluation and implementation cycles. Thus ensuring that each of these activities is carried out in a professional manner, and recognizing and drawing upon appropriate expertise as required. A further recommendation of Alexander and McKenzie (1998: 257) relates specifically to these issues:

> Staff development opportunities be provided in the areas of project management, working effectively in teams, evaluation of IT projects, and legal issues related to IT development, for current and potential project leaders.

Inadequacies in any of the above qualities commonly resulted in a project's failure to reach completion, or failure to achieve the intended outcomes, and were reflected in projects that:

- were overly ambitious in terms of desired outcomes for the budget and time available (roles and skills);
- commenced software development without adequate planning (roles and skills);
- did not have access to adequate technical advice, expertise and support (skills);
- acted on technical advice provided by people lacking in the necessary knowledge and skills to provide such advice, especially in relation to the selection of hardware and software (skills);
- did not change the assessment of learning to reflect changed learning outcomes (roles and skills);
- did not have access to adequate relevant expertise where projects involved significant software or multimedia development (roles and skills);
- had academic team members who felt they could perform all the technical functions, such as programming, graphic design etc, but were not able to do so (roles and skills);
- had staff on the project team who did not value the different skills required and available for the successful project completion (teamwork and skills);
- had project teams which were unable to resolve differing opinions (teamwork);
- had a project development team that did not include a member with responsibility for project management, and which did not foresee the need for project planning and/or documentation (roles);
- did not adequately prepare students for participation in learning experiences which they had not encountered before, such as working in groups (roles);
- over-estimated students' willingness to engage in higher level learning activities, especially when they were not related to assessment (roles);
- developed a project that was operational on the development computer only, and could not be run on the implementation computers because of inadequate memory, disk space etc, or because of non-existent CD ROM drives (skills);
- conducted evaluation (if at all) only when the project was complete, and discovered that changes were required for which funds were no longer available (roles and skills);
- conducted limited or poor evaluation of the project because of lack of time and/or budget and/or evaluation expertise (roles and skills);
- did not evaluate the project in the anticipated context of use, prior to implementing it (roles and skills).

Case study 1: The University of Wollongong

Examples of the implementation of staff development are seen at the University of Wollongong where the Academic Staff Development Committee established a working party to prepare a report on staff development for flexible delivery (Wills, 1997). Although flexible delivery does not necessarily entail the use of information technology, many of the modern techniques do assume a degree of technological literacy. The working party recognized that staff do not all have the same needs. The following grid was developed, as a thinking-tool to map the varying needs of staff involved in flexible delivery at varying levels.

Table 5.2   *Staff development for flexible delivery*

LEVEL OF USE OF INNOVATION	Finding out about flexible delivery	Planning for flexible delivery	Designing a flexible subject	Teaching flexibly	Managing and evaluating flexible delivery	Supporting flexible delivery
BEGINNERS: aware of innovation but little involvement						
GETTING STARTED: taking the first step						
ON THE JOB: implementing the innovation in their work						
ADVANCED: improving the innovation, demonstrating to others, and being rewarded						

The first column indicates staff level of use of the innovation (Flexible Delivery). The grid is based on the understanding that staff progress through four main levels of use of the innovation, from *Level 1 Beginners* through *Level 2 Getting Started* to *Level 3 On-the-job* to *Level 4 Advanced.* The shaded cells indicate the need for provision of staff development resources for each area.

Table 5.3 *Staff development for flexible delivery*

LEVEL OF USE OF INNOVATION	Finding out about flexible delivery	Planning for flexible delivery	Designing a flexible subject	Teaching flexibly	Managing and evaluating flexible delivery	Supporting flexible delivery
BEGINNERS: aware of innovation but little involvement						
GETTING STARTED: taking the first step						
ON THE JOB: implementing the innovation in their work						
ADVANCED: improving the innovation, demonstrating to others, and being rewarded						

The working party recognized that:

staff development is not only about provision of workshops and seminars but also about provision of information, resources and rewards. Flexible delivery may provide longer term rewards in terms of reducing the burden of time pressures, but it is important that academics who free up that time via innovations in their teaching, do not lose that time by having to take on other teaching commitments. Departments may need to review the way they calculate 'teaching contact hours'. Staff who innovate with alternative modes of delivery should also be rewarded with time release, encouragement to attend flexible delivery conferences and by publicity or other forms of recognition of their achievements in this area. Promotions procedures need to openly take more account of teaching innovations and academics need assistance in preparing Teaching Portfolios which demonstrate their achievements in this area. It also recognized that most staff development must be well-integrated with departmental plans rather than operating in isolation from the funding and support of the innovation.

(Wills, 1997)

Project LEAD

An example of a staff development strategy that goes past the traditional workshop strategy is Project LEAD. Funded in 1998 by a government grant, the University of Wollongong is implementing staff development in the team-based processes that underpin successful introduction of flexible delivery. The need for skills in management, leadership and team building has been highlighted above. Titled Project LEAD (for Leading and Evaluating Advancements in Delivery), it is an example of Action Learning as a staff development strategy. A further example in this chapter is the FLAG project at UTS, described in case study 2 below.

While workshops are only one staff development strategy, they are effective in raising awareness and motivation. One-off withdrawal workshops, in general, do not lead to sustainable change in teaching practices or management practices. Effective staff development programmes are collegial, problem-centred and outcomes-based, supported by the organization, and evaluated (Zuber-Skerritt, 1993a, 1993b; Elliot, 1991; Kemmis and McTaggart, 1988). Action learning programmes have these characteristics and make fertile ground for the proliferation of the learning community (Senge, 1990) within the University. Action learning groups link practice to research, setting new goals for collaborative research and learning (UQ, 1996). A community of reflective practitioners (Schon, 1987) encourages effective and ongoing personal and professional development. The University's staff development units in Project LEAD adopt a facilitator and co-ordinator role rather than a direct training role, a move from staff development to professional development.

The Project LEAD Co-ordinator has provided teams with tools and processes for:

- brief clarification and team cohesion (purposes, outcomes, roles; responsibilities);
- stakeholder analysis (interests, issues, benefits and risks);
- critical reflection for establishing the meaning and value of current practices;
- baseline measures of current practices and measures of change over time;
- information capture and information sharing;
- conceptual mapping;
- systems mapping;
- flowcharting;
- strategic use of communication strategies for team building;
- network-building strategies;
- debriefing and collaborative, strategic reporting as a leverage strategy for systems change.

Four LEAD teams formed themselves to focus on real problems that require real solutions:

- Faculty of Arts: South Coast Curriculum Developers.
- CEDIR Educational Development Team.
- Engineering Physics Curriculum Developers.
- Information Management Team: Flexible Delivery.

The latter team, the first to be formed, was a multi-functional group representing information management processes that constitute the design, development, production and delivery infrastructure for flexible learning environments. This team included representatives from:

- the Library;
- Interactive Media Production;
- Educational Development;
- the Academic Registrar;
- the Secretariat;
- Print and Distribution;
- Desktop Publishing;
- Administrative Information Services;
- Client Services;
- Infrastructure.

They achieved their initial goal 'development of a system for information capture and information sharing' within the very short span of four months. One of the factors critical to the success of this team is now seen to be the evolving role of the Team Facilitator, taken on by one of the team members, under the guidance of the Project LEAD Co-ordinator. This came about in order to ensure planning was taken forward into actionable steps, which could then be evaluated and if necessary reshaped.

Comments from members of this team included:

In hindsight I would admit that I had always been a supporter of the cross-functional team model to open up dialogue and implement change, but until Project LEAD, I had never had the opportunity to develop the necessary new skills and experience the cycle of personal development required to bring these goals to fruition. The staff development opportunity and experience for me was one which I doubt will ever be repeated in such an effective and satisfying manner and one which I will draw upon for a long time to come.

(Curtis, 1998b, Appendix 16)

We are not a committee – we get things done!

(Curtis, 1998a: 6)

If someone had asked me what we had achieved, I'd have said not much. But looking at the change in weightings, I can see that there has been an enormous change. We have re-positioned ourselves in light of not having clear direction and created our own.

(Curtis, 1998a: 6)

This team has been redefining the way the university will work in the future – the model is spreading because people don't have time to waste.

(Curtis, 1998b: 4)

The Project LEAD Co-ordinator in her Interim Report contends:

> There have been a range of benefits to the University from the work of this
> team that go beyond their impact on more effective systems, structures and
> processes for information management. Amongst these has been the building
> of strong and productive boundary-spanning networks, the development of
> satisfying and mutually beneficial social relations both within and across
> function areas and the building of intangible assets. While these assets will not
> appear in any institutional profit and loss balance sheets, they are the very as-
> sets that the university requires to assure its location in a higher education
> market-place which demands high quality and flexible teaching/learning en-
> vironments.
>
> (Curtis, 1998a: 11)

Pathways

As noted above, academics developing educational multimedia and subjects online
are usually not experienced project managers, and lack understanding of the overall
development process. Impart (1999), a government-funded Co-operative Multimedia Centre in which the University of Wollongong is a shareholder, has collaborated with Griffith University, Central Queensland University and New Media
Corporation to produce a development methodology, parts of which are freely
available on the Web as a staff development resource.

Virtual teacher training

If there is to be a paradigm shift in the way educational institutions deliver education, there will need to be a paradigm shift in staff development – not just personal
but also organizational. Delivery should be anywhere, anytime. Staff should be able
to put themselves into the learner's shoes and actively experience the learning environments that are advocated for their students. In order to mainstream these experiences for students, they need to be mainstreamed for staff professional
development. Only when staff are comfortable with using a variety of delivery
methods will they be able to incorporate them successfully in their own teaching.

Virtual resources

In 1995 the government provided to the PAGE consortium of distance education
universities funds for workshops for academic and general staff about designing and
delivering education at a distance. PAGE is a consortium of eight universities in
Australia and New Zealand collaborating to deliver Professional And Graduate Education (PAGE), at a distance. Originally using television, video and print as the
main delivery vehicles, PAGE providers are increasingly moving to the Internet and
CD ROM. It was recognized that the future success of the consortium, in bringing
distance subjects to the market, was largely dependent on quality training for uni-

versity staff, who in the main, have had little experience of distance education for their students' learning, nor for their own learning. Funds were also provided to build resources so that staff could learn at their 'own time and their own place'. Impart CMC, University of Wollongong, and Central Queensland University collaborated on the development.

The team decided to construct a hybrid CD: the resources were compiled in the Web format and pressed onto CD ROM. The advantages include:

- multiplatform delivery;
- speed of video and audio as the resources are being accessed from CD ROM rather than across the Internet;
- capability to easily update and expand the information by providing external links from the CD ROM to real Web sites;
- a familiar navigation interface ie the Web browser (Wills *et al*, 1997).

In addition to standardizing the Web navigation and frames, the team designed a graphical user interface to humanize the interaction with the resources. Beginning with a typical scenario in the Dean's Office (the mission assigned), the academic finds out what they need to know about distance education by setting up meetings with the:

- Education Consultant;
- Librarian;
- Enrolments and Enquiries Officer;
- PAGE Liaison person;
- Media Services Manager.

In addition, chatting with a colleague in the Staff Club.

Virtual-conferences

Universities in the National Council on Open and Distance Education (NCODE), recently collaborated to develop a Web site about Resource Based Learning, a project which was funded by the Committee for University Teaching and Staff Development (NCODE, 1998). Like the PAGE collaboration described above, its first objective is the provision of information. However, it has a second objective (in Stage 2) to provide opportunities for academics (the 'learners') to communicate and discuss at a distance the issues raised by the information in the Web site. A series of Virtual Staff Development Workshops are being run nationally to enable academics to experience distance learning, at first hand, using computer-mediated communication and collaboration, with the Web site as the focus. The first online workshop was aimed at staff developers themselves adopting a train-the-trainers approach. It was a combined onsite and virtual workshop – around 15 staff developers attending a national meeting in Darwin plus another 18 participating from their desktops around Australia – working as one virtual class. The themes were negotiated asynchronously online in the week leading up to the synchronous three-hour event. Nine people indicated they had never participated in an online discussion forum before. Some support was provided to these people, but the evaluation of the event indicated that more needed to be done in this respect.

What else was learnt from this experience? It was not completely satisfying for all the participants. Many commented that it was valuable 'to be put in their students shoes as participants of the forum' (Gilbert, 1998: 2). However, onsite participants became more interested in talking with each other and left the offsite participants hanging in virtual space waiting for some sign of activity. And not all offsite participants, who had registered in the week leading up to the event, actually participated on the day – something else more urgent took over their desktop. We do not have the discipline; yet, it seems, to set aside the time for our own professional development. It is a contradiction, but we still seem to find it easier to pack our bags, endure long flights, risk foreign food and unfamiliar beds, for days away, in order to attend an event face to face, rather than discipline ourselves to keep our computer desktop free for an afternoon to participate, at a distance, in a virtual event. It was recommended that in future 'The two aspects of the workshop could be viewed as supporting each other with the virtual taking place either prior to or after the face-to-face workshop. The two groups could "meet" online for a shorter period (1 hour) of synchronous communication on the specified day' (Gilbert, 1998: 2).

A similar story emerged at Teleteaching '96, an international conference attracting about 100 delegates to Canberra plus 100 online via video-conference or the Internet, depending on the event. Onsite participants in particular were very uncomfortable with the format. In the interests of practising what is preached as Teleteachers, the traditional conference format of papers delivered in half-hour parallel sessions was discarded, and seven half day interactive events were held in an Internet Café set up at the Convention Centre. To accommodate the participation of Australian teachers after school and international sites across numerous time zones, the video-conferences were held in the evenings, however, onsite delegates chose not to attend, because understandably, they preferred to go out to dinner and socialize. In reverse, the virtual-conference's social event failed to get onsite delegates rocking and dancing because it was held at 10.00 am in the morning and served coffee rather than the alcohol which normally helps make social events swing (Lefoe *et al*, 1996).

Everything in the Land Downunder was turned upside down and participants had no familiar formula to fall back on. We have a lot to learn yet about how to make virtual spaces effective. That is not to say all physical spaces are always effective – the traditional mode of delivery in universities and conferences is not very effective yet we stick with it because its familiar and everyone's role is well defined over centuries of use. Virtual spaces need the same sort of refining and polishing, and we as teachers, must certainly put *ourselves* in the learners' shoes *before* we inflict these new developments on our students.

Case study 2: The University of Technology, Sydney

Flexible Learning Action Groups (FLAG)

At the University of Technology, Sydney, 'Flexible Learning' was nominated as a strategic initiative. A decision was made to provide resources to six cross-university action groups, each of which was required to use the resources in a way which would benefit the university as a whole rather than benefit individual projects.

One of the six groups (comprised of academics from across the University) was asked to focus on the role of the Internet in flexible learning and the members (about 20 initially, but now around 60) selected three projects:

1. an investigation of the feasibility of and selection of, one Computer-Mediated Communication (CMC) tool for use across the university;
2. the feasibility of conducting online assessment;
3. and three pilot projects in each of these areas.

Members of the group took a keen interest in the first pilot project, and were kept informed of the successes and areas for improvement in the design of online learning in general, and the use of TopClass, in particular.

The critical outcomes of this group have been in the areas of contributions to policy and the rapid uptake of CMC in teaching across the University. In the area of policy, the recommendations of the group in the selection of a particular tool, the need for centralized hardware, software and support were accepted and put in place. The use of CMC as an integral part of teaching has risen from five subjects in 1996 to over 180 subjects in 1999.

A recent external evaluation of the group's activities (Moran, 1998) confirmed the important role the FLAG Group had played in raising awareness about the potential of online learning amongst academics across the university. It did this by promoting dissemination of good practice in the design of online learning, fostering inter-disciplinary collaboration and links within the University; and as a critical peer-support group for the 'early adopters'.

Alongside the range of strategies for the use of CIT in universities, and the development of new roles and skills are the all-important structures, which support the development and use of CIT in teaching and learning. Two examples of such structures are highlighted in the next section.

Structure

As identified by Alexander and McKenzie (1998), academics need access to adequate technical expertise, access to resources, as well as learning, teaching and evaluation expertise. This section will review the structures established within universities to respond to these needs.

Yetton *et al* (1997: 102) analyze approaches to the organization and management of CIT activities using a continuum: from a centralized model – to complete decentralization of control. They report that 'older universities have been shaped by a professional bureaucratic model, in which considerable operating autonomy has typically been devolved to faculties, departments and individual academics'. The newer universities, the authors claim, are characterized by more centralized bureaucratic structures. The major difference is said to be in the extent to which decision-making and budgeting is devolved. Further, the authors reported a trend to combine CIT services, library, multimedia production and staff development.

Case studies

At the University of Technology, Sydney two separate but complementary structures exist to provide the range of expertise required for the successful development of CIT projects. The Institute for Interactive Multimedia (IIM) provides support and advice on pedagogical approaches to teaching with communications and information technology, and the technological and project management expertise required for significant educational software development. Alongside IIM is the Centre for Learning and Teaching (CLT), which provides academic staff development in the areas of learning theories, assessment and evaluation. While this structure would be seen by Yetton *et al* (1997) as an example of a 'bureaucratic' structure, it is important to note that much of the decision making does, in fact, occur within a framework that is devolved. As noted earlier, the FLAG group on Internet use was the catalyst for the large-scale adoption of a Computer-Mediated Conferencing tool within the institution, and put forward recommendations (that were accepted and implemented) for funding for hardware, software and personnel. The role of IIM then, is essentially to implement the recommendations of this group, rather than determining the policy.

At the University of Wollongong, these two structures, originally separate, are now amalgamated in the Centre for Educational Development and Interactive Resources (CEDIR). CEDIR assists and develops university teachers to enhance the quality of education for students. Within the amalgamated unit, 'flexible delivery' is then positioned as just one of the priority areas for educational development, hopefully avoiding the danger that it will be viewed only as a 'technology' issue and in isolation from educational issues. Should subject flexibility entail development of educational materials, a structure like CEDIR's can provide a close coupling of staff development, needs analysis, design, and evaluation with technical production services. A key to the effective functioning of amalgamated units is the ability of multi-skilled staff to act as an interface between university teachers and technical production staff. CEDIR's educational developers each work closely with one Faculty usually via Faculty Education Committees.

The two case studies presented here, while clearly structured on a centralized model, also contain elements of a more devolved approach to the determination of both policies, and of budget priorities.

Management processes

The final piece in the jigsaw described in this chapter is the range of management processes necessary for managing the introduction of technology in teaching and learning. These include support for staff undertaking projects, time release for those staff, facilitating collaboration in projects, evaluation of project outcomes, and undertaking cost-benefit analyses.

The importance of providing support for staff undertaking CIT projects was noted by Alexander and McKenzie's study in which the lack of support from management was cited by almost 15 per cent of cases. The report notes the disappointingly high number of Heads of Department who felt that the project leader would have been better off devoting the time spent on the CIT project to research. As long as this view prevails, there is little incentive for academics to use CIT in teaching.

Time release

The second issue of providing adequate time release for academics undertaking CIT projects was also noted in the study:

> Comments about lack of time and teaching release appeared consistently in response to a range of questions... almost half of the project leaders reported time problems as a factor which hindered the project's development, and the most common piece of advice offered to new grantees was to 'be realistic about the time commitment and seek adequate teaching release'.
>
> (Alexander and McKenzie, 1998: 242)

Collaboration

While some CIT projects are developed by a single or small group of academics, the majority of successful projects appear to be collaborative. The ranges of the collaborations highlighted in the report include the following examples.

Collaboration between academics and private enterprise

An example of this collaboration was the development of the Japanese language learning project 'Kantaro', in which Fujitsu Australia Limited provided the technical expertise required for completion and extension of the project. This collaboration, as well as providing a boost in funding, allowed the academics involved to focus their involvement in the project on what they do best – determining and providing the content, as well as advising on particular learning activities which they know will promote high quality learning. Fujitsu Australia Limited managed the technical aspects of the project, handled copyright and intellectual property issues, packaging, as well as the marketing and distribution of the three CD ROMS produced (Alexander and McKenzie, 1998: 125–33).

Collaboration between academics at different institutions

One example of this collaboration is the development of a multimedia 'playground' by two academics, who were teaching statistics at different institutions – The University of Melbourne and La Trobe University. The project originated when the two academics realized they had surprisingly parallel views about the problems of teaching statistics, and about the ways in which it might be improved. They successfully applied for a series of grants and together developed the project that has become StatPlay. The collaboration was one in which they continually talked through ideas, options and strategies, offering different views but deciding together on a particular course of action. The outcome of this project has been the widespread adoption of the project outcome (StatPlay) at both institutions and more recently, since earlier copyright and intellectual property issues have been resolved, to the wider community (Alexander and McKenzie, 1998: 83–96).

A second example of collaboration between different institutions is an Internet-based political simulation of Middle-East politics. This project was only made possible through the collaboration of a Political Science academic and a Computer Science academic who, through serendipity, met when they were both working at the same institution (the University of Melbourne). When the Computer Science academic heard about his colleague's attempts to run an international simulation using faxes, he saw the potential of e-mail and the World Wide Web to enhance the simulation. Together, they were successful in gaining two grants to develop the software for the project, and despite the fact that they subsequently moved to different institutions in another state, the project continued. The outcome of this collaboration has been the development of a very successful and qualitatively different learning experience for students, one which was made possible by the complementary nature of the input of each academic (Alexander and McKenzie, 1998: 67–82).

Collaboration between academic development units at different institutions

The PAGE CD ROM described earlier in this chapter is an example of collaboration between staff development units. Central Queensland University, with its long experience as a distance education provider, had a number of existing staff development resources in print. The University of Wollongong, coming into distance education in more recent technological times, had a number of existing staff development resources, mainly in video. The two content providers collaborated to convert those resources to a digital medium using the multimedia design and production facilities at the University of Wollongong. Staff development is a task of such magnitude that the need for collaboration on developing resources is important. Mobility of academics means that any university that does expend funds on the development of their staff loses that investment in the learning curve to other universities, unless the investment is shared via collaboration. The development of student resources for generic skills, such as information literacy, statistical literacy, communication, career development etc is a task of similar magnitude. It is one that is best tackled by collaboration, for example, the UniLearning (1999) Web site under development by the University of Western Sydney, the University of Melbourne and the University of Wollongong.

Evaluation studies

Finally, the report highlighted the paucity of evaluation studies to determine the degree to which the original project intentions were realized. While in some cases the absence of evaluation data was reported by project leaders as being due to insufficient time and/or budget to undertake the study, in others project leaders reported a lack of access to evaluation expertise.

Of those who did conduct an evaluation, the study team noted the narrow range of evaluation methods used. There was a heavy reliance on student reaction surveys, and in some cases there is an apparent confusion between student reactions and student learning. While student reaction surveys are a useful component of any evaluation, they should not be the only component.

Evaluation needs to be part of all stages of the development and use of CIT. This evaluation needs to be informed by the rigorous models already developed, for example, by Kirkpatrick (1994) and Alexander and Hedberg (1994). It should involve academics in:

- developing their awareness of what is already known about effective evaluation of innovations;
- thoughtfully choosing evaluation methods to collect valid evidence at different stages of the project and for different purposes;
- critically analysing and synthesizing the evidence they have collected;
- using evaluation findings to inform ongoing changes to the innovation;
- and communicating about the innovation and its effectiveness to the academic community and the broader society.

This section has highlighted the importance of providing adequate time release for academics undertaking CIT projects, the benefits of a range of collaborations and the need to encourage a climate of thorough evaluation of projects. Other important management processes include establishing quality assurance procedures involving peer review of teaching materials, resolving intellectual property issues, and providing meaningful reward and recognition, for those undertaking the challenges of introducing technology in university teaching.

Conclusions

The outcomes of a 1998 national survey of academics leading IT-based teaching projects reinforce the outcomes of a 1997 national survey of management introducing technology in the delivery of education. Technology in itself does not change or improve teaching and learning. Attention to management processes, strategy, structure, and most importantly roles and skills, are the key to successfully introducing technology in university teaching and learning.

Chapter 6

Changing media, changing times: coping with adopting new educational technologies

Robert Fox and Allan Herrmann

Introduction

Universities are being urged to adopt new technologies to meet increasing demands on limited funds and to increase efficiencies in the teaching and learning process. These pressures to adopt the new technologies can be identified in the rhetorics found within such government-initiated reports as Dearing (1997) in the UK and West (1998) in Australia. Conventional media, such as print, telephone, audio and video are still the most popular in open and distance education settings. However, the growth of the Web and the dynamic potential of online teaching and learning are stimulating some staff to find new ways to engage their students in the learning process (DeLong, 1997). Digital media and especially the new communication and information technologies are creating new challenges for open and distance educators and their students.

Many teachers, however, are reluctant to take up the challenge to use the new online media. Some have deep-rooted concerns about changes in work practices, and others see the huge gap between the rhetoric surrounding technology and the realities of educational settings, while others boldly embrace new media with seemingly little critical pedagogical concern.

This chapter is based on 40 accounts of teachers' experiences of changing to teaching online. Six have been selected to inform the development of a framework to identify certain constructions of, and attitudes towards, online technologies in educational settings. Our aim is to stimulate debate on various constructions of technology and education and to help teaching staff and educational developers become aware of broad stances to technology adoption. By stances, we mean ways of thinking about the use of online technology in higher education. We want teachers to review various stances and to identify their allegiances to a particular stance or stances. Then by exploring why they identify with particular stances, we propose they become more aware, more critical users of technology. We want to provide educational developers, who take on a staff development role to help teachers design and develop learning resources and learning environments with a framework and a strategy to help teachers adopt the use of educational technology, in pedagogically appropriate ways.

Technology debates

The debates surrounding educational technologies and their roles in higher education are many and varied. Some concentrate on instructional technology and institutional change (Geoghegan, 1996; Bates, 1997a; Bates, 1997b). Some centre on discussing a binary divide between 'technophobes' and 'technophiles' and 'technological utopianism and anti-utopianism' (Winner, 1977). Other researchers point to the limitations of such discussions (Campion, 1991; Kling, 1996; DEETYA, 1997; Bigum and Kenway, 1998), the need for broader debate on various technological practices (Young, 1998) and stances (Bruce, 1997), and the flawed construction of 'technology' and 'higher education' as separate, distinct realms (Bruce, 1997; Law, 1998). This view of technology as autonomous or separate is what Latour (1991: 103) called the 'technology/society divide', where we perceive technology as being somehow 'out there', rather than an integral part of our way of thinking and doing. As Franklin puts it:

> It [technology] includes activities as well as a body of knowledge, structures as well as the act of structuring. Our language itself is poorly suited to describe the complexity of technological interactions. The interconnectedness of many of those processes, the fact that they are so complexly interrelated, defies our normal push-me-pull-you, cause-and-consequence metaphors. How does one speak about something that is both fish and water, means as well as end?
>
> (1990: 14–15)

We have drawn on these debates and definitions to inform our research in selecting and analysing these case accounts of university teachers changing to online approaches to their teaching.

Methodology and rationale

The general orientation of this research is within the qualitative, interpretative and critical domains. The empirical work undertaken was investigated through a case study approach. We readily acknowledge certain limitations to this approach. As Guba and Lincoln (1981) point out, case study does not lend itself to producing generalizations. However, we have taken as valid the notion of 'naturalistic generalisms', as described by Stake (1978: 5–8).

Case accounts are used to exemplify a range of online technology users and their attitudes towards the use of online approaches in two universities in Australia. Staff who took part in this study were asked to reflect on their experiences of using online approaches teaching. In addition to the interviews with both experienced and novice users, the authors collected data through e-mail and reviews of various online sites. From these cases, a number of archetypal stances were identified. In each case account selected individual teachers have expressed strong and varied views about the use of online technologies in teaching and learning.

Case accounts

Each case account outlined below tells a different story. In describing the various accounts, individuals provide insights into their attitudes to the use of technology in general, but in teaching and learning in particular. The accounts offer an approach to viewing technology, which impacts on how the individual will use technology in her or his teaching and learning contexts. Through studying these case accounts these consistencies were identified and grouped. These groups (five in all) we have called stances to reflect the fact that they are an 'outsider's' view and not a label agreed upon or accepted by the individual.

In the first case account, Paul is opposed to the inclusion of technology, while in the second account, Jennifer sees technology primarily as an efficiency tool, and as a way to improve communication with her students. In the third account, Jill, though sceptical of the rhetorical claims made about technology, is prepared to test various possibilities as long as they are not too disruptive to her work. In the fourth account, John sees the technology, as meeting his educational needs, but also realizes that it has the potential to change aspects of teaching and learning. In the fifth account, Keith indicates he understands that the technology transforms the teaching and learning environment and the content of his course. He is willing to rethink the curriculum of his course to include the work practices that the technology privileges make available. In the final account, Neil considers that new technology is the catalyst for, and a means of, changing the structure of his school quite radically to make significant cost savings and produce a variety of efficiencies.

Each case is unique with regard to issues and contexts. Nevertheless, the various ways of examining the use of technology as presented, reflect common themes that we have encountered as educational developers. We contend that these can be used to typify certain attitudes towards using online technologies.

Case account one

Paul was uninterested in using online technologies in his teaching. He used e-mail routinely to communicate with his colleagues, but he had no experience of using online communication with his students. His school, however, had developed an action plan for online teaching and his head of school had required all unit co-ordinators to place their unit (course) outline and study materials on the Web, linked to the school's home page. The school provided a standardized 'shell' which included computer conferencing between staff and students. Paul explained that he was strongly opposed to such action: 'I can't see the point of this... It's just a waste of money, resources and my time'.

Paul irregularly visited the site while his online component was trialled. He did not take part in the embryonic computer conferencing as he felt it provided a false sense of what 'real human communication' was all about. Students quickly realized that he was not interested in the site and they stopped using it. Paul described the site as:

> An electronic page turner, allowing students to print off a copy of the study materials; if they've lost their original copy. That's all it's good for. The important interactions between the students and myself are face-to-face... and with distance students... over the phone and in written correspondence... I can't see the value of substituting the real thing with this virtual thing. There's more to learning than just supplying information, there must be structure and guidance.

Paul's view is that the pressure to put all the course materials on the Web derives from a marketing initiative for potential students and to show competitors that 'we are keeping up with them', rather than from a desire to improve teaching and learning. Paul is happy to use his 'tried and proven' methods of teaching, along with print-based resources, but has little interest in 'learning through a machine'. He sees his own resistance as being educationally responsible, and his head of school's advocacy as irresponsible. Paul asserts that the dynamics of real classroom interaction is fundamental to genuine learning, and the extension and retention of ideas.

The key issue Paul raises reflects his concern that technology dehumanizes and reduces complex teaching and learning processes to simple mechanical processes. He also questions any real educational 'value-adding' by the use of technology in this context. He is also suspicious that this move to use technology is a management tactic to reduce the number of staff.

Case account two

Jennifer teaches a course in applied science. In previous years, she developed a print-based unit, which was received very positively by her students. She recently converted her print materials for use on the Web and has retained the same or very similar activities. She did this with the expectation that students would use the information in the same way they would if it were presented on paper. This she found was indeed the case:

> It has provided students with better and, for some, easier access to the study materials. Students who use the site seem to be working the same as before (and)… the quality of their assignments seems the same… .

She feels that the transfer to the Web has been a worthwhile task:

> I think the communications are better though. Whereas before I'd spend my time on the phone… often missing a student query… now students e-mail me and I always get their message.

Jennifer sees the technology very much as an efficiency tool: 'It's a convenience improvement too. I can answer e-mail messages when I want rather than having to answer phone calls all the time.'

Following a semester trial of the online component, Jennifer spoke of her experiences. She indicated she had started to discover some new options available to her.

> I'm often asked the same questions and have to reply 4–5 times with the same answer. If I put the answers to those questions… [on the electronic notice board]… I could save some time… and provide students with answers they're looking for when they need them.

Recently, Jennifer decided to open a discussion room online to enable her, not only to post answers to frequently asked questions, but to provide an opportunity to encourage her students to share their concerns and experiences, rather than individually sending all their messages by e-mail to the tutor. Jennifer believes that the online discussion room 'will replace the multiple e-mails that go just from one student to me and back… some of the things we talk about should be shared with all students'.

This case account exemplifies the possibility of the teachers' experiences altering their stance towards online technology. Initially, Jennifer approached the use of technology as a support for her teaching, as a convenience tool. She discovered that the Web made it easier to deliver the course learning resources. Jennifer felt that the technology itself would have no influence on her student learning, on the course content or the structure the course. Her experience, however, now leads Jennifer to believe that indeed there may be changes occurring in her course and that she needs to take account of how the technology is providing different opportunities for her students' learning and her teaching. Jennifer has changed her stance from seeing technology as a neutral convenience tool to acknowledging that it can significantly change the content and process of her course.

Case account three

Jill teaches an undergraduate distance course in a humanities subject. Her school has provided funding and resources to staff interested in developing online courses.

However, Jill is not convinced that online learning is as good as it is 'cracked up to be'.

> I've attended a short course conducted entirely online. I can't say I didn't learn anything, but I can say I think I'd have learnt the same, better... [and] quicker by attending a real class.

As a teacher, Jill is sceptical about the value of teaching online and she points to the gap between the 'hype' surrounding technology and the reality of using it for teaching and learning.

> There's a lot of talk about the advantages of teaching through the Internet... we can always make lists for anything, saying great things... but in weighing everything up... the costs, the maintenance requirements... the time it takes to develop worthwhile environments, the technical support we need as teachers and the access problems our students face... is it really worthwhile?

Jill speaks from her own experience of developing online materials. Despite her scepticism, she accepted funding and experimented with an online component to complement her print-based unit. It took time and effort to transfer and transform her materials for use online. She needed significant technical support and invested a considerable amount of her own time in developing the electronic component. She pointed out that her on-campus students required convincing that learning online was better, or at least as good as the classroom. Off-campus students experienced some technical problems and only half had access to the Web. Jill commented:

> Students were enthusiastic, once they got using it, though this could be the novelty of using the technology. I think we've got a long way to go before it's really useful. We're really busy and the idea of adding another technology to the string we've already got may not be worthwhile... [but] I'm prepared to give it a go, as long as I get extra help and money to do so.

This account highlights Jill's caution in using online teaching and, as an experienced teacher, she does not want to become reliant on it. She has previously experienced 'novelty technologies' which resulted in much effort for little reward. Jill is sceptical about the long-term cost-benefits and whether any improvements to student learning will occur.

Case account four

John is a course co-ordinator for a large first year programme with over 2,000 enrolments each year. The course is offered across three separate campuses and also at a distance.

> In reviewing our educational objectives, we decided to use the online facility, primarily for its conferencing capability, as collaborative work is of central importance to our students... that's how they'll be working in the real world. Students learn not only the course content but also how to access it and collaborate with fellow students through the technology... I'd like to make the

technology transparent… What is important is finding a way to meet our educational needs – the computer conferencing system fitted the bill… .

John is aware that new technology has the potential to affect changes in the content and the curriculum, but:

> There's been a deliberate attempt to minimize any changes to the curriculum… those lecturers who were used to face-to-face teaching environments would have less changes to contend with… the content remains the same, but the technology to deliver the programmes has changed… It's better to get people (the lecturers) used to the online environment first, before you start to experiment with doing things too differently.

In this account, John's view of online teaching is as primarily a labour saving, new tool for teaching and learning. However, he acknowledges the potential of online approaches to change the curriculum, teaching and learning, but he is not prepared to explore this full potential until all staff are 'online friendly'. In this sense, John holds several stances towards online technology. The first is one that sees online means as providing greater efficiency. The second stance concerns his belief in the transformative potential of online educational technology.

Case account five

Keith co-ordinates a postgraduate Masters course. The course team transferred the primarily print-based distance course to the Web.

> The units that make up this course can be entirely studied via the Web. Our on-campus, distance and overseas students can select to study this course… through the Web.

Transferring the Masters course into a Web-based environment provided the course team with an opportunity to rethink and even reinvent course content and how they wanted students and tutors to use it.

> We spent a lot of time in meetings examining new ideas, different structures to the course and reviewing the possibilities within the online environment… [both] conceptual and technical… The Web's ability to hyper-link disparate ideas and themes made us rethink our learning strategy too… rather than adopt an objectives model, we decided to use a more constructivist approach to structuring the course.

So, students are encouraged to work through various concepts and themes, based on activities they have been set. There is no prescribed way to work through the course; students need to complete tasks set in each of the units. The Web-based programmes have incorporated a number of interactive components.

> We've been able to incorporate new kinds of activities… a development on the old print-based in-text activities. We have an ability to provide immediate responses to student work here. These range from simple exercises to complet-

ing forms and conducting tests as well as requesting electronic copies of readings direct from the library.

Another planned component of this course is asynchronous conferencing for staff and students 'whether the students are studying on or off-campus or indeed, overseas'.

> We have also developed virtual reality field trips, which enable students to select particular tools and equipment and then use these to measure or record their findings in the virtual field.

The course also provides annotated notes and 'hot links' to significant sites. An online study skills component has been added. This offers students assistance with thinking about and using online research strategies as well as using various search engines. Basic technical support and answers to recurring questions provide a first line maintenance facility. The library is linked to the course site, enabling students to request electronically additional readings and to request library loans.

The use of the Web, in this example, has changed the course both in content and in the way it is taught. Keith has redesigned the course, taking into account new ways of working and thinking using online technology. In this sense, his stance can be described primarily as transformative: the technology is seen as transforming or changing the content and teaching and learning processes.

Case account six

Neil is a head of school whose vision for the school incorporates significant changes. He has adopted online technologies to help introduce 'major structural changes and new work practices'. As Neil explains '[now] we are highly productive, highly focused and we deal with our students in increasingly efficient ways'.

Within the last three years, his school has 'radically changed [the] staffing profile, in fact, we're running on two thirds of the [teaching] staff we had... teaching loads are lighter and we've got a lot of time for people to do research'. The school is working on transferring the entire school curriculum onto the Web, providing students, not only with the course and unit outlines, but all lecture notes and slides, 'handouts' and activities for completion prior to attending a reduced number of lectures and laboratory sessions. Students now do many of the laboratory preparations and practice activities, such as working with instruments in a 'virtual lab environment', on the Web. Students are given access to well-equipped computer laboratories to use either individually or in small groups. Open, distance and overseas students, are expected to have access to fast modems and powerful computers if they wish to participate in the school's programmes.

Although each unit has an online discussion facility for asynchronous interaction, we noted that no discussion had taken place. 'We've had to concentrate on getting things up', says Neil, 'and we've not seen this [discussion facility] as important... but we're always looking to find ways of doing things better and more efficiently'. Neil is open to suggestions and in general is keen to receive feedback on the school's whole-hearted use of online technology.

Neil has taken a very proactive stance to the introduction of online technology. He sees online ways of teaching and learning replacing both classroom teaching and also print-based distance teaching. Neil views online technology as providing the catalyst for solutions required in his school. Teaching staff would become facilitators, thereby releasing them to spend more time on research.

Stances framework

The above case accounts illustrate varied practices and different ways of thinking about the use of online technology in teaching and learning contexts. Based on our experiences as educational and staff developers we have drawn on these accounts to create a framework of archetypal stances. This framework draws primarily from Bruce (1997: 290–91) who outlined six stances to conceptualize ways of thinking about Internet technology in literacy education. These stances are: Neutrality, Opposition, Utilitarian, Sceptical, Transformational and Aesthetic. We have adopted and refined four of Bruce's stances and added one of our own to describe the people that we identified previously who adopt the archetypal ways of thinking about online technology in higher education. These are: neutralitarians, boosters (for example, Bigum and Kenway (1998)), oppositionals, sceptics and transformationalists. The people and their stances outlined below are not derived directly from the particular case accounts above. The reader may identify links between stances and the cases. It is important to note that these categories are not mutually exclusive, or sequentially ordered; rather they are archetypes around and through which many grey areas exist.

Neutralitarians view technology as being an unproblematic tool and, therefore, they do not think specifically about it. Neutralitarians accept various technological applications as being a means of introducing efficiencies, rather than a phenomenon that has the potential to change content and curriculum. 'It allows you to do the same things that you did before, but in a more convenient and more direct way.' (See http://tenb.mta.ca/phenom/phenom.html for nearly 250 research articles concerning the 'No Significant Difference' phenomenon.)

Boosters view the new and emergent electronic technologies, as being our 'salvation and our solace in a time of crisis and change' (Bigum and Green, 1993: 5). Their stance values technology as all powerful, efficiency as the primary goal of human labour, and technical calculation is superior to human judgement. Hence, educational technology unquestionably has the capacity to improve education. Boosters always look for the next wave of technological innovation to solve their problems.

Those who take an **oppositional** stance display a resistance to the use of new technology. They argue that new educational technologies reject human values, reducing the complex educational process to a simple mechanistic one. Technology is seen as replacing teachers with machines.

Unlike Oppositionals, **Sceptics** do not see any great dangers in technology itself, but rather in the 'hyperbolic rhetoric' surrounding new educational technologies. Sceptics cite the huge gap between rhetoric and reality, which sometimes deludes 'researchers, policy makers and informed practitioners', to believe in new technological means 'superiority as a teaching tool' (Cuban, 1986: 14). Sceptics acknowledge the potential usefulness of technology, but are hesitant about engaging new technologies unless they can see confirmed advantages in doing so.

A **Transformationalist** accepts that new technologies are replacing or transforming teaching and learning environments in terms of curriculum and pedagogy. The Transformationalist sees the end result of this transformation as essentially positive, 'though the process itself is not without difficulties along the way' (Bruce, 1997: 291). Transformationalists see their task as discovering, understanding and guiding this transformation. Figure 6.1 summarizes our arguments above.

Stances

Neutralitarian   Online approaches make no significant difference to learning or curriculum. Online teaching is a tool that can improve efficiency.

Boosters   The new online approaches will improve learning and make education more effective and efficient. New developments in educational technology are inherently good and non-problematic. New technologies offer solutions to many teaching and learning problems.

Oppositional   Technology over-simplifies complex teaching and learning processes and practices. The danger is that ultimately, machines will take the place of teachers.

Sceptic   There is a significant gap between the rhetoric and reality of online practices. Sceptics are hesitant to use technology unless the advantages in so doing are obvious.

Transformationalist   Online approaches radically change teaching and learning processes and curricula

---

Figure 6.1 *Educators' typical stances about online educational technology*

Using stances to effect change

The stances we have identified are significant for planning and effecting staff development, and for effecting change in teaching. A common staff development issue is whether a 'one-fits-all' approach is appropriate. In the context of online teaching and learning our experiences suggest that it is not. If staff have broadly varied stances to the use of online technology in teaching and learning, it follows that any staff development strategy should also be broad and varied. Asking staff to identify a stance that most closely reflects their way of thinking makes it easier, for educational developers, to view technology change from the perspective of their clients right from the start of their partnership. Online technology in teaching and learning contexts requires new ways of working, not only for teaching staff, but also for educational developers. The stances are a useful device to monitor, not only the attitudes of teaching staff, but also the views and beliefs of educational developers themselves and the changes in stances they take.

A common technology we use for staff development is the workshop or seminar. In these, we use the stances to help participants uncover their own attitudes toward the use of online approaches to teaching. At the beginning of a workshop, broad statements outlining the stances are explained. Participants are asked to identify a statement that most closely reflects their ways of thinking about a particular online project, resource or learning environment. They are then asked to form groups of people with similar stances and discuss why they identify mostly with a particular statement describing a stance. Groups report back to all the participants on their reasons. This exercise encourages a more open and critical discussion of the adoption of online approaches in different contexts. Staff are often surprised by their colleagues' choices of stance and their rationales. This can be enlightening and revealing, particularly for those who are working as a team on collaborative projects. Discussions may be expanded to include what stances students might adopt and how these may affect their learning. Subsequent meetings between educational developers and workshop participants may reveal shifts in their stances with experience.

As educational developers, we increasingly work with teachers, while programmes are being used with students. It is often only through working with specific online teaching and learning contexts that we discover how the change to online approaches privileges certain practices, and also how people's stances influence the manner in which they (both teachers and students) respond. Understanding stances helps us to interpret those responses to change which are described by Sproull and Kiesler (1991: 4–5) as second level effects.

More broadly, in planning and decision-making processes, not only those who positively support technological developments (Boosters) should be involved in decision making, but also people with other stances should have opportunities to influence decisions. Our University community is more likely to view decisions as credible and balanced if they are derived from committees and processes where ownership is across disciplines and different stances are understood and included (Noble, 1998). It has been demonstrated that different disciplines favour certain technological practices (Matthew and Zeitlyn, 1996) and epistemological frameworks (Taylor et al, 1997). Therefore, in planning change strategies for online teaching and learning, such cross-stance and cross-discipline representation is particularly important. Through this more inclusive approach, we hope to effect changes to teaching within the wider University culture.

Rogers's five adopter categories are used widely in describing adoption of new technologies in higher education (Geoghegan, 1996). Rogers and other Diffusion Theorists use the terms: innovators, early adopters, early and late majority and laggards to describe the range of technology adopters. 'Stances' described in this chapter, provide another perspective for viewing approaches to technology. Rogers' adopter categories imply linearity, a sequence and chronology, whereas the stances described, are more context-sensitive and are grounded in the understanding that people may change stances to reflect changes in the context in which they are working.

The new computer and information media provide resources and also environments in which teaching and learning takes place. It could be argued that educational developers need to offer a broader, more holistic level of assistance and development to staff. This should encompass the design and development of a course, in addition, to support for students, teachers and other participants as they work within the new teaching and learning environments. We have discussed this matter in greater detail elsewhere (Fox and Herrmann, 1997). Any changes in teaching practices can be threatening, even frightening, to staff when it takes them beyond their accustomed practices. Identifying stances and encouraging open debate about them, together with recognising that stances may change with experience and in response to a given context, may have the effect of making change less painful and less imposed.

The educational developer must help staff to understand that online and especially Web environments provide opportunities to link various parts of a university (for example, the library, study skills support) and beyond. Understanding people's stances may help provide meaning to the way in which they respond to change. In fact, understanding such stances may assist in anticipating responses and provide possible 'solutions'. By using the framework in Figure 6.1, it is intended that educational developers, who are called on often to act as project managers, will be able to respond sensitively and constructively to the extensive range of needs and perceptions of staff.

No simple template or checklist can hope to predict and resolve complex interactive processes. However, we have outlined a framework, based on empirical evidence, which can support the activities of educational developers in their work in online contexts. The five stances described provide opportunities to investigate perspectives and rehearse and test responses to them, thus reducing misunderstandings, friction and conflict within team environments. Given the pressures emanating from management and other sources, the opportunity to reduce stresses and facilitate the smooth functioning of teams can have positive effects.

Chapter 7

Opening up new teaching and learning spaces

Michelle Selinger

> Better learning will not come from finding better ways for the teacher to instruct but from giving the learner better opportunities to construct.
>
> (Papert, 1991)

Introduction

Text based computer-mediated communications has allowed the introduction of a new mode of education discourse: it brings isolated or disparate groups together; allows the less verbose the opportunity to contribute in discussion and debate, and offers an alternative medium sitting somewhere beyond academic writing and academic debate. It is a medium that has potential for enhancing collaboration between tutors, between students and between students and tutors; and as such, has implications for teaching. Structures can be established that offer potential for group tasks, collaborative learning and peer assessment, and potential for increasing contact time between tutors and students. The chapter draws on wide-ranging personal experience, in using the medium in conventional university settings, and in distance education with students and with colleagues, in a range of academic situations from formal teaching opportunities to collegial support. This support comes in the form of listservs, which encroach, sometimes intrusively, into private e-mail space, to conferencing systems, which separate group forums from e-mail. It is my belief that although there are positive advantages in the introduction of a new form of communication, like other forms of more traditional communications, there will be some that find it a difficult medium to use. However, as its structures, etiquette and limitations are realized, some may prefer to, and be allowed to, select the medium that best suits the task in hand.

In this chapter the possibilities introduced by text based electronic communications are explored in some depth. Starting with a discussion of models of teaching and learning, and of the different learning spaces that have become available to students and teachers, ways of exploiting the medium to provide opportunities for greater peer collaboration, in the form of group tasks, collaborative learning and assessment are explored. Contact with tutors and other academics is also considered, as are issues surrounding participation, maintaining dialogue, and the role played by the moderator. The chapter draws on the personal experience described above, but particularly, in the field of distance taught pre-service teacher education and considers the merits and difficulties that arise in both distance taught and conventional teaching situations. I shall argue that text based computer-mediated communications is just one of a number of learning spaces that must suit both the task and the individual if it is to be effective.

Models of teaching and learning

That said, then the traditional model of teaching and learning is being, or about to be, radically challenged. The image of a teaching situation, in which a tutor is in a room or a lecture theatre with a large group of students, or in a tutorial with a small group of students, is no longer the only way in which teaching can or does take place. Of course, distance learning institutions have employed a range of alternatives for many years. They have used a mix of printed materials, television broadcasts, audio and video materials, and face-to-face tutorials. Latterly, they have started to make use of the Internet for Web-based teaching, and encouraged communications through electronic text or video, and these media are rapidly moving into all educational establishments, albeit, some with more haste than others.

Much has been written about learning styles (for example, Gardner, 1983; Harding, 1985) and the resulting considerations by teachers. Additionally, Bruner (1996) in a discussion of folk pedagogies, looks at how rarely teaching is matched to views of the learner, and how most frequently the teacher perceives all learners as homogenous. This concurs with my own research where teachers I have interviewed appear to have a single view of learning – often not articulated, but possibly based on their own learning experiences – and, accordingly, teach their students from this perspective. Walkerdine's research on holistic and serialistic approaches to pedagogy also indicates these phenomena, and she discusses the merits and drawbacks of these approaches on different types of learners (Walkerdine *et al*, 1989).

The focus of the debate, however, is largely on teachers; how they match teaching to learning, and seldom about enabling the learners to make their *own* choices about where, when and how they learn. This was brought to my attention in an informal meeting of tutors, prior to making a distance taught course for a Masters in Education programme in which we discussed how we learnt from a printed article. The differences in styles were so marked and revealing that the resulting discussion was recorded and used in the introduction to the course (Open University, 1996). It drew attention to the fact that the students, as learners, had choices that they were free to make about how and when they learned, and that no one way was the 'right' way. If this diverse range is apparent through the one medium of text, then the diversity afforded through a range of media must be even greater. I learn best from talking to the author of an article, and then reading their paper, or reading the article and discussing it with a colleague. Reading on its own, for me, is not enough. With the emergence of the Internet, I can now have those discussions with an author or a colleague who has read the article at a distance; either prolonged over a period of time, with built-in time for reflection through electronic communications, or in the moment, in an online chat.

Learning communities and learning spaces

Universities, of any description, are sources of learning communities. Learning communities have been defined by Bruner (1996) and others (for example, Johnson-Lenz, 1991). Bruner sees the idea of the classroom as community as a radical proposal that has developed from the cultural-psychological approach to education. He defines a learning community as one that:

> models ways of doing or knowing, provides opportunity for emulation, offers running commentary, provides 'scaffolding' for novices, and even provides a good context for teaching deliberately. It even makes possible that form of job-related divisions of labour one finds in effective work groups: some serving pro-tem as 'memories' for the others, or as record keepers of 'where things have got up to now', or as encouragers or cautioners. The point is for those in the group to either get the lay of the land and the hang of the job.
>
> (Bruner, 1996: 21)

A learning community has traditionally been associated with a physical location; a school, a college, a university, an evening class, a laboratory. With the advent of new technology the notion of the learning community has moved into virtual space. Distance learning institutions' programmes have developed from the correspondence courses of the past, where students were sent printed text to guide their study, and written assignments had to be completed and sent to an anonymous tutor. They are now institutions that have put a human element back into the equation with the addition of video and audio, and face-to-face tutorials and seminars. Now with the advent of telematics, communication can take place across locations and time and the whole notion of a learning community has changed. Students can learn with others anywhere in the world. They no longer have to be registered with a distance learning institution, as traditional institutions encroach on distance learning through new technology. Students engage in learning activity through e-mail, computer conferences, Web-based discussion forums and video-conferencing – collectively referred to as *telematics*. The early pioneers of telematics were based in Australia, beginning with the 'school of the air' radio broadcasts, and now using the new technologies linking remote families and communities to bring education to their children.

To form a learning community, I have suggested that students need to have a number of common goals (Selinger, 1998). There needs to be ownership of the learning process, a sense of purpose, and a sense of audience. The community needs to have shared aims, goals and interests, and learners need to have ease of access and use of whatever learning medium is available in both place and time; and, this access includes the student feeling comfortable with this particular use of technology. These factors give rise to the notion of *learning spaces*; places where learning occurs in time and/or location, and with or without others, such as a lecture theatre or a corridor conversation, or an e-mail discussion. Johnson-Lenz (1991) defines a learning community as one that require 'rhythms, boundaries and containers' for interaction (Harasim *et al*, 1995: 277). Containers and boundaries can be in the form of classrooms and learning institutions, or in the form of electronic forums determined by 'a combination of software features, facilitator actions and instructional designs or metaphors' (Harasim *et al*, 1995: 277).

The definition of possible learning spaces arose during an International Federation for Information Processing (IFIP) working group discussion in Israel in 1996, where the notion of a three dimensional model was proposed with time, location and group size as the three axes (Nicholson *et al*, 1997). 'Location' is defined as the place in which individuals or groups meet. These can be where participants are together working face-to-face (defined here as same location), or where participants are working together, but are separated by distance (defined as different location). 'Participants' are defined as groups working together or as individuals. Taking the traditional model of teaching and learning, a lecture is defined as 'group' whereas a tutorial between a tutor and a student is defined as 'individual'. Each of the resulting eight spaces represents a place where learning can take place. Figure 7.1 defines the parameters of each space and suggests the type of activity that can take place therein.

From the table, it can be seen that the opportunities provided for teaching and learning are increased when electronic communications are made available. The traditional spaces of synchronous time and location are simply one context in which to learn. The opportunities open to learners to select those spaces where they can learn best are increased, providing the learning institutions make them available. However, for this to happen, students need to be aware of the dimensions of each, and they also need to have easy access to the medium, to test it out and to make decisions about the opportunities that present themselves. Not all will 'take to' an electronic medium. For others, the opportunity of asynchronous discussions allows those more considered thinkers the time to have their say without interruptions from those for whom face-to-face discourse provides the energy with which to

TIME	LOCATION	PARTICIPANTS	ACTIVITY
same time	same location	individual	tutorial
same time	same loction	group	lecture, seminar
same time	different location	individual	online discussion, video-conference
same time	different location	group	online discussion, video-conference
different time	same location	individual	computer-conference listserv/newsgroup
different time	same location	group	computer-conference
different time	different location	individual	e-mail
different time	different location	group	computer-conference

Figure 7.1 *Learning spaces and related activities*

think and react in the moment. The asynchronous nature of electronic discussion creates structures whereby thinking time can be imposed on participants to allow all those involved to consider their contribution. A further time delay can also be incorporated, and a paper can be posted on a conference or on a Web site, a week or so before any electronic discussion is allowed to commence. An example of this was in a discussion between trainee teachers of mathematics and science. The paper examined the problems of students using mathematics in science lessons and posed some questions on the issues for electronic communications (Benson and Selinger, 1998). The students, who were all following a distance education course, were exposed to a debate that was not explicit in the course's teaching materials, but was one that had emerged in some of the informal conferences the students were using (see below). It was interesting to note that in this situation a different set of students were responding in the specially set up discussion area; although, the waiting time was not explicitly followed up as a possible contributory factor.

The distance learning experience

The following case study provides an example of electronic communications within a distance learning environment. In 1994 the Open University (OU) in the United Kingdom launched the first large-scale use of FirstClass©, a text based computer-conferencing system based on a graphical user interface, in the context of a teacher education course. This was the first 'non-technology' course, in which the OU had used computer-conferencing, as an integral part of the course structure and hailed the beginning of large-scale use across the university. The students involved were training to be teachers, and were enrolled on a postgraduate certificate in education (PGCE), through distance learning. Over 1,200 students, teaching part-time at either primary level (4–11) or secondary level (11–18), were enrolled.

The students were loaned computers to support them in becoming confident users of information and communications technology (ICT), and the teaching materials included elements, to help them consider the integration of ICT in their curriculum specialisms. As the member of the course team responsible for ICT across the curriculum, I had to ensure that the students had a coherent and valuable experience of ICT, and were prepared for teaching with new technology. In addition, we were also aware that beginning teaching can be a stressful experience, and that considerable support would be needed, particularly, during school experience. Many students, because of the nature of the course, could feel isolated since they would only meet formally with other students on five occasions during the 18 months of the course, and potentially they might be the only student teacher in a school. Therefore, they would need peer support, in addition to the support received from other teachers in their schools. The stresses and demands on student teachers on school placements is well documented, and this research evidence was used to convince the administrators of the need for a communication mechanism, in addition to the traditional support from a personal tutor.

As a result, we loaned students a modem and invited them to join conferences, according to their subject specialism, age range to be taught and their physical location. The medium was not to be used, at this stage, as a direct teaching mechanism, since the course was already well into production, and it was too late to embed the electronic element into the materials. Instead, it was structured as a forum for support and for keeping students informed about recent changes and development in educational policy and issues. For example, it was used to encourage discussion on new legislation; it provided a forum for critiques of reports and articles in the educational press; it alerted students to new research findings, and encouraged debate of some of the course-related issues or extended the materials, as observations were made that had not been included in the printed texts (such as the use of mathematics in science teaching). In other words, it was intended to supplement and enhance the teaching materials, whilst reducing students' feelings of isolation.

The metaphor of a campus map was used within the structure of FirstClass and discussions were held in individual folders. For example, secondary mathematics teachers would find items of interest in their tutor group (15 students and a tutor from a geographical location), their regional group (comprising all the tutor groups in one of 12 OU regions into which the country is divided), the mathematics conference (to which all students had access), a general course conference (for course related issues), and a chat forum (for informal conversations) (Selinger, 1996).

For many students, the modem proved to be a valued lifeline. It enabled them to have electronic contact with other students struggling to complete the course whilst juggling many of the other commitments that had prevented them from studying to become a teacher through the conventional route – a full-time, one year course in a face-to-face initial teacher training institution. Traditionally, lecturers at the Open University had very little contact with their students because of the nature of their distance learning courses. However with the provision of electronic communication this model changed, and lecturers now have contact with students across the country and can offer support, stimulate debate on teaching materials and point students to additional resources.

A number of themes have emerged over three years of working with students in this medium:

- the length of time students used the system was in direct proportion to the inter-textual responses – a phrase coined by Howell-Richardson and Mellar (1996) – to previously posted messages;
- the participation rate increased the longer students had access to the medium;
- tutors were able to respond to issues arising from the course that had not been anticipated at the time of writing study materials;
- recent news items relevant to the students could be woven into the course and inform students' thinking;
- the members of the course team were able to gauge the course pressure points and make adjustments for subsequent years;
- cross phase and cross curricular discussion was facilitated;
- sustained dialogue on a particular topic rarely occurred.

Inter-textual messages

Perkins and Newman (1996: 165) suggest that there is 'a tendency for messages to be a series of monologues and statements of opinions rather than an exchange of ideas'. This was certainly true in the early stages of teaching as students tested out the medium, and they tended to take little or no notice of comments that had gone before. However, as time went on, the messages began to take heed of what others had said, indicating the need for a familiarization period, wherein, students adjust to these novel means of communication and to new technology. At the beginning of the course less than half the students reported any substantial level of confidence and competence with computers, let alone electronic discussions. For some, the computer loaned to them was the first they had ever used. Russell (1995) describes a six-stage model for users new to e-mail and computer technology, which takes it from being intrusive to becoming invisible and assists in the understanding of the experiences of these OU students using the technology:

1. awareness;
2. learning the process;
3. understanding and application of the process;
4. familiarity and confidences;
5. adaptation to other contexts;
6. creative applications to new contexts (Russell, 1995: 175).

In the early stages, students needed support and modelling of good practice. Tutors drew conclusions from students' contributions and suggested ways forward for students to agree or disagree with, or asked for further comments to specific points. There were positive and negative outcomes from this. On the positive side, the students appreciated someone summing up and making suggestions for further discussion, but the negative aspects were that students began to expect it, and were less inclined to reference others' comments. This dependency needs to be withdrawn once the familiarization period is over. Using a student to do this proved very helpful, and often sets the ball rolling. Finding a student, who is willing to a take lead, proves relatively easy as they can be selected from the 'virtuosos' in the group (Perkins and Newman, 1996). These are the more verbose students, who contribute frequently and lucidly, and who are highly regarded by others. One virtuoso was an educational researcher and was taking the teaching course to gain qualified teacher status so that, if necessary, he could teach legally as part of his research. He was an obvious choice, as a 'plant', and there were numerous exchanges between him and the moderator about his potential and subsequent contributions. This 'hidden intervention' appeared to provoke the moderator's desired reaction from other students, and inter-textual references started to increase and discussions were slightly more prolonged. The moderator wanted the discussion to be between students, and when she intervened with a comment, it appeared to her that the students took this as 'gospel'; and once such comments were made the discussion was closed. She felt her presence was an inhibitor to sustained debate; it felt more like the classroom situation she was trying to avoid.

From interviews with students, it would appear that a good deal of inter-textual referencing did take place, but outside the conferences. One virtuoso, who posted messages regularly, reported that she had a good deal of discussion with students in her private mailbox. FirstClass provides all users with private e-mail facilities in addition to the conferences to which they are subscribed. This particular feature appears to encourage and support the contributions to conferences.

Current events

The last decade has seen an increasing amount of government intervention in the UK educational process. The introduction of a National Curriculum for schools, national testing programmes, new school inspection procedures, the introduction of literacy and numeracy targets are just some of the multitude of initiatives. Any initial teacher education course has to ensure that students are well prepared for teaching, and this includes a capacity to respond quickly to changes in the educational process. But conventional distance learning courses, by necessity, involve a time lag as they go through the writing, editorial and printing process. FirstClass, therefore, provided an optimum forum for informing students about new curricular and other arrangements as they were received. Students' attention could also be drawn to media coverage and debates were initiated about the issues. In the mathematics conference, for instance, there was a debate about a proposed calculator ban in primary schools. Sometimes the students were alerted to these issues by tutors, other times by the media.

A discussion of whole class teaching and related class sizes, prompted by a television programme, engaged students in one of the fiercest online debates. The immediate access to FirstClass from their homes allowed students to go online within moments of the programme finishing. In fact, the discussion provoked the largest number of messages experienced in any of the PGCE conferences – 53 messages in four days. The discussion was started by students and was very much peer led, and peer supported. The authenticity of this situation was a factor in the success. This was a 'real issue' and one that they could see would affect them. One student summed the discussion up succinctly by referring to material from the course, talking about social constructivism, and observing how they – the students – were constructing knowledge from this discussion. The debate was successful because students were able to respond, in the moment, in the knowledge that there would be an audience who wanted to share the same issues with them. This knowledge encouraged students to go online, to post and respond to messages with others whose concerns and goals were similar. The same student reported that if he had waited until the next day he might not have wanted the discussion, and he believed that he would certainly not have engaged at the level he did. This event highlights the importance of ease of access and the need to find authentic issues that will encourage students to engage in debate.

Pressure points

Combining professional placements with distance learning materials was an innovation within the OU. The timing of assignments was radically restructured after the first year, responding to students' conversation aired forcefully through FirstClass. The nature of the discussion was also indicative of students' concerns and moved from discussion of the course itself, to the practical issues of dealing with disruptive pupils when on school placement. Conferences were most often used was when assignments were due in and during school placements. Towards the end of the course discussion moved to gaining employment and conversation ranged from what to wear at interview, to questions asked and responses given that gained them employment. Other discussions helped in adjusting timings for completing assignments, the nature of the assignments for subsequent cohorts and tutors began to become familiar with appropriate timings for injecting particular issues into discussions. It became clear that there would be little response to debates on learning theories in education, when students main concern was how to get an unruly class to sit in their seats and engage in the lesson, at any level. Later, when the students had finished the school placement, some of these theoretical issues could be dealt with and the relationship between theory and practice could be debated, away from pressing and often stressful teaching demands.

Cross-curricular possibilities

There are few opportunities for collaboration between students following different courses or different subjects within the same course in face-to-face institutions. However, through computer-conferencing this can be readily set up and can raise students' awareness of cross curricular issues that they might not otherwise consider. In the OU PGCE course a conference was set up to discuss the issues of teaching mathematics in science lessons, and using science contexts in mathematics lessons (Benson and Selinger, 1998). A mathematics student commented how reading the discussion in the science-mathematics conference had suddenly, many years after leaving school, helped her to realize why she had such a bad experience at school doing her science and mathematics examinations.

Integrating electronic and face-to-face settings

Implementing electronic communications in face-to-face settings is a very different story. On-campus students may use e-mail, but mainly for social purposes and to access people away from campus. There has to be a rationale for setting up electronic communications in a learning context. This can range from facilitating collaborative projects, to setting group assignments, offering students easy access to visiting speakers from anywhere in the world, allowing students to participate or 'eavesdrop' on expert debate, or providing access to authentic learning situations. It also provides tutors with paperless access to students, to inform them about lecture and tutorial details, to change class or assignment arrangements, or to engage them in one-to-one, or one-to-many, dialogues. As students come from an increasingly diverse range of backgrounds and more mature students engage in higher education, the campus resident student is no longer the norm, and access to tutors, as students live further from the university, becomes more difficult. One tutor reported that since the faculty relocated to a more remote part of the campus, he sees far less of his students, and they of each other, resulting in the loss of valuable informal conversations. Cuts in staffing also mean that academics have less time to meet with students, tutorial group sizes increase and hence, tutorials become more like seminars. The dynamics of interaction change as group sizes grow, and students have fewer opportunities to contribute to the discussion, or to direct the discussion in favour of their particular concern or interest.

In a pilot project at Warwick University, staff are seeking to use electronic communications to explore a number of possibilities and challenges facing the faculty in teaching undergraduate courses. The academics involved cite large group teaching, seminar assessment, the management of multi-group/multi-teacher courses, the encouragement of student participation, and linking to electronic resources as major issues for discussion. They believe that the use of a conferencing system will facilitate course planning, co-ordination and monitoring of students between tutors, as well as encouraging peer collaboration and more student autonomy.

As stated earlier, in any discussion forum, there are those who react and speak in the moment, and those who need time to consider their responses. This is indicative of the necessity to provide a range of learning spaces in all learning institutions. Students who are articulate in class may not be those who are articulate in an electronic discussion forum. In recent seminars with a group of 27 students, who met for eight hours a week for seminars, there were always eight or so who were most verbal in discussions; the others had to be invited to speak by the tutor, or group activities were set to encourage wider engagement. When these students were given the opportunity to discuss issues online this was encouraged by posting seminar notes electronically, and by being posed a question related to the themes of the seminar. The overlap in those contributing online and those contributing in the seminar was small; the electronic forum provided a mechanism for wider participation. There were still some students who contributed to neither, although their assignments revealed a depth of thinking and consideration sometimes in extent of their more verbose peers. From this experience, there is evidence to suggest that there are at least three mechanisms for students to demonstrate or increase their understanding: listening and writing, discussion in seminars and contributing to an electronic conference. All contributions are equally valued, and should be accredited in some way in student assessment.

Assessment

Whether or not to assess online discussion is an issue that has created a great deal of debate in the projects I have been involved with. Evidence suggests that once debate is assessed, students will only use the medium for the assessment period and then disregard it. It is perceived as an assessment tool (Pearson and Mason, 1992), and not as a tool for collaboration and peer support.

However for group assignments, electronic communications can be a valuable and effective mechanism. Students can be assessed according to the nature of their contribution to an electronic debate. Certain parameters can be set, such as engaging with and discussing the ideas suggested by others within the debate, thus encouraging inter-textual references. Conferencing can also be useful for collaborative writing, where subsequent drafts are circulated for comment and change by each group member in turn. Little research in this area is available in order to make a valid judgement on the relative merits of such assignments; given the increasing use of electronic groupwork in the workplace, this form of assessment needs to be researched further.

Collaborative learning

The workplace increasingly seeks employees who are able to work in teams and who have good problem solving capabilities. There is evidence that electronic communications do support this. Sproull and Keisler (1991) found that people who were unwilling to converse in groups become more willing to do so after spending some time actively participating in electronic conferences. Recent evidence from a cohort of PGCE students on a face-to-face course bears this out. Three students, who said very little in seminars, made significant and valuable contributions on FirstClass while on school placements. On their return to the university, they became amongst the most frequent seminar contributors. A number of pilot projects at Warwick University are being set up because lecturers want students to engage more actively with their peers. In one department a tutor expressed concern about the lack of student engagement in tutorial activities; he saw the use of electronic discussions as one way of increasing this. He proposes to set students group tasks that they first need to discuss electronically or otherwise outside the classroom and, subsequently, to have them present their arguments to the rest of the tutorial group for further discussion. He sees this as potentially enhancing peer discussion and collaboration, and as a way of enhancing tutorial time.

Access to experts

As the body of knowledge in a discipline grows, then, even within large faculties, expertise in all areas can rarely be available. The access to expertise in the field, therefore, becomes vital especially when students select to work on theses that may be outside the domain of the faculty, or when the work in the field is dynamic and there are known experts on the most recent developments in other universities, nationally or internationally. These people can be enlisted to run guest discussions with students without the vast expense of bringing them to the faculty. Alternatively a number of experts can be invited to engage in a 'fishbowl' debate in which students can 'eavesdrop' in the first instance, and then become involved in a question and answer session or further debate. Guest conferences were trialled successfully in the OU PGCE course; students reported that the discussions broadened their thinking beyond the course material, and gave them the opportunity to articulate their understanding and engage personally with their 'bibliography'. For individuals engaged with theses, the opportunities to engage in dialogue with international experts and others researching in the field can prove to be one of the most productive and exciting elements of electronic communications, and begins to form the basis for the 'global university'.

There are concerns, however. Traditionally academics are contracted to work on research, which is credited to their home institution and to teaching students registered there. The explosion in e-mail has meant that the physical constraints to movement between institutions are lost, and the electronic access to expertise opens up the notion of the virtual or global university. This is a feature of the developing megauniversity structure proposed by Sir John Daniel, Vice Chancellor of the Open University in the UK (Daniel, 1996). He defines the megauniversities as the 10 distance-teaching universities that each enrolled over 100,000 students a year. Whether the traditional universities link up with the mega-universities waits to be seen. What effect will this have on traditional modes of teaching, which still have validity and a place in the education system?

Lessons to be learnt

The role of the tutor in determining the mode of communication for students depends very much on the nature of the subject, the context in which it is being taught, and the resources available to them. It also relies on tutors' views of learning and their perceptions of their role as a teacher. Distance learning brings new demands, and staff in traditional universities trying to incorporate an element of distance learning into their courses, find that their workload increases in the first instance, as the old continues; while they prepare to integrate the new. Preparing material to go online and writing Web pages is only one such element. There are decisions to be made about assessment processes. How to organize tutorials – considerations of whether these should be face-to-face or online, or a mixture of both. The issues of access to technology for both staff and students are absolutely fundamental. Offering choices to students may mean that face-to-face sessions will run alongside electronic discussions where students can engage in either or both. How will that be managed and is it feasible? These are issues that will have to be resolved, but they will not be resolved until tutors have time to become more familiar with, experiment with, and become comfortable with, new communications technologies. For some, the new media may suit their learning and teaching styles or their beliefs about the teaching and learning process. Where practicals are involved, for example, online discussions may only form a small feature of the teaching, or none at all. The possibilities of offering Web-based simulations prior to a practical session in a laboratory, however, may speed up the work in the laboratory, allow time for discussion about changes to experiments and procedures to be followed, and may mean that time spent in the lab is more productive. Training for staff is vital, not only in the use of the technology, but in the uses to which it can be put, and in the changing role of the tutor. Moderating electronic conferences and discussion groups is an emerging set of skills.

The introduction of electronic communications does not mean that teaching has to change completely; rather, it can be enhanced and extended. Students and teachers can make choices as more opportunities for spaces to share learning are developed and made widely available.

Chapter 8

Fears and ambitions: adopting audiotape and compact disc approaches to teaching at the University of Papua New Guinea

Samuel Haihuie

There are two questions that practitioners of university education should try to answer. How can new technologies help to 'push' the skills of course developers in conventional and distance education programmes to produce better quality learning resources for study at tertiary level? Have we attempted to use existing or new technologies effectively to make university education available to as many people as possible? This chapter focuses on the struggle to adopt the use of audiotapes and compact discs in university teaching at the University of Papua New Guinea (UPNG). These new approaches can be seen as a way of extending university education in developing nations, such as Papua New Guinea (PNG), where the infrastructure and resources are very limited. However, changes to traditional approaches to university teaching often encounter problems and resistance. This chapter describes a case study of two attempts to improve teaching at UPNG which were aimed at enhancing the learning experiences of off-campus, and often remote, students.

Distance education in PNG and at UPNG

Distance education began during 1952 in PNG with the establishment of the Correspondence School, now called the College of Distance Education. The development of university education in PNG is very recent compared to some nations in the developed world. UPNG enrolled its first intake of students in 1966 and the University of Technology in Lae was given university status in 1974. These are the two longstanding universities in the country and they offer a limited number of programmes through distance education.

The University of Papua New Guinea's distance education roots have been traced by various authors to the *Currie Commission Report* of 1964 (Currie, Gunter and Spate, 1964) that made external teaching one of the five objectives of the UPNG. However, for more than a decade the objective of external teaching remained dormant. In 1974, the *Report of the Committee of Enquiry into University Development,* the Gris Report (Gris, 1974), provided details on establishing an outreach programme, including the development of provincial university centres, and the appointment of a Director of Extension Studies in 1977. The first significant staffing and subsequent enrolment of students in Extension Studies took place in 1985 (Kema and Guy, 1991; Van Trease, 1990–91). The organizational and academic context for university-based distance education at UPNG has remained that of a small outreach effort within the conventional university environment.

A postcolonialist interpretation of the Currie Commission's objective of external teaching could see it as the separation and segregation of people that is a feature typical of colonial administrations. In this sense, distance education was used as camouflage for colonialist intentions. Such intentions were to restrict natives from coming to the towns and cities for education due to the fear that it would encourage rural to urban migration, thus 'contaminating' colonialist dominated urban settlements. Distance education enabled native people to be kept in their rural villages 'where they belong'. From another perspective this critique also highlights the issue that the word 'distance' in distance education is more than just spatial distance, but an element of social and economic separation and parity between the provider or the source of knowledge and the recipient.

In 1994, the Institute of Distance and Continuing Education (IDCE) replaced Extension Studies, adopting a broader mission with new funding and reporting processes. The mission statement elaborated the objective of the Currie Commission and emphasized that if the people cannot attend the university then the university must be taken to the people. The IDCE remains to accomplish this objective. However, virtually all of the staff recruited to IDCE have little or no distance education background, and so the capacity to achieve it is not high.

Enrolment in the distance education programme at UPNG has increased annually, with growth in all programme areas and at most centres. In 1998, there were approximately 16,000 course enrolments throughout PNG. The programmes offered by the IDCE include:

- pre-matriculation and adult matriculation courses;
- first year university level foundation courses;
- diploma in primary school teaching;
- some course units in the bachelor of education (in-service) which is now offered at the University of Goroka;

- a Diploma in Commerce;
- and a Diploma in Social Administration.

In 1999 the PNG government, through the Office of Higher Education, announced major policy initiatives on distance education. Distance education has been discussed in the past in major government policy documents such as the Higher Education Plan (Commission for Higher Education, 1990) but the prominence of distance education has never been greater.

On 15 January 1999, the *National* newspaper carried a front-page article titled 'Green light for correspondence degrees' which stated that the national government was planning to make all universities and colleges offer their degree and diploma programmes through distance education. It was reported that this was a bid to make higher education cheaper and more accessible. The plan is also a part of the government's efforts to extend higher education opportunities to people who are unable to gain direct entry.

At a higher education summit meeting in early 1999, the Vice Minister for Higher Education, Research, Science and Technology emphasized four important areas for a framework for the higher education sector (Waiko, 1998). The first area he named was cost-effective, relevant and appropriate modes of delivery. He argued that it was wrongly assumed that education only occurs at a place where teachers and students are together. At the end of the summit 17 broad resolutions were adopted, including one directly related to the expansion of distance education.

It is worth pondering why the PNG government is driving higher education in this direction. In recent times higher education has experienced drastic budget cuts whereas there has been increased funding of primary and secondary education. The director general of the Office of Higher Education has stated that since the government could not provide the full amount of funds required by tertiary institutions, like UPNG, the idea of offering degree and diploma programmes through distance education would alleviate the financial burdens these institutions face. This provoked strong criticisms of the government's policies and assumptions about distance education. Prominent among the critics was a professor at UPNG, who argued that in order to have a centralized distance study centre that would co-ordinate the degree and diploma programmes of various universities and colleges, the basic infrastructure, communication network, libraries, laboratories and other facilities have to be provided. He argued that the degree and diploma programmes offered through distance education would be down graded and may not be recognized by other universities and colleges internationally.

Even before this increased attention on distance education, organizations such as IDCE have continued to increase the provision of university education through open and distance education. Attempts have been made to bring changes and innovation into the practical aspects of such university teaching using new technology. Such attempts preceded the government's recent enthusiasm for distance education and the resistance that is emerging in some quarters. However, the future of distance education in PNG can only be cost effective if the approaches used and the technologies drawn upon are appropriate for the circumstances of PNG. What follows are two cases of steps toward using non-print approaches at UPNG. They are part of a project that has the following objectives:

- To introduce non-print technologies into an otherwise conservative and very restricted print-based culture of distance education.
- To gauge the views and reactions of both teachers and learners on the use of audiotapes and compact discs in distance teaching.
- To identify from both the IDCE staff and students, the factors seen as hindering advances in developing and employing non-print technologies.
- To provide this information to the UPNG authorities, course developers and co-ordinators and to others interested in the provision of university distance education in PNG.

The introduction of audiocassettes

This case is based on the 1998 DSA (Diploma in Social Administration) programme of which the author was the coordinator. Out of a total of 16 course units that make up the programme, 9 have been *written* for distance education, while work on the other units is under way. The project concerns both the use of audiotapes to supplement the print materials in one of the course units of the DSA programme, and also an assessment of the reactions of staff to a proposal to acquire equipment to record and produce compact discs for the course.

Both the use of audiotapes and the proposition to use compact discs represent a challenge to the print-based culture of distance education at UPNG. It is an attempt by 'grassroots' teaching staff to initiate changes to the University's teaching. The focus, first is on the experiences of the use of audiotapes, in the DSA course unit entitled *Social Administration*. We begin by looking at the background information on the DSA programme.

The brochure advertising the distance education DSA includes the following information:

> The Diploma in Social Administration is offered by the Department of Anthropology and Sociology through the IDCE. Courses are the same as those in the internal Diploma in Social Administration programme.

> Social Work is the study of how to work with people and the focus of its concern is meeting the social needs and improving the social lives of people in both rural and urban communities. The study of social work is intended for students who wish to obtain a professional preparation for careers in individual and group work, community work, and social policy administration in both government and non-government agencies.

> Upon completion of this programme you will be better equipped to perform duties related to social work.

Course delivery is restricted to print and this medium is limited in its capacity to fulfil some of the objectives of course in terms of social work skills and practice. For example, those skills requiring interactivity and participation in social, community and group work. More broadly there is also the question of using the best available educational media to produce appropriate high quality teaching materials.

Among the seven compulsory course units in the DSA programme include those entitled: *Working With Communities* and *Social Development*. The course description for *Social Development* in the 1997 Arts Faculty Course Handbook reads:

> This course will provide opportunities for the student to examine the concept of social needs and changing ways of meeting these needs. The development of education, health and social services in Papua New Guinea will be compared with the experiences of other countries and against the background of traditional approaches to meeting social needs in Melanesian societies. The course aims to provide a critical perspective of development for students preparing for careers in education, law, planning and administration, research and social work.

The task was based on two assumptions. First, as the DSA programme envisages to produce a competent social worker who will live, work and interact in a social environment, it is assumed that the print-based teaching materials prepared by the IDCE are too restrictive to facilitate effective two-way communication between the teacher and student. The printed materials do not facilitate the necessary social and interactive experiences. Second, a type of conservatism reigns in IDCE, and there is a lack of imagination and creativity in the use of new media and approaches. The introduction of non-print approaches is seen as a disruptive wave to the smooth sailing of IDCE.

The use of audiotapes in distance teaching is not new and falls within the 'second generation' of technologies used in distance learning (Garrison, 1985; Nipper, 1989). Lappia and Kirkland (1989), drawing on the work of Mcdonald and Knight, summarize the advantages and disadvantages of audiotape as follows:

Advantages

1. Simplicity; audiotapes are easy to use; they can be rewound, paused briefly or stopped for a period. As well, play back machines with counters enable listeners to locate selections fairly quickly.
2. Flexibility; tapes can complement a variety of other media.
3. User control; listeners can choose when to listen.
4. Humanizing instructor-student relationship.
5. Stimulating and motivating people by using another sensory modality; variations in phase, amplitude and frequency provide cues to highlight aspects of the content.
6. Variable concentration; listeners can elect to pay close attention or listen with 'half an ear' whilst carrying on other activities (like driving, or household chores).

Disadvantages

1. Time; unless the producer indicates tape duration, listeners have no way of knowing how much time to set aside.
2. Access; although counters help it is often difficult to locate a specific item on a tape.
3. Printed articles can be browsed more readily.
4. Individual preferences; some people do not like learning with their ears, others have hearing disabilities.
5. Quality; distorted audiotapes are extremely distracting (Lappia and Kirkland, 1989: 278–79).

Two audiotapes, each with an hour long live recorded lecture, were prepared to accompany the printed course materials for the Social Development course. The course materials consisted of one introductory booklet containing assignments, one study guide, two books of selected readings, two supplementary textbooks, a newsletter and the two audiotapes. The two taped lectures covered two topics of the course. There are no properly equipped studio facilities either for audio or video production at UPNG. Therefore, no editing of the tapes was undertaken, nor was an introduction or conclusion provided. Students when covering topics five and six were required to listen to the tapes as supplementary to the notes in the study guides.

Registration in semester one of 1998 saw three students out of an expected five enrolling for the Social Development course. Only two students completed the assessment by submitting all course work assignments and sitting the final exam. This situation was expected for three main reasons: many of the students in the DSA programme were police officers and withdrew due to work commitments; a sponsorship arrangement collapsed; and IDCE failed to provide sufficient student support. Of the students who completed, one was a male police officer based in Port Moresby, and the other a female information officer with a non-government organization based in Goroka. Discussions were held with these two students about their experiences of using audiotapes for their study of the Social Development unit.

Although both students received the two audiotapes, the student in Goroka received one that was inaudible. An offer was made to send her a replacement copy. However, she replied that there was no need if the assessment was not based on it! Here we confront an obvious limitation when audiotapes are used as supplementary material only. The students were not motivated to use the audiotapes unless they directly related to their assessment.

The nature of the tapes was also a problem. One hour of listening to a lecture on tape can be boring. There are more effective ways to use the medium. However, unless students are bounded by set tasks, or responses are expected for assessment purposes, it may be difficult to ascertain whether students use, or find the tapes useful, at all.

Again, the student from Goroka brings another concern to light. She said in a discussion:

So far it has been good. The introduction booklet directs us to contact the social science coordinator should we have any queries. For me it's OK, I have a telephone. If I ring and you are not there I will try again and again until I get you, but how about someone who does not have a telephone or who travels in from outside of Goroka to make a call. If there is no response it kills the interest.

Despite the attempt to supplement and 'bring to life' the print media with the use of audiotapes, it fell short of facilitating interactivity in the social process of learning. In this case, the student was looking to use the telephone for her interaction. However, nowadays, there are other media to be explored, such as the new computer-mediated communications media, which may promote the notion of learning, as a social process, in distance education.

The proposal to use compact discs

Compact discs can facilitate forms of 'virtual' interaction due to their capacity to store large amounts of text, graphics and audio media. The second case to discuss here concerns IDCE's responses to a proposal from a staff member to acquire a compact disc writer. Staff views on the acquisition varied, but generally there was little enthusiasm. The proposal included a rationale and justification as follows:

When UPNG started offering courses by distance education it has been restricted to the print media for distance teaching. The IDCE has not been innovative in adopting new and affordable technology to deliver quality instructional material to students.

While compact disc will not completely replace the print media it has certain advantages and can be complementary to existing print media. One notable being space and volume, for example, one CD can easily contain all the five social science matriculation courses. It has the advantage of 'writing on' pictures and diagrams with the use of additional equipment such as the under utilized scanner that IDCE already has. It can also record sound or music, which makes it all more exciting for downloading material from existing compact disc encyclopedias and other reference books and the Internet for course development.

This is an affordable new technology, which only costs K1,600.00. If IDCE is to use more advanced technology such as audio conference (radio talk-back), or satellite communication in future then it might as well start now with some affordable technology requiring little or no specialist technicians.

The IDCE has occupied its new purpose-built building for more than a year now and the media wing is the least utilized part. Two of the air-conditioned rooms are idle. Nobody else will come and tell us how best to use this part of the building but us. This proposal is one step in that direction.

All IDCE staff were given the opportunity to respond to the proposal. One response, for example, commented:

> What is the possibility of a demonstration by [the supplier]? Have you sought views from the CSU [Computer Services Unit]? It's affordable, but certainly expensive, half the cost of a brand new computer. How much would each blank CD cost? For student use? We should do more research on what we have [print] and what [we] should get.

These comments reflect those of a conservative culture, perhaps tinged with ignorance and fear of using compact discs.

Reasons relating to costs are ones grounded in the economics of the developing world versus the developed. Developing countries are on the periphery of global economic and political decision making. The desire in developing nations to use the latest in educational technologies is confronted by lack of funding and the lack of expert skills. It is more within the means of the developed world to have the resources to change university teaching than it is for those in developing nations. The 'trickle down' of new educational technology to the remote corners of PNG, for example, may take about five years or more, by which time they may be obsolete. Even though the ambitions might be high to acquire these technologies, the fears are real and will endure.

The most encouraging and positive comment supporting the purchase of a compact disc writer came from an influential senior administrative staff member. He said that, 'Anything that enhances teaching and learning is a plus but [again] money should be the eventual ruler.'

In contrast, a senior member of the course development staff was sceptical:

> Have you surveyed the [provincial] centres to see if they have compact disc drivers? I don't know for sure, but I suspect most do not. I support this in terms of advancing our ability to produce quality course materials etc. My main concern is that computers must be made available to students/staff who will be using the CDs [compact discs]. We don't have any available [in the National Capital District] for students and [many of] our staff still do not have CD drives. And, as questioned above, I doubt many of our centres currently have even one CD drive for staff use. Money for new computers is scarce. And training for using new computers and equipment is also scarce, especially in the centres.

One might expect that advances in the use of new technology in distance teaching at university level would come from a person such as the senior course developer quoted above. Such persons are typically appraised of the latest developments in educational technology to produce quality learning materials. However, here there is evidence of resistance, using economic arguments of cost and lack of technical facilities. These fears are shallow when considering the demands for interactive teaching to promote the social processes of learning at a distance.

A print culture of conservatism and fear: the difficulties to break free

New forms of technology are rarely received with unanimous enthusiasm. In some cases, it instils fear and insecurity, usually due to an inability to adapt to the new technology.

There have been many innovations in communication technologies for educational purposes. Some of these have been effectively used as a sole medium of instruction or, in others, as part of the media used to present a course. Garrison (1985) and Nipper (1989) categorize three generations of distance education, which are linked historically to the development of production, distribution and communication technologies. 'First generation' distance learning is correspondence teaching and the medium in this case is written or print material. Multi-media distance teaching that has been developed since the late 1960s is the 'second generation'. This generation integrates the use of print with broadcast media, audio and video media, and some computer media. The 'third generation' uses the digital communications systems with computer-based software to provide real and virtual interactive learning materials.

The arguments against the use of print have not been well received at UPNG. The perceptions and limitations of the print media in distance teaching and contesting issues of what is knowledge, who owns knowledge and should the source of knowledge be questioned have been raised in earlier studies (Guy, 1994; Guy, Haihuie and Pena, 1996). Though the print media have 'opened the classroom', there are local practices that undermine that openness of the classroom.

Work done by Guy (1994, 1995) with a group of 25 educators engaged in a distance education programme offered by the IDCE brings to prominence these issues of knowledge, power and pedagogy in distance education in Papua New Guinea. Guy states:

> The increasing prominence of post colonial discourses encompassing indigenous voices, local perspectives and epistemologies, together with the post modern shift within Western academic disciplines that define the field, open up new possibilities and opportunities for understanding and organizing distance education in the South Pacific. Theoretical borders have been eroded, conventional wisdom challenged and fundamental questions are raised about knowledge and the relationships of power within distance education initiatives and programmes with the South Pacific.
>
> (Guy, 1995: 79)

Traditional Melanesians have always lived in a communal society of doing things together, be it planting, feasting, warfare or learning. Any media used for distance teaching must be conscious of this important underlying feature of a people's culture. Guy's (1994) research in PNG with a group of educators using print media for professional development, for example, brings forth such issues as structural and pedagogical barriers on the IDCE's part. It shows how these educators were able to reflect critically and transform their study and teaching over time in ways that are consistent with the social, cultural, and political contexts in which they lived and worked.

Whatever means is used to deliver university teaching at a distance in PNG must recognize emerging local theories and practices. Knowledge must be seen to be a shared experience, one that is interactive, participatory and 'real', that reflects PNG and Melanesian culture and social life. All events affecting the way people live is done with a communal sense of being together, doing it together and sharing the success and failures together. This is the 'wantok way' (common kinship).

The push to introduce new technology is to 'bring life' into the learning process. The study guide and book of readings in the written media are 'cold' and to the Papua New Guinean/Melanesian learner may seem idiosyncratic as a learning medium if not well structured and presented. Distance education in PNG has to cope with the traditional culture of distance education (and academic life in general) being one of reading and writing. However, the traditional learning cultures of PNG are ones of observation and orality. A boy learns to fish by going out with his father, observing, being spoken to by the father and this culminates in confidence for the boy to try fishing by himself.

Conclusion

Distance education presents itself as an alternative to conventional teaching at universities. In recent times, distance education has been catapulted to new prominence with advances in computer and communications technologies. Additionally, education is being vigorously applied as a solution to social and economic problems in nations such as PNG. Limited classroom space and other student amenities do not allow for an increase in numbers of on-campus students.

Distance education can make universities and university education available to a greater number of Papua New Guineans. From the reported cases at least two broad conclusions can be drawn. First, to make available university education to many people, staff perceptions and existing practices need to change. Second, to make such changes, there is a need to explain the theoretical underpinnings pertaining to using new and appropriate technologies in distance teaching that will bring about effective student learning. At UPNG we need to explore all opportunities and possibilities for using new technology in distance education and decide what is appropriate for local contexts.

While desires and ambitions may have been genuine to change university teaching using new technology there are obvious inhibiting factors. Print will continue to remain as the dominant medium of distance teaching in PNG, while at the same time, other technologies do present new opportunities for combination or supplementing other distance teaching materials. New innovations are bound to meet some resistance as reported in this case study.

Acknowledgement

I would like to acknowledge the initiative of Aileen Natera who was the Social Development course writer who pushed for the use of audiotapes with the study guides.

Chapter 9

Lions and merlions: critical reflections on the introduction of new technologies in higher education in Swaziland and Singapore

Neil Hanley and Stewart Marshall

Introduction

In this chapter, we compare and reflect critically on our experiences of the introduction of new technologies in higher education in Swaziland and Singapore. In Swaziland, we use as a case study the first two years of operation of the Institute of Distance Education at the University of Swaziland. In Singapore we use as our case study the first two years of offering an Australian degree by distance education.

In our reflections, we find that it is impossible to fully understand the experiences, and especially the difficulties, without considering the broader social, cultural and political contexts within which the innovations are located.

Singapore and Swaziland achieved independence about the same time, if you count Singapore's 'independence' to be when it broke away from the Malaysian Federation. In Swaziland the King is symbolized as a lion. Singapore (or Singa Pura – Lion City) uses the merlion as its symbol. But little else (other than the fact that their names both have the same initial consonant) appears to be same. Singapore is an island; Swaziland is landlocked. Swaziland has less than half the population in an area 30 times as big as Singapore. No one has a mobile phone in Swaziland, whereas in Singapore everyone appears to have one. Very few people in Swaziland have computers, and even fewer are connected to the Internet, whereas Singapore is one of the world's most connected societies.

The two countries appear to be considerably different in their reactions to the global diffusion of modernity. Similarly, in the case studies that we discuss below, we find that the two countries differ considerably in their reactions to the introduction of new technologies in higher education.

The first case study is based in Swaziland. After a brief description of the context, Stewart tells the story of his experiences during the first two years of operation of the Institute of Distance Education at the University of Swaziland, and then reflects on the major issues that emerge. Similarly, after a brief description of the context of the second case study, Neil tells the story of his experiences during the first two years of offering an Australian degree by distance education in Singapore, and then reflects on the major issues that emerge.

Case study 1: Swaziland

The context

Swaziland is a landlocked country that shares borders with Mozambique and South Africa. It was founded by Bantu peoples from Mozambique in the 18th century, and became a British protectorate when colonial rule was established in 1903. Sobhuza II led Swaziland to independence in 1968. In 1973, proclaiming the rejection of colonial influences and the re-affirmation of Swazi tradition, Sobhuza II repealed the independence constitution, banned political parties and assumed supreme power in the kingdom (Matsebula, 1988: 260–61). The country continues to be ruled under this 1973 decree as a dual monarchy with a King (currently King Mswati III) and Queen Mother. The system is described by the ruling aristocracy as Swaziland's 'unique form of democracy'. It is this system that the 'progressives' in Swaziland are seeking to overthrow.

The population of Swaziland is approximately 1 million people (IRRC, 1997). Subsistence agriculture, which occupies more than 60 per cent of the population, contributes nearly 25 per cent to the GDP. English (in which government business is conducted) and siSwati are the official languages. Sixty-seven per cent of the population aged 15 and over can read and write.

There is one university, the University of Swaziland (UNISWA), with an enrolment of about 3,000 students. It was to this university that I was appointed to assist in the establishment of distance education at the newly formed Institute of Distance Education (IDE). Unfortunately, IDE and I arrived at a time of political, social and economic upheaval in Swaziland.

The mission of the IDE is to create educational and training opportunities for qualified individuals who have been unable, for one reason or another, to undertake conventional university education programmes. The programmes offered by IDE are the same as those offered on-campus.

IDE programmes comprise six to eight subjects per year, and use two modes of teaching: printed materials and face-to-face tutorials. The printed material is specially written by IDE Course Writers who are usually the UNISWA lecturers teaching the on-campus version of the programme. Students also have approximately 25 hours per subject of face-to-face tutorials. Ten to 15 of these hours occur when the students attend the university for three one-week intensive study sessions with the IDE Course Lecturers (who are usually the UNISWA lecturers teaching the on-campus version of the programme). These 'Study Weeks' are similar to the 'residentials' offered by other universities, except that owing to shortage of bed-space at UNISWA, they are not residential. The remaining tutorial hours are conducted in the Regional Learning Centres (RLCs) in Manzini and Mbabane by Course Tutors (usually high school teachers) specifically appointed for this task by IDE.

Stewart's story

IDE enrolled its first intake of students in August 1996. A total of 150 students registered for the three programmes: BA Humanities (Languages), Diploma in Law, and Diploma in Commerce, offered by IDE. These students were taught by approximately 25 UNISWA lecturers and 30 external tutors. I arrived in October 1996.

As Co-ordinator of Academic Studies, I was responsible for the teaching/learning operations of IDE. This included co-ordinating the recruitment, admission, and assessment of students, and establishing and maintaining records in these areas. The job also involved organizing the face-to-face teaching sessions, time-tabling, the recruitment of tutors, and organizing and running staff development workshops for tutors and lecturers.

It would be not unfair to say that the secondary and tertiary teaching methods in Swaziland tended to create dependent learners skilled in surface rather than deep learning. We (the members of staff in IDE) wanted to change this. We saw the role of academic and other staff employed by IDE as *facilitators of learning*, not *deliverers of education*. So in our early staff development workshops for tutors and lecturers, we endeavoured to engage the participants by using the student centred methods we favoured. We stressed to the participants that we wished them to be 'dialogically involved' (Freire, 1982) as co-researchers in the distance education project in Swaziland. We wanted them to reflect on their ways of thinking and acting, because 'through this process of investigation, the level of critical thinking is raised among all those involved' (Freire, 1982: 30). We tried to establish our roles as 'critical friends' (Kember, 1998: 57). Unfortunately, although most of the tutors attended, it was difficult to get the UNISWA lecturers to attend these workshops.

Attendance by staff at their teaching sessions was also a problem on many occasions. For one of the Saturday Study Days at the University campus, I was dismayed to find that for the Law Year 1 programme only four of the seven lecturers turned up, and in each of these four classes the students were given a test.

The creation of effective information and communication systems proved to be a major problem. I decided that I would use written communication (newsletters and mail-merge letters) both for information purposes, and also to try to create a sense of 'community' amongst all those staff and students involved with IDE. Since I had no computer in my office, all this had to be done on our home computer and printer. Three weeks after the first mailout to all students, I was surprized to find how few of them had actually received my mail. Subsequent mailouts confirmed that mail was taking at least two weeks to get to those outside the university, and that in far too many cases it never arrived at all.

In March 1997 I wrote my first e-mail to a colleague in Australia, and tried to explain why I had not written earlier:

> For the last month the country has been at a standstill because of the mass stay-away organized by the Swaziland Federation of Trade Unions (SFTU). We had to stock up on food, water, candles, paraffin stove, etc in case the shops were closed, and the electricity and water services were all cut (as happened last year during the mass stay-away). There were several power cuts and some violent incidents around the country, but we managed to stay out of trouble.
>
> A major problem is that I still do not have a computer at work and I do not have an outside telephone line. We have a computer at home, but we have no telephone line (nor any chance of getting one because of the shortage of lines) so cannot e-mail or get on the Internet.
>
> I have only just now been able to get an e-mail account through the Computer Centre. Unfortunately, that means competing with students for a machine and sitting in a crowded and very hot room to work on a computer with a disabled a-drive and a very slow connection (in theory 9,600 bps, but in practice about 200 bps) to Johannesburg for e-mail access.

In August 1997, IDE registered its second intake of students. As in the previous year, registration was conducted at the beginning of the first Study Week. But this particular registration exercise was a disaster.

As a few students in the 1996–97 cohort had not paid all their fees, the University Senate decided that for 1997–98 the full fee of E2500 (instead of the half-fee, as before) should be payable 'up-front' at registration. Unfortunately, this decision was only communicated to the new and continuing students a couple of weeks before registration by means of a notice in *The Observer* newspaper. Since most students did not read this paper, they arrived to register with only half their fee. They were told by the Registrar that they would be allowed to register late, but that they would have to pay a late-registration fee of E50 per day (one week's pay for a Swazi housekeeper, half a week's pay for a gardener). Furthermore, they would not be allowed to sit in classes or receive teaching material until they had registered. This meant that the majority of the IDE students missed the first Study Week entirely, and did not receive their DE materials for several weeks.

In this same month, in a letter to a colleague in Australia, I wrote:

> I am so sorry that I have not written for so long. Did you get my e-mail in March, and the latest one sent in July? Our University system sometimes has problems and the users are not notified that their e-mails are not going anywhere – but when it is working it is probably the best means of communicating. The post is very unreliable.

A major problem and source of extreme annoyance is that I still do not have a computer to work on at the University – and a great deal of my work must be done on one (try enrolling and keeping track of hundreds of students, writing to them, calculating their results, presenting the data to Faculty Board and Senate, etc, without a computer). So I am still using our computer at home to do my work – usually in the evenings after I get home from the University – which doesn't give me much time for letter writing. We had to buy another computer so that the three of us wouldn't fight over this one.

November 1997 was an exciting time for everyone in the IDE. UNESCO donated the much-needed educational technology hardware: computers, printers, scanner, television, videocassette recorder, and video camera. At last I had a computer on my desk.

But communication remained a problem. Although I now had an outside line, this was no help for maintaining contact with most of our students. In December 1997, I wrote the following to my colleagues in Australia:

> Every day I seem to be more and more enmeshed in issues, which are directly or indirectly linked to the political machinations of the day. One example: to communicate with our DE students I used to place notices in the *Times* as well as announcements on the radio. Now the government has forbidden parastatals using the *Times* for advertising (they say it is a cost cutting exercise but it is really an attempt to close down the *Times* because it is always outspoken and reveals much of the corruption and abuse). The other newspaper (the paper basically owned by the Royal family) has a very small circulation and so it is not really worth putting notices in there. So I now have difficulty communicating with the students at short notice.
>
> For example, a couple of months ago the Graduation ceremony was postponed at short notice by one week (because the scheduled date coincided with a traditional Royal ceremony). The new date for Graduation coincided with our IDE Study Day. So we announced on the radio that the new Study Day date would be one week earlier than planned. You can imagine the chaos – people turned up for the Graduation on our Study Day, and students turned up for the Study Day on Graduation Day. More recently, the teachers' strike (which lasted over four weeks) caused the schools which we use as Regional Learning Centres to be closed. I found it extremely difficult to inform the students of a change of venue at short notice.

Critical reflection is helped by obtaining the perceptions of others. At the end of 1997, I asked students to comment on any aspect of their studies with IDE. I received comments from 64 of the students. I used NUD★IST (*Non-numerical Unstructured Data Indexing, Searching and Theorising* – a computer programme written by Qualitative Solutions and Research of La Trobe University in Australia) to analyse the students' comments.

Twenty-two per cent of the respondents were concerned about transferring to the on-campus programme. All these students were enrolled in the BA programme and had originally applied for the on-campus programme, but owing to a shortage of places had not been successful.

Over 40 per cent of the respondents were concerned about Course Tutors and Lecturers missing sessions. Forty-eight per cent of the respondents were concerned about the perceived attitude of staff to the students. The students expressed their need for feedback, and their concern at the staff attitude, which was implied when such feedback was not provided:

> Please see to it that all the lecturers see us during our Study Days when we have to meet them because some do not even bother coming, they just send assignments to us. Some bring them back but they do not even guide us on how we should do things. Some do not even bring back our assignments.
>
> Humanities student

Over 30 per cent of the respondents expressed their need to be treated better by the University and staff:

> Be considered as the University of Swaziland students in the following: be treated as equal to those who are on-campus.
>
> Humanities student

Other students wrote of their concern about the lack of consideration and respect from some staff:

> Some of the lecturers cannot listen or cannot seek our ideas, as how best can we understand the subjects. They don't want to compromise or feel we are committed adults.
>
> Law 2 student

> Lecturers announcing that they are doing us a favour by giving us lectures.
>
> Law 2 student

Ten per cent of the respondents commented on communication problems between IDE and students, for example:

> Sometimes we are not informed on time of changes of RLC dates. This becomes expensive because we travel for nothing. IDE must use even the *Times* of Swaziland since some of us don't buy the *Observer*.
>
> Adult Education student

The chaotic nature of things in the last four months of 1997 had made it difficult to communicate with the tutors, let alone organize development workshops. It was as a result of this that I decided to publish a newsletter specifically for tutors and lecturers that would contain their critical reflections on their practices. I hoped that this would facilitate their dialogical involvement with the project and assist in their personal development. I did not obtain a large number of responses (those from lecturers were very few), but was able to produce and distribute two issues of the *IDEAS Newsletter* before I left Swaziland.

Some of the lecturers, who were very committed to the distance education project, always attended meetings and responded to requests for information or involvement. One of these lecturers wrote:

I do not know of another university that has as high a turnover of staff as UNISWA. This can stunt the growth of disciplines/departments, etc, with implications for DE, amongst others.

Humanities lecturer

Another lecturer told me about a student who was not really doing as well as she was able. When challenged by the lecturer, she said that there was no point in her trying hard. This was because however well she performed she 'had the wrong surname to be able to get a good job or sponsorship for further studies' (ie that she was not connected to royalty, the royal surname being 'Dlamini'). In support of their privileged positions, one prince said that 'a Dlamini is closer to God'.

My contract at IDE finished at the end of June 1998. Shortly before that date, I e-mailed the following to Neil:

One thing that strikes me is the reluctance of staff to commit themselves in writing. I have to communicate with about 45 lecturers in the university. I do this by means of mail merge memos and letters. Over the time I have been here I have sent out hundreds of written communications, but have received back only a handful of replies. Example: lecturers were asked to tell me the dates and titles for their assignments. Nothing returned. When the students come for one of their face-to-face tutorials, the lecturers announce the title and return date. All those students who do not attend that tutorial (because of illness, deaths in the family, work, etc) don't get to know these essential details. I can't mail the details out to them because I don't know either.

Now, is this a function of this being an oral culture? Or something more sinister. One lecturer said to me 'don't put anything in writing'.

Reflection on major issues that emerge from this case study

The administrative and academic culture of UNISWA is like that of so many single mode universities of yesteryear. For example, the administrative and teaching functions presuppose that students with government scholarships will attend university for five days a week between 9.00 am and 5.00 pm for approximately 35 weeks of the year. In its operations, IDE challenged all these presuppositions. But the students too showed their desire for (dependence on) face-to-face teaching.

Throughout my time in Swaziland, communication with students and staff remained a major problem. I was unable to find an effective way to transmit information to the students; I was unable to get effective feedback from the lecturers; and, I was unable to create an effective mechanism for communication between lecturers and tutors. To some extent, these communication problems resulted from inadequate communications technology or infrastructure. But the communication problems with and between staff were largely due to the attitudes of the human participants.

Establishing effective communication between staff and changing the culture of an institution require levels of motivation and goodwill, which are not apparent in UNISWA. In order to understand this, we have to look further afield than the university administration. I believe that the attitudes that I have described, and which are also apparent in many organizations throughout the country, are largely a reflection of the system of government. The complaint by the majority of people is that they will get nowhere in life, no matter how well educated they become, because they do not have the correct surname.

Case study 2: Singapore

The context

Monash University's Gippsland campus has been the focus for delivering subjects and courses through the Distance Education Centre (DEC). The DEC has always encouraged, within budget constraints, a mix of technologies, strategies and materials to support flexible learning. These include printed materials (Subject Guides, Subject Books, Readings), audio and video tapes, CD ROM and software for online class access.

Singapore is seen as a 'mature market'. The economy is well-developed, communications infrastructure continually being updated, the English language is studied throughout school, promoted through the use of English in print, radio and television media. While traditional cultural practices remain in the various cultural groups, it can be argued that these cultures have also 'westernized' through processes such as colonization and economic developments linked to advanced western economies. Additionally there has been a strong value placed on obtaining education in places like the United Kingdom, United States of America, Canada and, more recently, Australia for those families who can afford to send their children overseas for education.

Potential students can, in general, be assumed to be fluent in several languages, including English, and relatively comfortable with the cultural contexts on which the subjects they study are based.

Singaporeans place a high value on education and, indeed, continuing education, as a way of gaining advantage in a competitive society. Material affluence and education are important indicators of success. Educational experience has been face-to-face and teaching, rather than learning, has been the pedagogic focus.

While Monash campuses have attracted increasing numbers of students from Singapore studying full-time in Australia, staff members on the Gippsland Campus recognized the numbers of potential students in Singapore who, for reasons related to work and family, would not be able to study a degree programme in Australia. It was also recognized that some students might wish to choose a mix of Singapore-based education and study in Australia. In formulating an approach to offering such education in Singapore, the concept of 'flexible learning' was adopted.

Singapore is a relatively small land mass. As it has developed advanced technological capacity through government and business initiatives (the country is currently being cabled) and given its desire to be a 'communications hub' for Asia. The option to utilize new communications technologies, such as online classes, e-mail, and the Internet as a tool for research was evident.

The Schools of Computing and Information Technology, Applied Science, Business and Electronic Commerce, and the School of Humanities, Communications and Social Sciences offer degree programmes at Technology Management Centre for Advanced Seminars in Singapore (TMCAS). These programmes are similar to programmes based at Gippsland campus, and offered through Gippsland campus at other Monash campuses. The most recent campus offering programmes from the School of Humanities, Communications and Social Sciences is in Malaysia.

Flexible learning means recognizing and communicating with differing student populations and the differing needs of students within these population groups. Cultural, social, political and economic concerns are crucial in considering access to and usage of new technologies.

In this case study of 'new technologies' in higher education, the focus is on TMCAS. The 'new technology' in this case is online learning, but there will be reference to other teaching technologies.

Neil's story

The School of Humanities, Communications and Social Sciences first offered the Bachelor of Arts (Communications) at TMCAS in Singapore in 1995. Degrees in Computing and Business were already established and the Communications degree was designed to mesh into these offerings. Additionally, students in Computing were using NetFace (later WebFace) for online class activity, e-mail and, in some cases, assignment submission.

The School of Humanities, Communications and Social Sciences had an efficient print-based curriculum and infrastructure to deliver DE materials. This was built on in offering the Bachelor of Arts (Communications) in Singapore at TMCAS by incorporating various mixes of audio, video, online classes, and e-mail. Fundamental to our approach and use of technologies was a 'learning' rather than 'teaching' model of education. This pedagogy highlighted basic differences in cultural practices of educating.

In the first year communications stream two subjects were offered: 'Introduction to Communication Studies' and 'Media Studies', both offering online access through TMCAS or by alternative Internet access. This was also the case for a second year subject I offered titled 'Public Relations and Mass Communications Technologies'. The print medium was organized to structure a semester of study in weekly modules based around a Subject Book, Readings and Activities. Audio and video materials were utilized. Online learning was seen as a support tool in the first year subjects, but a key part of the second year subject.

Online learning activities and an e-mail option were based on software developed by the (DEC) at Gippsland. Initially DOS-based software titled NetFace was used but was then replaced by graphics-based software called WebFace with Internet access so TMCAS students could participate in their online classes, access various Monash and other newsgroups, do library searches, 'visit' the chaplain or the student union, and use e-mail. These online classes were 'closed' rather than 'open'. This meant only students enrolled in the subject could participate in the online class. Implicit in this approach was a belief in the value of asynchronous education, virtual classes – bringing students together by technologies that would assist in overcoming the 'tyranny of distance'. It was believed that this asynchronous contact would increase the sense of belonging and decrease the dropout rate (Kember, 1995).

There have been and remain limitations to available facilities for online classes at TMCAS. However, students usually had fortnightly contact with a subject co-ordinator, although they were identified technically as distance education students. This meant that they had more face-to-face contact options than other distance education students, who were given the choice to attend three or four weekend schools at Gippsland campus. Many of this second group could not attend because of travel, family and financial constraints. In effect, for TMCAS, a model was developed 'in between' on-campus and distance education practices. There were occasional visits by staff of the School of Humanities, Communications and Social Sciences to meet students and talk with TMCAS staff. The School also appointed a Student Administrator – International Students, and liaised closely with the DEC on production and distribution of various subject materials.

GSC2410: a closer look at the TMCAS Experience

The subject Public Relations and Mass Communications Technologies (GSC2410, 1998) provides modular week-based study topics based on a Subject Book and TMCAS unit co-ordinator support. Integral with print material at TMCAS is the face-to-face contact, with online class options plus e-mail access to the Subject co-ordinator at Gippsland.

There was almost no online contribution from TMCAS students in this subject to the online (virtual) class in GSC2410. However, TMCAS students in this subject were the heaviest users of e-mail directed to the Subject co-ordinator in Australia. These imbalances suggest a number of factors based on cultures of educating, communication practices, work and domestic considerations, which vary from those of other Monash Gippsland students. Few TMCAS students utilized TMCAS facilities for any form of online activity, even though many attended classes at TMC on a regular basis. There is no evidence of TMCAS students being 'sleepers' and reading the contributions of others to the online class. Many of the questions they asked in e-mail and answers to them were available online or already available in the Subject Book.

Many TMCAS students had alternative access to e-mail, either as individual Internet subscribers or through facilities available at their places of work. Many students were working long hours and clearly prioritized 'what do I have to do to get a good grade' as more important than contributing to an online class, and becoming involved in online collaborative learning activities, even when these online activities were identified as of value to discussing assignments. Trial topics had been placed in the online class for responses focusing on what might be appropriate models and strategies identified in the Subject Book and prescribed text.

However, numbers did appear to form their own study groups and choose the option to work in a small collective to complete their major piece of assessment. This was also observed in the approach of Singapore students to studying in this subject at Gippsland campus. TMCAS students also placed high value e-mail contact with the Subject co-ordinator, although much information provided would have been available from the TMCAS Unit Co-ordinator. This again suggests differing social and cultural conditions and past experiences in how education can occur. It also suggests no difficulty in asynchronous communication, but that this is clearly preferred at the individual level rather than in the 'public' virtual class environment.

Another noticeable difference in comparing both on-campus and distance education students with those at TMCAS was that students from both groups posted responses to trial topics in the virtual class and discussed possible major assignment responses, either as individuals or as part of an often evolving group. External students were limited by access to appropriate computing equipment, but many of those without other means of access used regional study centres, accessed the microlabs at weekend schools and, occasionally, used cyber cafés.

Reflection on major issues that emerged from this case study

It was evident that TMCAS students relied on the Subject Book, face-to-face sessions at TMCAS and e-mail to the appropriate Subject co-ordinator at Gippsland campus. The comprehensiveness of the Subject Books, textbook, associated audio/video materials in the subjects identified indicates that 'stand alone' materials in these subjects were perceived to be the major source of information for responding to subjects and examinations by TMCAS students.

Attendance at face-to-face sessions at TMCAS was clearly preferred to being part of an online class. The available facilities at TMCAS and student time to use them may have been factors, but given e-mail activity it would appear that participation in an online class was not deemed valuable by TMCAS students. This may have to do with the weight given to the value of online learning and perceptions about this value. The higher rates of usage in Australia indicate more structured and, at times, creative uses of online learning.

Online learning, if perceived as an 'add on' in curriculum, is unlikely to be seen as an appropriate area for students to invest learning time. However, if built into to curriculum, there is better opportunity for developing learning experiences.

This approach needs to account for available technologies, educational facilities and practices, social and cultural contexts. The preference of TMCAS students (with access to appropriate technologies) for e-mail rather than online class activity reflects a student-teacher response which might be identified as culturally 'natural'. They did not engage the virtual community available to them.

The desire to chat on the Internet (being private rather than public) is not confined to Singaporean students, of course, but chat seems to have been a way of approaching the Subject co-ordinator, initially and usually, with a formal approach about subject matters. Some students became less formal as e-mail transactions increased, particularly those who developed understandings about applying the informality of e-mail to student-teacher frameworks. Some went beyond this relationship to make contributions better suited to the online class.

Many factors impinge on the choice to participate in an online class. For TMCAS students it would seem that access to appropriate technology and software is not, generally, a problem. Facilities at TMCAS and opportunity to use them may be factors. But it is more likely that TMCAS students regard private access as desirable and convenient and find online classes with students remote to them as not so attractive.

This example of perceived 'tyranny of distance' and 'irrelevance' of online classes poses problems for how to better integrate Monash's expanding campuses, technology options, and understanding of diverse student populations. Students, academic and administrative staff need more chances to be effective participants in the process of online learning.

Concluding remarks

In order to understand the changes in so many of the world's higher education institutions, we must take into account the broader economic, political, social and technological changes. There is recognition by many that African institutions of higher education also need to transform in response to these broader world changes (Otaala, 1997), but more particularly that they need to change to be in line with the continent's new political and socioeconomic environment. In the case of the University of Swaziland, the necessary transformation is not helped by the political situation in Swaziland.

In Swaziland, education is seen as a way to earn a living in a society, which rewards birthright rather than ability. In Singapore, education is seen as a way of gaining significant advantage in a competitive society, which values academic success. In both countries, educational experience has been face-to-face, and teaching, rather than learning has been the pedagogic focus.

The cultures within which students learn, and how to fit these factors with distance education pedagogy and curriculum are issues on which academics must continue to work. Administrative staff, too, need to work with distance education structures that are more 'user friendly' and better integrated with academic requirements.

Chapter 10

To be *or* not to be:
technological change in the University of the South Pacific

Richard Wah

> All of us in the practice of education have an interesting and important role to play. We have the knowledge to deliver lifelong learning to users at their location of choice, we have the technology to support us in our endeavours, and we even have governments and their leaders urging for more and more education. What remains to complete the cycle is the imagination and will of those in education to bring it all together.
>
> Gajaray Dhanarajan

The University of the South Pacific (USP) serves 12 island nation states (INS) with a combined land area of roughly the size of Tasmania, but smaller than Ireland, stretching over a tract of ocean larger than the Australian continent or the United States mainland. The USP's charter requires it to serve it students within the contexts of their own countries and, consequently, its distance education (DE) programmes are of fundamental importance. These programmes require the best communications infrastructure available in a context in which most member countries struggle to provide a reliable public telephone system. Furthermore, funds are limited by the size and limited development of the economies of the co-operating nation states and the aid available from donors such as Australia, Japan and New Zealand. How is it possible to employ modern communications and telecommunications technologies to serve the distance education programmes in the USP?

This chapter is written from the perspective of an 'insider' who is currently an 'outsider'. I have worked at various levels within the DE system at the USP for over 10 years, as an associate lecturer, lecturer, Director of a National Extension Centre (NEC) and, finally, as Head of Distance Education. In some of these positions, I was in a position of power and influence, and in others, I was in a subaltern position (Spivak, 1988). I do not write from the perspective of the Head of DE at the USP, but from the various perspectives listed above, and as a student who has been engaged in postgraduate studies with the University of Queensland for the past three years. This has given me some time to stand back from the system and to compare notes with colleagues – innovators, conservatives, radicals and others – from Asian countries, Africa, North America and Australia. From this, I have now acquired a broader theoretical and practical basis in my understanding of the system, how it has shifted and matured, how it can be changed and possible directions for change.

After providing some relevant background information about the USP and its DE programmes, I will discuss the various phases of development of the university's communications network, and then proceed to an analysis of its effectiveness in the light of government and university policies and relevant literature.

The University of the South Pacific

The USP was established by 12 South Pacific INS which, in various ways, were formerly subject to British colonial domination: the Cook Islands, Fiji, Kiribati, the Marshall Islands, Nauru, Niue, Samoa, Solomon Islands, Tokelau, Tonga, Tuvalu and Vanuatu. The USP's geographic area extends about 6,500 kilometres from east to west and more than 3,000 kilometres from south to north. The USP consortium countries have populations ranging from less than 2,000 (Niue) to over 800,000 (Fiji). It is within this context that the USP is chartered to provide tertiary education for the Pacific peoples, without the need for students to attend one central campus. The USP's DE system serves the charter by taking the university to where the people are. This poses many practical problems, due to the large areas covered by the USP, the limited funds to provide tertiary education in each of the INS, and the inadequate telecommunications and transportation infrastructure that are essential for DE. However, despite these conditions, the consensus amongst those concerned with DE at the USP has always been that communications technologies are essential for DE within the region.

John Chick (1981) described the USP as 'an incredibly complex institution, multi-national, multi-ethnic, multi-lingual and one which had to work under enormous political pressure'. A decade later, Renwick and his team of consultants wrote:

> There can be no other part of the world with as many challenges to the development of effective distance education as the region covered by the USP... The problems that other institutions have to some degree, the USP has on a massive scale.
>
> (Renwick, Shale and King, 1991: 14)

There are around 60 cultures and 235 languages practised and spoken by 1.6 million people in the 12 member countries of the USP. The USP reacted to the tyranny of distance and other barriers, by setting up National Extension Centres in 11 of its 12 INS. These Centres are the USP's eyes and ears providing the university with tools for surveillance, response and control within these countries. A Centre Director, one or more Centre Lecturers and some clerical staff usually staff the Centres. The NECs also have libraries, computer and science laboratories, telephones, faxes, e-mail hookup via dial-up and teleconferencing systems for communicating with the University Extension Head Quarters (UEHQ) at the USP's main campus in Suva, Fiji. All interactions between the students and their lecturers at the main campuses are via the link between the Centres and UEHQ. Thus the students must travel to the Centres for teleconferencing tutorials. It is pertinent that I point out that the costs of travel from a student's residence to a Centre can vary considerably from less than a dollar to a few hundred dollars.

The USPNet

When the term the USPNet is used it usually refers to the telecommunications links between the Centres and the campuses. However, I would like to broaden the meaning of this term. I like to think of the USPNet as the communications system that keeps the USP DE system functioning. It consists of five parts. First, and most important, is the USP's private mailbag system. This is a system of mailbags that transports all documents (learning packages, assignments, examination papers, notices to students and local tutors, administrative information and directives, and all manner of memos) between the Centres and the campuses. Without it the USP's operation as a regional university would be greatly diminished. Second is the USP's tele-conferencing system. This is the system that enables online tutorials and online staff meetings and discussions between staff and students at the Centres with staff at the three major campuses. This system has been supplementary to the teaching conducted via the learning packages; it was an add-on, a 'luxury'. For the period that it was absent (1983 to 1986), it was missed, but administrative communications continued via telephones, faxes and memos transported via the mailbag system. The third part of USPNet is the e-mail system. This system is mainly used for messages about assignment queries, transference of student database records between computers at the main campus and those in the Centres. This system became functional and operational in the mid 1990s, and was a crucial element in devolving back to the Centres the responsibility of validating of each Centre's students' records. Prior to it, commissioning this responsibility lay with UEHQ administrative staff. The final part of the USPNet is the telephone and fax links between the Centres and main campus. These systems are reliable but their high operation costs have discouraged substantial reliance on them. The USPNet is thus a combination of various communication systems.

Outside the public telephone and fax systems, the USP is very reliant on electronic technologies based on computers and telecommunications. For our purposes, computer technology relates to all kinds of computers and peripherals including a diversity of software. Included within computer technologies are: various computers, including PCs and servers, printers, modems, scanners, compact discs, zip drives, multimedia systems, operating systems, applications, communication and utility packages. Telecommunications technologies include computers, communications software, modems, Internet providers and the communication channels – cables, microwave links, high frequency transceivers and satellites. In DE, these technologies are used for teaching (audioconferencing, videoconferencing, videotapes, audiotapes, audiographics, e-mail and Internet) and for administration (all of those mentioned in teaching and including computer systems like databases for students' records, assignment tracking, student support tracking, etc). The former I prefer to call 't-technology' and the latter 'a-technology'. I hasten to add that within DE, the divide between administration and teaching is not as clearly defined as it is in face-to-face teaching situations, and I have chosen to use these categories in order to better present my arguments.

The development of the USPNet can be seen in four stages or phases. Currently, the university is planning the next phase, which is due to commence in 2001. Of course, the USPNet is based on the telecommunications infrastructure of the USP region. These infrastructures are owned and operated by telecommunications companies, usually partly owned by government and multinational companies, and the major carriers are the communications giants Cable and Wireless and IntelSat. Thus, to negotiate a link between Fiji and Cook Islands, for example, the USP must hold discussions with Fiji Telecom (which provides the in-country telecommunications services) and FINTEL (which provides services external to Fiji), Cable and Wireless and IntelSat and Cooks Islands Telecom – five different corporate organizations. This process must be repeated 12 times. Only after agreements are reached can the systems configuration be finalized. If one country does not agree, the whole system is in jeopardy.

Phase One: NAS ATS-1 Satellite 1972–83

This system used earth stations located at each of the NECs. The system enabled half-duplex audio teleconferencing and slow scan video-transmission, using Apple 2e computers. The system was maintained from Hawaii, under the auspices of PEACESAT, and it was used for administration and online tutorials. An experimental e-mail system was installed in the early 1980s. Unfortunately, because of its minimum functionality, un-friendliness, and lack of staff training, it was put to very little use. This e-mail system did not have a connection to the outside world.

Phase Two: IntelSat 1986–96

The ATS-1 satellite drifted out of useful range for the USP's purposes, so from 1983 to 1986 it did not function. In 1986, transponders on an IntelSat satellite were used for another series of telecommunication experiments. The ATS-1/PEACESAT earth stations at the Centres were dismantled. Unfortunately, not all the NECs could be connected to this satellite. Therefore a hybrid system was commissioned.

The system consisted of three different telecommunications schemes. Some Centres were connected via satellite linkup (Cook Islands, Fiji, Solomon Islands, Tonga, Vanuatu) others were linked via High Frequency (HF) transceivers (Fiji, Nauru, Niue, Samoa, Tuvalu) and the third group was linked by telephone calls and patched into the system (Fiji, Kiribati, Marshall Islands). The last system was seldom used. The satellite links also used leased lines between the National Centres and their local National Telecom earth stations. Tokelau students were not connected as their contact was through the Samoa Centre. Cable & Wireless and IntelSat subsidized the satellite linkup. The quality of audio in the satellite linkups was much better than the previous ATS-1 system, but the quality of HF communications literally depended on the weather.

The e-mail system was via dialup to the Centres and the rest of the world. A computer at the main campus 'called' the computers at the Centres and downloaded their e-mail every weekday. This system was mainly used for the downloading and uploading of student records for the student information systems that were kept at the Centres. The link to the outside world was only possible via the Suva campus, and a dialup link generously provided by and through the Waikato University in New Zealand. By the late 1980s the International Development Program (IDP) subsidized the cost of a leased line from the Suva campus to Melbourne. This service, a 4.8 bps line, cost the USP around $100,000 pa.

Phase Three: leased lines 1995–97

The Fiji Centre, the largest National Extension Centre, which accounts for more than 55 per cent of the DE students of the USP, moved from its location in Suva to Lautoka, a distance from about two kilometres to more than 200 kilometres from the main campus. Thus the telephone costs between the Fiji Centre and UEHQ would increase phenomenally, since the increased distances meant that the telephone calls would be trunk calls rather than local ones. A case was put to the policymakers to install leased lines between the campus and Fiji Centre. The leased line option was cheaper and provided more functionality than estimated costs of trunk calls between Suva and Lautoka. A 64 kbps line comprising four voice and one data channel was leased to maintain affordable telecommunications between Suva and Lautoka. The e-mail system is an integral part of the leased line system.

Phase Four: the interim system 1997–present

Leased lines are now in place to all the NECs previously connected to the satellite, and the HF system continues to operate. The leased lines to Centres outside Fiji have videoconferencing capabilities. Both options for e-mail are used, with dialup facilities in some NECs and permanent connections for those Centres fortunate to have a leased line. The link to the outside world extended to a 19.2 kbps line from the Suva campus to Hong Kong, which costs $8,800 per month. The Melbourne link was discontinued.

Phase Five: plans for 2001

The preferred option of the USP is given below. Justification of this system was in terms of specified functionality and presumed economies of scale. Video-conferencing options are to enable lecturers located at one of the three campuses to lecture students at other campuses, Centres and/or institutes. There will be direct e-mail links between all the Centres and campuses. The USP hopes to have its own earth stations in each of its INS. This system will be similar to the ATS-1. The Hub (Fiji) and mini-hubs (Vanuatu & Samoa) will have the capacity to transmit video, audio and data simultaneously. The system will also be able to conduct two separate simultaneous videoconferencing sessions. The only barrier to this system is the obtaining of licenses for the USP to operate its own earth stations. E-mail will always be connected and is planned to be an integral part of the system.

Using electronic technologies at the USP

The 'hard facts' about the development of the educational technologies within DE at the USP are presented above. In this section, I attempt to discuss them from another perspective. This perspective is in line with sentiments raised by John Herrmann, the Centre Director (CD) for the Cook Islands, in 'Swimming against the tide: The case for keeping the human face of education'. Herrmann's major point is that the human subject is very important within DE. Furthermore, the implementation of technologies must be mindful that many of the technological strategies being proposed and implemented were 'developed in countries with wholly different social, cultural, economic and physical structures... our focus should always remain on the actual students who have an educational need' (Herrmann, 1997: 39). I have reconstituted the notion of 'educational need' to that of 'lessening the transactional distance'. Transactional distance is the space that is inherent in DE, a space that emphasizes the differences in the psychological makeup and communication skills of the learners and the teachers – 'a space of potential misunderstanding between the inputs of the instructor and those of the learner' (Moore, 1993a: 22). Herrmann implies that there is 'an' educational need and tends to assume that the student body is homogeneous. The concept of transactional distance allows us to understand that students have different needs, learning styles and motivations based on their cultural, economic and educational backgrounds. Selecting affordable and appropriate technologies that will allow for the most effective communications between teachers and students is the key issue.

The push for technology

There is a feeling within the institution, its sponsors and its clients that electronic communications technologies will increase the educational efficiency of a DE system that is spread over the three major campuses, 11 NECs, eight institutes and two teaching units located in the different countries of the USP consortium. Unfortunately, this feeling has not been conclusively supported by research or practice. In fact, there is evidence that the USP and other DE providers in the Pacific Islands with their 'low tech' approach to DE have had more success in relation to throughputs and dropouts than institutions with more developed technologies (Hendey, 1994). At the USP, the improved technologies will aid the process of DE and also provide for a more efficient communications system amongst the various outposts of the USP community. Thereby the USP has jumped on the bandwagon to emulate the DE institutions in developed countries. Unfortunately, the USP has neither the financial nor the human resources to implement these technologies successfully. Over the years, the USP's approach to the implementation of technologies in DE has shifted from *ad hoc* patchwork to long drawn out planning focussing on the functionality of a preferred system, with little regard for the needs of isolated students who need these communications facilities most. For example, when Kiribati was feeling left out of teleconferencing system phone patches were instituted. When some Centres agitated about the lack of computer technologies, the USP provided makeshift computer laboratories and dial-up e-mail facility.

The policymakers had to address two questions: why use electronic technologies, and, which technologies to use? They had to deal with these in a context in which 'growth', 'equity' and 'economic rationalism' were key terms. In this context, growth to refers to expansion in all areas:

- number of students enrolled;
- increases in numbers and variety of courses taught;
- increases in the interaction between the students and teachers and amongst students;
- increases in throughput;
- increases in the prestige of the institution within DE systems at a global level;
- and increases in the variety of knowledges and methods of teaching.

Equity, on the other hand, is rather loosely defined, including within it notions of: parity, fairness and even distribution of the commodity being considered. Economic rationalism relates to the notions of efficiency and effectiveness, it is concerned with getting more done with less resources.

The implementation of the technologies has been driven from the highest levels at the USP, in line with the Dhanarajan's quotation at the head of the chapter. Unfortunately, during the deliberations about technological implementations, the voices of the students and the Centres were the weakest. So in practice, at the USP, the technology implementation catered for the margins through the requirements of the centre. The Vice Chancellor's Telecommunications *ad hoc* Working Group dealt with the technocratic aspects of the implementation of technologies for regional communications including DE. With hindsight, I suggest that the preoccupations of the Working Group were too concerned with growth, with functional efficiency and effectiveness and based on the fallacious assumption that the USP's students were a homogeneous group.

The policymakers believed they had no choice but to agree to implement t-technologies since the three considerations mentioned above favour that decision. The issues related to the usage and benefits of the technologies to the students were not systematically resolved since equity, growth and efficiency issues tended to favour the implementation of fordist-type technologies – technologies that allow for economies of scale. This approach to t-technology constructs the DE students as a homogeneous group, and provides a single technological approach to which all students are expected to react to in similar fashion. Those students who could not or preferred not to respond in the expected manner are ignored/silenced. Unfortunately, as has been the case at the USP, the vast majority of students have been ignored/silenced.

The issue of growth could also have been dealt with by implementation of a number of different technologies – post-fordist technologies – technologies that allow for variety in the commodity, and more and different ways of responding to the variety of needs of the distance education students. These strategies would attempt to deal with the variety of students and staff needs. Based on understandings of transactional rather than geographic distances, broader categories of students could be constructed through negotiation with the students and other key players – persons who understand the technologies, the contexts and the contents of the teaching/learning wherever they occur. This road appeared harder to travel, and in the USP's case was not considered because of the assumed large financial and human costs of implementation and maintenance. In 1999, this approach appears so logical to me. With hindsight, I can now see that we were after more of the system that we were familiar with. An analysis of the preferred option will show that it was basically a more efficient configuration of the ATS-1 model. More of the same is being requested, yet research into reasons why the current system is not adequately used was never carried out. The assumption was that because the system was half duplex it was not user friendly. Questions that we have been avoiding to ask include: would a user friendly, full duplex system teleconferencing system be used more than the current one? Would its use, through online synchronous teleconferencing, become obligatory to justify the huge capital and recurrent costs?

In addressing these issues the following realities have to be taken into account:

- The USP depends on overseas donors for around 10–20% of its recurrent budget and most of its capital expenditure, and its consortium consists of 12 INS's that cannot be expected to have identical technological and developmental agendas.
- The amounts of money available to students, to allow them to take advantage of the increased technological support that would only be present at the Centres, varies considerably from one country to another. The purchasing power parity across INS varies immensely and transport costs can be high.
- There is an enormous scarcity of personnel who have experience with the technologies that are being implemented. To further complicate the problem once trained many of these skilled personnel leave region (Ogden, 1992).

- The closest many students have come to computers or telecommunications technologies are in movies or magazines. Most students lack 'technological literacy' and they have difficulty dealing with abstract notions of 'virtual' and 'real', time and space compressions and expansions, 'body-less' interactions, divergence and convergence of technologies, iconography, new mindsets, new vocabularies and new communities of learners (Bruce, 1997; Bruce and Bruce, 1997; Luke, 1997).

Problems of implementation

As the USP's 'eyes and ears', the Centre Directors and their staff have enjoyed some autonomy from UEHQ and the teaching staff at the main campuses. But as the technologies implemented became more sophisticated the Centre staff began to lose some of that autonomy. So, the technologies helped in re-establishing the Suva campus as the centre and the Centres as the margins of the USP's DE system. Furthermore, the technologies allowed the central administration to extend its eyes and ears to its member countries through the technologies rather than through the Centres. The human communications that the CDs desired was being eroded. Thus they could not be expected to have the 'will' to support technological implementation that could erode their control. But is this desirable? Many on the main campus would say 'yes', but those in the outposts will probably vote 'no'. Thus, the new technologies could bring about more divisions between the centre and the outposts, with the outposts feeling that the centre does not understand the situation on the ground and the centre feeling the outposts are inefficient, costly units. However, the technologies could just as easily be about a fusion of these perspectives of efficiency and catering for the locals 'by and with the locals' rather than 'doing things to the locals'. While technological implementations (especially t-technologies) will keep the DE of the USP up with technological developments in other DE institutions, it needs the participation of the 'locals in the margins' (Centres) to sustain the system's economic viability. Economic viability and sustainability are fundamental to the policymakers and sponsors and, therefore, it is clear that local involvement 'warts and all' must be encouraged and nurtured rather than silenced or ignored.

On the other hand, the Centre senior staff sense the passing of an era and a 'moving into the technological age'. A time when the decisions that directly affect their students' eligibility to study, approval of a programme of study and diversity of support are decided from outside their country, through telecommunications, rather than being defaulted to them because of their better knowledge of their students' situations. The CDs' presentations at the 1994 Regional Centres Conference show that they were seeking more human communications with their colleagues, their communities and students, rather than technological ones (Fiefia, 1997; Herrmann, 1997; Tuza, 1997; Va'ai, 1997). However, if the technological linkups helped the human communications then the CDs would ensure that they were utilized and remained functional at the Centre level. This last point is of crucial importance. The users of the technologies must experience first hand the benefits, to themselves and their students, of using the technologies before they will fully support them. If this experience is achieved they would then display the 'will' that Dhanarajan wrote about. I have experienced this with staff at the Fiji Centre, initially, they were wary of the a-technologies, but after experiencing their benefits, they developed the required will.

From the perspective of junior staff – the silent workers who make the DE system tick – new technologies can be an added burden. For instance, within the Pacific, a student's name can change from semester to semester; the a-technologies have difficulties handling this, especially when the students do not remember their student numbers or deliberately mis-fill their enrolment forms to a new ID number. There are many examples that show the inflexibility of an a-technology system that was designed for an environment that does not experience many of the idiosyncrasies of the INS cultures and which could be more easily handled by non-technological systems. When the student database system was being implemented in the Centres, the major question that was asked was who would operate the system. It was very clear that many Centres' junior staff felt that they were already overworked, and that the technologies would just add to their already very heavy workload. They could not see any advantages to using the technologies accruing to them personally, in fact, many saw them only as extra work.

Contrary to expectations the synchronous audioconferencing tutorials held in the Centres have always been poorly attended. Sometimes this is simply because of transport difficulties and costs. However, the technology also puts students off. The unreliability of the system often caused frustration for the students and staff at their first few online sessions. There are also scheduling difficulties since the USP services four different time zones. The system is based on simultaneous two-way synchronous communication. Unfortunately, the latter means that the students and the staff must meet at set times and there is only a very small 'time window', a maximum of four hours within a 24-hour period, which is available for teleconferencing, because of the four time zones: Zone One: Solomons, Vanuatu; Zone Two: Fiji, Kiribati, Tuvalu, Marshalls, Nauru; Zone Three: Niue, Samoa, Tokelau, Tonga; Zone Four: Cook Islands.

Students mainly come from everyday cultures where oral social interactions are paramount. Computer technology requires 'silent readers'. Yet, the students learn best with their ears and eyes, but in this medium, learning is stimulated mainly with the eyes, even with sophisticated multimedia software. The textual language and iconography of the technology is also foreign to the students. So the technology places another layer between the students and the content, or problem solving skills that they need to learn. Also, they are usually not 'in the content', the language used to learn the content is not theirs. So the students need to learn the language of instruction and the technology before they can get to the purpose of the learning. Two way communications that were supposed to be enhanced by the t-technologies did not eventuate as the majority of audio conferences were mostly tutor talk. Another t-technology that has been used was e-mail for students in remote sites, unfortunately, the students and staff underestimated the difficulties in support for the DE students via e-mail and the students dropped out. In both cases the functionality of the t-technologies was the focus rather than the actual needs of the students.

Searching for solutions

How can the USP justify 'sparing' staff to conduct the required technological needs analysis? Where are the interested staff who can do the work of conceptually constructing various technological solutions, to cater for the needs of various groups of students? How does the system retain staff once they become technologically proficient and prefer to move to greener pastures, especially overseas, or to other regional organizations or the private sector, for better salaries and working conditions? What about the long serving, loyal staff, who cannot adapt to the a-technologies?

As mentioned previously, the capital costs of the hardware and software, will probably be provided by donors. But the cost that institutions such as the USP find hardest to meet relates to training. Training for technology implementation, I contend, has two major strands: technocratic training – the 'how to do it' training and critical training – educating towards a different mindset, one that will encourage imaginings and creativity.

At the USP, it is assumed that the institution's major role is to provide the technologies, and the students and staff were to find the time to learn to apply it usefully. Minimum training and the maintenance of the system are funded from the various units' recurrent budgets, and only technocratic training is provided. From my experience as computer teacher and student this is inadequate and inappropriate. Critical educating has not been undertaken so much of the work – at the coal-face level – continued as though the technologies were not being used. Thus, the assumed benefits of technological implementations were not realized. The staff generally knew the 'how to', but had a negative attitude to the technologies, and so were not keen to allow it into other areas of their work; they wanted to continue to control those areas. For these technologies to be effective, supervisors, general and teaching staff, and students from various groups must be encouraged to suggest improved a-technological and t-technological solutions in their working areas, links between their areas and others, and not to be content with the status quo. Similarly, the managers must provide the space for these creative expressions and imaginings to be discussed and tried as appropriate.

For instance, audiocassette recordings of missed online tutorials could be sent to the students who have difficulties coming to the Centres. Modems could be provided for e-mail queries to a discussion group operated by a Centre at a national level. These kinds of suggestions are an example of possible outcomes of a change in mindsets – imaginings and creativity that results from positive critical training and a clear understanding of the context and the contents. Can the university support the Centres in their drive for more technologically based solutions to lessening the transactional distances? Will all parties lobby the telecommunications companies for concessions to the education institutions for the use of t-technologies? Will communities provide the extra funds required by their members who need to access these technologies? How can the communities be encouraged to support these initiatives?

Conclusion

This chapter has discussed the development of the basic communications infrastructure that is necessary to support teaching and administration of the DE programme at the USP. It deals with a real world that is quite remote from 'the virtual university'. This is a world that has to adapt technologies created for other purposes to its own. Geographical distances are an immense challenge to the USP. The mailbag system remains as an efficient and cost effective foundation for the USPNet, but its time delays contribute substantially to the transactional distance between staff and students. Electronic communications have much potential to decrease these transactional distances, but only if they are effectively built into the educational system.

Technological implementation should be made on the basis of needs of the students, needs that have been identified through research – 'by' and 'with' the students and other keyplayers that have close interaction with the students – needs that become more evident when one considers transactional rather than geographical distances. In this way, the scarce resources of the organization will be spent in the 'areas' that they are needed most, rather than in geographically distant areas per se. In this way economies of scale (unit cost per student) will definitively be achieved, as more needy students will have access to the telecommunications. I do not have empirical data to support my suppositions, but have formulated them on my experiences at various levels of working in DE at the USP, my teaching and working with technologies and the luxury of reflexivity that has become available to me during my studies away from my office at the USP. I now offer them as an alternative perspective for implementing technologies in post-colonial countries like most of those served by the USP.

Chapter 11

The ultimate disorienting dilemma: the online learning community

Chere Campbell-Gibson

'On death and dying: a distance learner's reflections' – the title of a student's required reflective paper – certainly aroused my curiosity. What followed were one learner's reflections on learning online and her journey as a distance education student which, from her perspective, resembled Dr Kubler-Ross's (1969) stages of dying. These stages, as she reminded me in the paper, include denial, anger, bargaining, depression and acceptance.

What transpired between the first attempt at denial through the final stage of staring death in the face, represents, I believe, a transformational learning experience as defined by Mezirow (1990) as a result of a disorienting dilemma – that of being in the online classroom for the first time. While the flair for the dramatic was certainly unique to the writings of the learner quoted above, the journey was not. What follows is a short walk down memory lane – reflections on a three credit graduate class entitled *The Adult Independent Learner* that I have taught for the last twelve years with the last five years exclusively online. It was this course that elicited the opening quote.

The course, originated by Charles Wedemeyer in the early 1970s, provides an introduction to the theory and practice of distance education. It utilizes a compendium of readings, consisting of selected book chapters and research articles on distance education, as well as the learners' experience as a foundation for discussion on distance education – all conducted solely via computer-mediated conferencing. Moving the course to the online environment was a strategic teaching decision, allowing both teacher and learners to 'live the content' and 'more fully appreciate what it means to learn at a distance', as the course syllabus duly noted. In retrospect, more seemed to be happening as learners reflected on their experience! I felt the same way.

If we are to embrace educational technologies as part of the changing university, we must do more than examine our teaching. As Harasim has argued in her many publications and presentations, educational technologies not only enable but require us to teach and learn in different ways. We need to recognize the transactional nature of teaching/learning, and the impact of this changing collegiate environment, on both teachers and teaching *and* learners and learning. Teaching and learning online represent a growing trend in post-secondary education, but not one without its challenges to teacher and learner alike, as we shall soon see.

Learners' initial expectations

Learners are attracted to the online class in question for a variety of reasons. Like any other course, many learners are attracted by the content, be it required or an optional course selection. Others are attracted to the flexibility afforded by online teaching and learning. As one student (Lynn) noted:

> to complete three traditional classes in Madison, which would mean 12 hours of drive time to Madison, was unthinkable. So when one of my classmates recommended this distance education class, I looked into it and decided to enrol.

For others like Patsy it was the process itself:

> For me I guess it boils down to the fact that I seem comfortable in a [distance education] setting.

Another student (Karen) noted:

> As an advisor of students who are studying at a distance, I was curious about how it felt to be a student at a distance. What issues could one plan for in advance, what were the surprises, how did the medium affect the process or the product of learning, and how might I feel in those 'shoes'?

She was soon to find out!

There were also emotional aspects to the decision to enrol in an online class, perhaps summed up best by one student (Caroline) who noted, 'I faced this semester with both the anticipation and apprehension inherent in a new learning environment'. Interestingly enough the majority of the apprehension related to anticipated technology problems and an inability to resolve these problems. Others expressed concern about the process of using the Internet and related software. As one learner (Valerie) noted, 'I initially was focused… make that obsessed… with the technology'.

With few exceptions, issues of teaching and learning were not considered initially. However, one learner (Jill) did wonder:

> Without a lecture how would I identify the key points in the readings? Could the rambling insights of other learners be as effective as the voice of the expert/teacher?

Interestingly, as a faculty member, issues of teaching and learning were foremost in my mind when I made the decision to teach online. And I had some very similar questions!

Few knew I felt the same! But they soon were to find out as, with few exceptions, we found ourselves confronted with the reality that teaching and learning online was not the same as that we had experienced over a lifetime! Our old patterns of response to the teaching/learning transaction were not going to work in this online environment. From a teaching/learning perspective – we were faced with the ultimate disorienting dilemma!

The phrase 'disorienting dilemma' appeared repeatedly in learners' online writings as well as reflective papers and was one that kept surfacing in my thinking as well. The concepts of perspective transformation and disorienting dilemma were not introduced in the online course, but many of the learners had been exposed to the concepts in other educational experiences in their graduate studies. I found it interesting that the concepts seemed to truly resonate with the learners, and I had to ask – to what extent had many course participants, myself included, actually engaged in a perspective transformation?

The theory of perspective transformation

Jack Mezirow (1985, 1998) has suggested that learning is more than simply adding to that which we already know. More specifically, he defines learning as 'the process of making a new or revised interpretation of the meaning of an experience, which guides subsequent understanding, appreciation and action' (Mezirow, 1990: 1). He notes the importance of the personal theories, assumptions, beliefs, propositions and prototypes that make up our higher order thinking schemata that undergirds our habits of expectation. Familiar role relationships, such as employer–employee and teacher–student, are examples of habitual expectations familiar to everyone. Mezirow contends that our key role as educators is 'to help learners make explicit, elaborate, and act upon assumptions, premises… upon which their performance, achievement and productivity are based' (Mezirow 1985: 148). This perspective transformation begins with a disorienting dilemma that calls into question the effectiveness of previously held beliefs, values, and assumptions and is theorized to progress through a 10-step process. This 10-step process includes the following:

1. a disorienting dilemma;
2. self examination with feelings of guilt or shame;
3. a critical assessment of epistemic, sociocultural, or psychic assumptions;

4. recognition that one's discontent and the process of transformation are shared and that others have negotiated a similar change;
5. exploration of options to form new roles, relationships, and actions;
6. planning a course of action;
7. acquisition of knowledge and skills for implementing one's plans;
8. provisional trying of new roles;
9. building of competence and self-confidence in new roles and relationships;
10. a reintegration into one's life on the basis of conditions dictated by one's new perspective (Mezirow, 1991: 168–69).

A critical component in the transformative learning process is critical reflection, more specifically critical reflection on assumptions, that is, 'reassessing of the presuppositions on which our beliefs are based and acting on insights derived from the transformed meaning perspective that results from such assessments' (Mezirow 1990: 20).

One can certainly raise a number of issues and concerns related to this 10-step process, including its linearity and its seemingly individualistic and cognitive bent. However, the theory might provide a frame to examine learners' and faculty's online experiences that many, myself included, would contend are indeed transformative from the perspective of personal definitions of teaching and learning. To what extent had transformation occurred in many of my online classes? How had I changed? How could I, or should I, facilitate learners' perspective transformations? What were my responsibilities to learners? What were their responsibilities to each other?

I began to re-read learners' papers prepared for an assignment that had simply asked them to reflect on their experience learning at a distance with no further guidance, allowing their experience to structure their comments. Most reflected on their learning online as it was their first distance education experience. I decided to use Mezirow's 10 steps to organize and analyse their comments, I began to consider their reflections from several perspectives – the extent we shared similar dilemmas and how I might modify my teaching in the future in light of these revelations. In retrospect, I found I had assigned no responsibility to the learner, that is, I had not asked how learners, as individuals or as small group members, could enhance the teaching/learning transaction for all. Remnants of old paradigms, roles and responsibilities obviously still linger for me. Corrections are in order! My findings follow.

Enter the disorienting dilemma

The online environment posed many challenges for us all. One student (Jean) noted:

> the transition from lecture style to distance education has been challenging. The first challenge I faced was time management.

Another (Kristy) echoed a concern I was feeling:

> The lack of a specific schedule has been a major obstacle for me to overcome
> in this new educational format.

The net result for many in the first week were summed up by a learner (Sara) who
noted:

> The emotions I have experienced so far are fear, a floundering feeling [maybe
> it's actually the feeling of being overwhelmed commented on so many times
> in Reflections] and anger.

Sadly, many were dealing with symptoms, not the 'real' problem at hand!

Others began to realize that they were encountering a very different experience
than they had anticipated. One learner (Anne) indicated she experienced true denial. She wrote, 'I was now aware of my misconceptions of distance learning, however I continued to deny that the experience would be any different than my
traditional face-to-face encounters'. She continued noting that she had made some
initial attempts to 'convert' the online class into her traditional learning style with
the net result of moving into the Anger stage in week two. As you might guess, as I
read this reflections paper I was dying a bit myself. What should I have done to save
learners this pain?

Others seemed to have avoided the anger (or perhaps were less candid) yet still
exhibited similar struggles:

> I like to hear what the authority has to say. For years I have learned by reading
> and listening… hearing what the instructor has to say then rereading those ar-
> eas stressed as important. How easily can one change their learning style?
> Sometimes I feel like I'm missing something. Then I wonder if this is just a
> paradigm shift I need to make in the way I learn. Maybe I'm experiencing
> some resistance to learning this way because of its unfamiliarity.
>
> (Rachel)

I must admit, what she longed for, I missed a bit too! How easily can one change their
teaching style? Even as committed as I was to social constructivism, there were times
when I longed for the familiar old chalk board and rapt attention of learners hanging
on my every word (and yes, we only remember the good teaching experiences)!

The journey continues

The second stage of Mezirow's perspective transformation, that of self-examination
with feelings of guilt or shame, seemed evident in the writings of the student who
wrote the last statement above regarding her personal resistance to embracing new
ways of teaching and learning in the online environment. Again Rachel noted:

> I had to look really deep inside myself and find out why I was blocked from
> learning or accepting the responsibilities and advantages of distance educa-

tion. *It was a painful struggle* [original emphasis]... It revealed the attach-ment/dependency I had placed on my teachers, my hearing and my visual observations to facilitate learning. It revealed my feelings of inadequacy and intimidation in working with others who have more experience with educa-tional theory and processes.

Another added:

My final revelation this semester has been the evolution of my personal learn-ing style this year. While describing my personal approach as either 'surface learning' (Morgan, 1995) or 'obedient purposefulness' (Gibbs, Morgan and Taylor, 1982) would be an exaggeration, the reality was near enough for com-parison... I assumed that my professors perceived more clearly the informa-tion/skills necessary to my success in the 'world of work'. I duly memorized materials and reproduced it in papers and on tests.

(Carol)

Reflecting on her academic self-concept, Carol continued, 'My lack of confidence in the worth of my ideas was, initially, an inhibiting factor in my performance'. An-other student (Sara) suggested, 'My trouble (learning online) had been a failure to recognize that alternative processes and approaches existed'.

Yet another reflected on her personal development as a learner and her ability to engage in learning within the environment created in class.

While interactions with the materials, other learners and the technology are a part of the interaction process, for me the interaction with the instructor is key. For those of us who need the support, the challenge, and vision to get to that deeper learning, and have not fully developed those skills to learn effec-tively, this guidance and challenge is critical.

(Valerie)

Valerie continued noting:

While feedback and replies to comments from fellow learners are valuable, that [feedback] received from the faculty... was highly regarded based on my developmental stage as a learner... I would have revered a bit of loss of control for some scheduled 'tutorials'.

Painful revelations, I would suggest, and again, I personally felt the pain as I read the comments. The decision to teach in a new way obviously had broader repercussions than I had anticipated.

It caused me to reflect on the work of Kitchener and King (1981, 1990), and their reflective judgement model. This seven-stage model suggests that there are as-sumptions about:

what can be known and how certain one can be about knowing it... these as-sumptions can be inferred from how individuals approach problem solving, their expectations of instructors, their beliefs about the certainty of problem solving, and so on.

(Kitchener and King, 1990: 161)

Re-reading Kitchener and King helped me identify my covert goal in the course – that of helping learners move to Stage Seven in their model. This stage is where individuals recognize that knowing is uncertain, situational, subject to interpretation, and that epistemically justifiable claims can be made about better or best solutions to the problem under consideration. Perhaps my expectations are unrealistic. Even Kitchener and King (1990: 167) suggest from their 10 years of research that 'individuals have difficulty understanding epistemic assumptions more than two stages higher than they typically use'. Valerie's quote above suggests a Stage Three learner. More food for thought. Perhaps, this is why some learners were willing and able to be reflective, while others simply over-intellectualized the reflective activity and/or focused on the surface issues, failing to reflect in any deep way. Moreover, it did raise the question in my mind once again: how do I, or should I, try to minimize the pain?

Another explanation for the lack of depth of exploration of their online learning experiences, may have been that I failed to ask them to engage in a critical assessment of the epistemic, sociocultural, or psychic assumptions that undergird their understanding of teaching and learning in adulthood – the third step in Mezirow's transformational learning process. While some learners, for example Sherry and Doreen, echoed the following themes: 'This (online class)... increased my awareness of my own learning'; and 'This has been a very thought-provoking learning encounter and an adventure I am grateful for having had the opportunity to experience'. Few took the reflective process any deeper. One learner commented:

> CAVE 643 has been an especial challenge for me because of its divergence from my usual educational approaches. Ideas rather that facts are the focus; no one opinion is seen as the 'legitimate', definitive answer – in fact no real answers are given.
>
> (Carol)

However, there is no sign that she realizes that there are no real answers.

In contrast, a medical professional in the class noted:

> I often had thought that knowledge was something like property: a person could own it and give it to someone else. Through the process of reading, reflecting, dialoguing, reflecting action, I was able to transform my conception of knowledge into something deeper than I had held previously... I came to know and understand my new conception of knowledge as a deeper intuitive and more inclusive process, as opposed to a transferable product.
>
> (Gordon)

Yes, there was hope!

Struggling alone or together

Recognition that one's discontent and the process of transformation are shared and that others have negotiated a similar change represents Mezirow's fourth stage of perspective transformation. As I construct online learning environments, I always design a space/corner of the conference for reflections on the process of teaching and learning online. Perhaps this is one of my small contributions to the process of perspective transformation. It becomes a place to discover that one is not alone in his or her struggles. I was reminded that one of the longest 'threads' in a recent online course carried the title 'Overwhelmed'. The title said it all! As one learner (Fern) noted, 'Lastly, the process file, which I discovered late in the semester, is useful in identifying and considering process issues that I may otherwise just internalize'. It did serve a purpose it appears. I am reminded that the 'reflections on process' portion of the conference is always most active (and I believe most helpful) when learners themselves raise questions about learning online, and strategies for effective and efficient are openly shared among and between group members, myself included.

Exploration of options, forming new roles, relationships and actions; planning a course of action; and acquisition of knowledge and skills for implementing one's plans, constitute the next three steps in the transformational process. However, I am not sure that I can see evidence of these steps, at least, as discrete entities. Learners in my online classes are required to take on the role of an active participant in a learning community. I passionately describe this learning community as a community linked for the purpose of making meaning out of our shared experiences, our unique past and present experiences, our personal knowledge and understanding, and the literature of distance education and training. I voice the hope that as a result of the efforts of the learning community, we will all be better able to take carefully considered actions, to enhance teaching and learning at a distance. The many roles of community members, some new and some not so new to the learners, include discussant, moderator, summarizer of small group discussion and/or problem solving activity, evaluator of other small group projects, etc.

These roles are not optional – they are expected. To some extent, I have provided some guidance including suggestions for participation in online discussions, moderating online discussions, and netiquette. Learners, however, seem pre-occupied in their reflective comments with logistical concerns that facilitate individual learning rather than the process of learning itself, although several do illustrate a perceived connection between the two. These quotes provide a flavour of their actions:

> I am a connected learner – seeing how things are connected in order to learn. An example of this was my need to 'see' the other students when I read their comments. I began the class frustrated that I could not keep people and 'their voices' separated from each other. But, by the second week, I had adapted my traditional learning style... by replacing my sight with copies of everyone's résumé and posting them above my computer so I could refer to them when I was reading comments.

> (Lynn)

While one learner struggled with her need to see her fellow learners others struggled with time and stress management:

> The lack of a specific schedule has been a major obstacle for me to overcome in this new educational format... I have decided to schedule my online time

directly into my weekly calendar. While I mentally know it's a trick to get me to the computer, I also understand why I am using this trick. If my online time is already scheduled into my life, I know I have time for it and am able to allow my self to fully participate in it during that time.

(Jean)

Jean continued:

Despite the frustration of millions of messages... I have developed a strategy of skimming messages first for content, then returning to important ones later. That way all messages get read in a timely fashion and I am able to gain insights from them.

What was I hoping to read? I think statements that suggested 'if we do X, then we'll all be able to do Y' – some flavour of a sense of interdependence, of helping each other through our struggles. There was a bit of that, for example, comments about linking messages, and using reply functions to keep a logical thread of messages, but not on the actual process of meaning making as a group. And perhaps this suggests I, as a member of the online learning community, need to raise more questions online to elicit such discussions. But I am reluctant, wanting the initiative to be taken by others. I think that would make it more meaningful! Or am I just shirking my responsibility under the guise of social constructivism again.

New roles and responsibilities

Perhaps the greatest struggle for us all occurred in the area of responsibility for learning and, as Mezirow might add, our personal habits of expectation. I have struggled with my changing role. Initially trained as physical scientist, I am quite at home lecturing and writing on the board, certainly more so than sitting on my hands reading learners' perspectives on the research articles of the week and their applicability to their world at large. I overstate the case perhaps, but trying to move from an espoused theory of constructivism to acting upon this theory is easier said than done. I did take heart as I read the following comedic but insightful comment, 'I think the most radical change in roles occurs for the classroom leader or *The Artist Formerly Known as Teacher*' (Kent). Someone appreciated my struggles. But the elation was short lived. New roles and responsibilities seemed unexplored in the minds of many.

For example, when a group member failed to contribute during the early stages of a problem solving exercise, a student, who had previously identified herself as 'an autonomous learner, who knows what she needs and wants to learn', noted:

I felt stymied. I considered telling him in a personal message that he had contributed nothing compared to everyone else and that we would appreciate his help. But this seemed to be taking on the teacher's role and I was uncomfortable doing so.

(Kim)

Another student (Rachel) noted, 'There are also times when I want a response (from the teacher) and it doesn't happen'. However, as she later notes, 'Instructor feedback on my personal progress in the course is mostly my responsibility and I'm working on this'. Examining traditional roles and responsibilities happens to varying degrees, even with a course exercise designed to promote it.

Perhaps my expectations and actions are incongruent! A part of me is still the traditional teacher. Helping learners enter and examine a body of content is still my foremost agenda. For this particular class I have a second agenda, that of positioning the learner in the environment of distance teaching and learning so they can live the content as I note in the syllabus. That content includes a focus on how people learn in general and at a distance in particular, with consideration given to the changing roles and responsibilities of teachers and learners. Perhaps a self-examination of one's own learning is an unspoken agenda item, but the assignment alone provides a clue. Perhaps the assignment to reflect on one's learning at a distance needs more structure. Perhaps formally introducing the concepts of disorienting dilemma and perspective transformations, as well as Mezirow's 10-step framework would encourage deeper reflection, but that somehow seems too directive, too teacher-centered.

Perhaps it is enough to begin the process, to help learners begin to reflect on how they view teaching and learning through a disorienting dilemma. Perhaps serving as a catalyst is sufficient. Critical reflection and the resultant perspective transformation may take more time as the following quote suggests:

> I see how de-emphasizing structure and emphasizing process and trusting the resulting outcomes... changes the motivation for learning and the quality of the results of an educational experience for adults too. This appreciation has been enhanced through taking time to reflect on my own interpretations of the experiences I have had and the feelings I felt before and during the learning process.
>
> (Tom)

But once again, more questions than answers emerged in my mind. To what extent are learners really beginning to question their conception of knowledge and their conception of learning? How does this impact their learning processes or the learning strategies they employ? What impact does this have over time and across various teaching/learning experiences? The following quote from a student (June) gives me cause to believe that longitudinal research that begins to address these questions will be fruitful – 'While these challenges [of online learning] create stress in the short term, I am certain that they are lessons I will remember in the long term'.

I have to acknowledge that there are some encouraging signs that learners are engaged in a provisional trying of new roles – Mezirow's eighth step in perspective transformation. For example:

> I seem to be younger than many other students in the class, and I have less experience to relate to the issues of distance education. As a result I have felt that my perspective was not valuable and that I couldn't grasp the significance of the assigned articles... was able to experiment with different participation

strategies. Ultimately I found that contributing more to discussions led to more feedback from other students which helped me feel like I 'fit in'.

(Ellen)

Others noted:

After just one month of participation in a distance education class, I am beginning to understand how this medium can promote intimate and meaningful learning.

(Jill)

I have also increased my appreciation for the idea that learners actively construct their learning experience.

(Karen)

I use my fellow distance learners much more than in classroom learning to understand the material and I'm surprised to find myself so actively involved in the discussions.

(Jackie)

The class… helped me finally understand how adults can direct their own formal learning when given the opportunity… .

(Ellen)

Mezirow suggests that the building of competence and self-confidence in new roles and relationships is yet another important step, the ninth of ten, in any perspective transformation. A particularly apprehensive older adult learner came to an interesting revelation in the process of learning online. She exclaimed proudly:

It is now very clear to me that I can read the same material as someone else in class and have it impact [on] me totally differently because of the moment I'm in and the experiences I have brought to that moment.

(June)

June continues, noting after being told by another student that her interpretation was not what the author intended:

I realized how much I had matured as a learner. It didn't bother me to be corrected… I was totally happy with what I had gotten from the reading. In the past, my academic self-esteem would have been devastated.

Another learner (Gordon), who had previously taken a similarly structured online course with me, noted 'This year I'm a lot more confident and comfortable with the learning process'.

Of course there are quotes that will remain in my mind and heart for those discouraging times when all seems lost – quotes that seem to suggest that for some a new perspective has emerged, and that this new meaning has been integrated into their very being. These include such gems as:

Through the experience of this new learning process I have discovered new ideas and reflections on what learning is all about and how, when and where learning takes place... education/learning takes place within oneself.

(Gordon)

I have also increased my appreciation for the idea that learners actually construct their learning experience.

(Caroline)

Revelling in the constructivist environment, another confessed:

In response to this lack of prescribed schedule, authorizing leader, limited time frame and static information, I am filling it up with my own agenda and experiencing what it means to structure my own learning and constructing my own knowledge.

(Jackie)

Perhaps they have discovered and internalized new roles for themselves as learners, as others noted:

I think I've actually matured as a learner. I'm finding satisfaction in learning for my own needs... I have realized that I don't need validation from an external source to feel successful about learning something.

(Jean)

The introspective nature of the first two writing assignments has forced me to take a deeper look at myself as a learner. I came away from this exercise with a more positive outlook on myself than that with which I began.

(Carol)

But not all learners end up at the same place at the same time. One has to smile as one reads:

Though I long to be the ideal humanist, the postmodern poster girl of 1996, to be one who '... chooses stimulation... develops a capacity for joy... seeks inter-dependence rather than independence...' (Peters, 1993: 45) I fear that I am not totally apart from some behaviourist cravings (Moore, 1993b). Though I embrace collaboration and learner to learner interaction I still long for my instructor to pose a question, stand at the chalkboard, and help me and my classmates to clarify and synthesize the meanings we have begun to construct through our readings and discursive collaboration. (OK, so I grew up with 'Leave it to Beaver'.)

(Pam)

And her instructor still feels a bit the same way as the reader can discern. ☺

The changing university community

Teaching and learning online represents, for many, the ultimate disorienting dilemma in higher education. Emerging new roles and responsibilities for members of these online learning communities call into question definitions of teachers, learners, what it means to learn both as an individual and as a group, and what is means to have learned. Past values, beliefs, and assumptions are challenged. Some teachers and learners are changed by the experience forever and I would contend for the better. Others remain unchanged while yet others, I would contend, are left with self-doubt about their flexibility and capabilities as learners. Some may see me as failing in my role as teacher. I too struggle a bit with that label of failure. A little niggling bit of guilt creeps in. I have not provided answers. I sleep because I know I have provided an environment for learning albeit a tad more structured than even I prefer. I design an online environment, select texts and research for the learners to read that certainly share many of my biases. I provide advanced organizers (which many don't read, I'm pleased to say), raise questions to begin conversations on the readings (often ignored late in the semester – a good sign I believe) and set general parameters for assignments leaving room for multiple agendas. To help both learners and teachers transition expediently to this new environment with its new roles and responsibilities, I try to provide not only logistical 'hints', such as information on learning online and netiquette, but also a place to discuss the process of learning online. And I try to be candid about my own personal struggles teaching and learning online. I truly believe that there is much to be gained by the collective reflection on both teaching and learning online and by the sharing of hopes, fears, struggles and victories.

But what are the costs? Boud, Cohen and Walker (1998) suggest that learning builds on and flows from experiences and that these experiences are central to all learning. The experience of participating in my course has scored very high (7.98 on an 8.0 scale) on impact of the course on the learner – a measure in our standardized evaluation form. The course does impact learners' lives – but how? I worry that some still feel they are a failure as learning online was a challenge that was not overcome to their satisfaction. Dashing a learner's academic self-confidence is hardly a desired outcome. Why even worry? It is because we are educators that we feel responsible and accountable, and this too needs to be examined. We may say that we want to create constructivist learning communities, but the question is, do we really? And does everyone have to be a constructivist? Perhaps, it is enough to give learners an opportunity to engage in a teaching and learning environment that may stretch them in some ways, but not necessarily change them. I do know it has changed me!

It has also changed the student who was negotiating the five stages of dying. She ended her paper with the following quote, a tad more upbeat than its opening:

> By living distance education, I have also come to 'know' distance education…
> I have started at a very low level of Pratt's (1987) competence, commitment
> and confidence in my abilities as a distance learner and through

self-reflection, have arrived at a much higher level, and will continue to build on this with any future distance education encounters. Lastly, I, once again, have survived the stages of death in academia.

(Ann)

Chapter 12

Using new technologies to create learning partnerships

Ron Oliver

Introduction

There is a growing trend in education across all sectors to move from a focus on teaching to one of learning (Ramsden, 1992; Bates, 1995). Evidence of this trend is reflected in many aspects of emerging educational reforms including:

- moves in many countries to outcomes-based curricula;
- the emerging use of technology as an instructional aid;
- the development and increased use of student-centred learning environments.

The higher education sector has not been spared from these trends and strategic plans and policies have been developed, or are being developed, to ensure that university teaching reflects the mainstream (Laurillard, 1993). The various factors that are currently shaping and forming the nature and style of university teaching include public sector reform and the globalization of the economy (Bennett, 1997). These have led to a more client-centred mode of operation, with universities assuming business principles and practices to attract and secure markets for their educational products. Many universities that were predominantly funded by operating grants from governments are now seeing increasing moves by governments to remove much of the cost of higher education from the public purse. This economic rationalism has created new forces in the funding process as evidenced by such reviews as the Dearing Report (1997) in the United Kingdom and the West (1998) review in Australia, both of which propose new forms and policies for university activity in their respective countries.

Increasingly a significant component of public university budgets are now being derived from other sources, such as student fees, commercial courses, external consultancies and industry partners. Universities are creating partnerships with their stakeholders. The issues of partnerships and the various roles of stakeholders in the learning process are becoming more prominent in the planning and implementation of university courses and curricula. Stakeholders in this process include the governments funding education, the business sector and employers employing the graduates, the professional bodies setting and maintaining standards, the academics designing and implementing courses and the students enrolling in the courses. While there have been many partnerships developed among these stakeholders in the past, one area where the partnership has been less evident has been in the learning process itself, that between the teachers and students.

University teaching and learning

There has been a tendency in this reform process to question and reflect on the general roles and functions of universities and, in particular, to revisit the question concerning the importance and place of teaching. There have been many critics of university teaching (Levin, 1998). University teaching is often claimed to be too content-oriented, employing transmissive modes and providing knowledge, which is narrow and limited. There has been no shortage of advice and guidance on what good university teaching entails. Ramsden (1992) suggests effective teaching and learning is characterized by a number of critical features including:

- clear learning goals;
- appropriate assessment tasks and strategies;
- appropriate work loads;
- an emphasis on learner independence.

Contemporary research has revealed much about the nature of the university student and the adult learner. Knowles (1990) and others describe a number of distinguishing characteristics of adult learners. These include:

- being motivated primarily by intrinsic factors and being driven to perform and succeed by personal forces related to needs such as seeking to improve the quality of life and enhancing self-esteem;
- tending to be problem or task-centred with orientations stemming from the need to use information meaningfully to improve aspects of their lives or work situations;
- integrating new information most effectively when it is presented in the context of real-life situations;
- coming to the learning situation with a wealth of accumulated life experiences;
- often fearing the loss of self-esteem in classroom encounters and student-type exchanges;

- having a strong sense of how they learn and being able to exercise high degrees of self-regulation in the learning process.

This knowledge of adult learners and contemporary learning theories has led in recent years to a proliferation of innovative learning environments, and a re-engineering of university courses (Collis, 1997). Some of the types of learning experiences that students can now expect to meet during their life in a university include:

- student-centred modes of teaching where the teacher plays a facilitating role supporting learner autonomy and self-regulation (Hannafin and Land, 1997; Taylor, 1990);
- constructivist environments providing students with active and engaging learning experiences which enable them to construct personal understanding of the content (Candy, 1991);
- problem-based learning, whereby learning occurs through a systematic inquiry of tasks and problems with 'solution spaces' within the academic content (Raidal, 1997; Sage and Torp, 1997);
- situated learning, wherein learners are exposed to the content in realistic and authentic settings and the learning activities reflect the way in which the knowledge is intended to be used in real life (Herrington and Oliver, 1997);
- collaborative learning, in which the learners develop knowledge and understanding of content through interactions and joint activities with other learners (Freeman, 1997).

Characteristic of these new forms of teaching and learning is the transformation of the learner from a traditional passive mode to one which is more active and self-regulated, involving high degrees of reflection, personal judgements and heightened responsibilities for one's own learning and academic progress. Several writers, however, caution against the uniformed use of these changed environments (Candy, 1991), and suggest the need to create learning environments that are flexible in their approaches and that cater more fully for the various needs of individual learners. It seems clear though that these active forms of environment are able to provide substantially enhanced forms of learning, and to provide students with strong prospects of making meaningful use of the learned knowledge. The challenge for university teaching is the exploration of the opportunities, within and across, all teaching domains and a meaningful reflection on the outcomes achieved in relation to the costs incurred.

The role of new educational technologies

One of the more obvious signs of change in university teaching has been the extent and scope of uptake of new technologies in programme delivery. The new educational technologies make use of the developing multimedia and communications technologies, and this book provides a wealth of evidence that demonstrates the various uses and applications of these technologies in higher education. The new educational technologies support highly interactive student-centred learning and provide many new opportunities for both learners and teachers. There appear many reasons why the new technologies are developing important roles in contemporary teaching systems. Some of the advantages and opportunities attributed to their application include:

- provision of improved access to education (Oliver and Short, 1997);
- support for customized educational programmes to meet the needs of individual learners (Kennedy and McNaught, 1997);
- the provision of increased opportunities for learning in authentic contexts (Laffey, Tupper and Musser, 1998);
- the provision of opportunities for active and engaging learning environments where students are able to communicate and collaborate (Freeman, 1997);
- the provision of tools able to enhance students' cognitive powers and processes (Jonassen and Reeves, 1996).

As with most tools, however, the methods of implementation play an important role in determining success, and there are many examples in the literature where unsuccessful implementation strategies have led to less than successful outcomes. Many writers caution users of educational technologies to focus on learning issues and to be guided by educational imperatives, rather than those associated with the technologies. For example, Alan (1995) suggests that in choosing educational technologies teachers should consider those that are 'state of the mind', rather than 'state of the art' and those that are inclusive as opposed to exclusive. But the new technologies tend to be very attractive and appealing entities and have pervaded the university education scene in significant ways.

Open and flexible learning

One very visible sign of the restructuring and re-engineering of university programmes in response to the various forces of change, and prompted by the opportunities provided by the new technologies, has been the expansion of open and flexible modes of course delivery. This development has seen a move away from the more transmissive modes of education characterized by teacher-led content development and mass lectures, towards education where learners play more prominent roles in their learning. In the student-centred forms of flexible and open learning, the learners are given many freedoms over the form and pace of their learning. The focus changes from the content being delivered to aspects of its use and application. The process of learning becomes as important, if not more important, than the product. These changes are potentially very powerful. We are informed, and all the evidence suggests, that such changes have the prospect to considerably enhance the quality of learning, and to make learners more independent and capable of sustaining their own lifelong learning.

But nothing comes without a cost. Student-centred learning can be a difficult process for learners. It aims to promote understanding and deep learning as compared to the alternative shallow or surface learning (Biggs and Telfer, 1987). It places the onus onto the student to explore and inquire, to reflect and articulate, to collaborate and co-operate, in active tasks requiring enhanced degrees of initiative, interest, motivation, and cognitive and physical effort. In schools, students and parents tend to accept the will and judgements of the teachers and activities of this type are usually accepted and encouraged. In universities, however, where the learners are often questioning clients, and have many ways to influence outcomes, learners may be reluctant to accept the teachers' definition of their needs.

Students come to universities for many reasons. Some come to gain credentials, others to pursue learning, in its own right. Some are highly motivated and clever, while others require motivation, and find learning a much more difficult process. We know that among adult learners, many are already aware of what helps them to learn and have preferred styles for dealing with the information that they are required to learn (Knowles, 1990). We also know that adult learners are not nearly as docile as school learners, for instance, when the learning is not seen as in their best interests or in their preferred ways, they will make their feelings known and expect to have their concerns listened to and dealt with. In contexts such as these, partnerships hold strong prospects for ensuring that the needs and interests of students and teachers are met.

A case study in the local context

To more fully understand the needs of learners and the issues associated with developing computer-based student-centred learning environments, it is useful to consider a case study from my own teaching, recently undertaken among students in a postgraduate course. The students were enrolled in a unit from a graduate course in interactive multimedia technologies. This unit explored the use of multimedia, as a tool for distance education and open learning, and it was appropriate that much of the design, planning and implementation of this course should reflect the values and content being delivered. This course was presented in a face-to-face mode but made extensive use of technology-based and student-centred learning activities and processes.

The unit contained a variety of teaching and learning activities and used technology in a variety of ways to support student inquiry and learning. The principal forms of learning activity used in this class included:

- the World Wide Web (WWW) as an information and reference source;
- focussed reading and inquiry from the textbook;
- WWW-based inquiry tasks ahead of class meetings;
- co-operative WWW-based inquiry tasks as part of formal class activities;
- personal and informal browsing on the WWW;
- reading printed notes prepared by the teacher;
- preparing notes for weekly face-to-face seminar sessions;
- use of a bulletin board to share useful WWW sites;
- classroom-based seminar activities;

- classroom-based collaborative and co-operative group activities;
- open-ended assignment tasks and topics;
- teacher-led class discussions and seminars;
- informal interactions with other class members.

From week to week, students were given a variety of problems and issues to pursue through their own inquiry and research. Open-ended problems and contextual settings were used to provide contexts for the student research and inquiry. Weekly seminars and group activities were used to provide students with opportunities to reflect on their findings, and to articulate and organize their ideas through discussion, communication and collaboration with others. To this extent, the unit made sound use of the best features of student-centred learning to encourage student activity and to promote and enhance learning as discussed above. The 18 students in the group became well-known to each other and, by the end of the semester, face-to-face classes were characterized by the free and open exchange of ideas based on quite detailed research and inquiry.

As part of the evaluation of the course, students were asked to complete a detailed description of their impressions and opinions of the various components of the course and their feedback, while predictable in many instances, provided some interesting insights concerning their impressions of this changed form of learning environment. The students' responses provided interesting information in several areas, in particular, their impressions of the impact of the various activities on their learning.

Table 12.1 provides a descriptive measure of the students' perceptions of the impact of the various learning activities undertaken during the course on their learning. The students were given a list of these activities and asked to rank each with a number between 0 and 4 indicating their impression of its impact on their learning. A zero score was used to indicate a very low impact while a 4 indicated a very high perceived impact on learning. Thus, the possible range for each activity was between 0 and 72, there being 18 students in the class.

Table 12.1 *Students' perceptions of the impact of the learning activities on their learning*

Learning Activity	Score	Perceived Impact	Rank
completing Assignment 1	53	high	3
completing Assignment 2	57	high	2
reading the textbook before class	46	high	8
reading the teacher's printed notes	51	high	4
completing written notes prior to class	47	high	7
teacher-led class discussions	60	high	1
class group activities and discussions	51	high	4
WWW searching and reading prior to class	39	medium	10
WWW searching and reading during class	34	medium	12
finding relevant WWW pages to post	38	medium	11
reading relevant WWW pages posted by others	34	medium	12
interactions with other students in the class	51	high	4
personal browsing on the WWW	44	medium	9

The table provides some interesting insights into students' impressions of the value of the various learning activities. Those activities that they regarded as having the most bearing on their learning, were the two assignments and the teacher-led discussions. Those activities which they saw as having the least impact were: WWW searching and reading during class, reading WWW pages suggested by other students, finding WWW pages to submit to a public bulletin board and WWW searching and reading as a preparatory activity for class seminars. All these activities were planned by the teacher to be student-centred, active and engaging forms of inquiry and information seeking and were considered to be vital components of the learning process, yet students perceived them as having lesser learning value when compared to the other activities.

There is a distinct pattern in this table which shows that the activities the students valued the most were those with higher degrees of structure and teacher direction, and the tasks which students valued the least were those that provided the higher degrees of autonomy, personal choice and direction. Further information was gained from interviews with the students, in which specific questions were posed to discover reasons for their various preferences. Their responses are instructive for a teacher interested in using WWW technologies to facilitate active forms of learning.

Students' perceived value of WWW information

An initial inquiry was made to explore students' perceptions of the value of the WWW as an information source for the course. Feedback from the students provided strong support for initial expectations that they would find this information source valuable and useful. Most students were very positive in their responses to questions concerning the value of information obtained from the WWW sources contained in the course materials. The various links provided a variety of information and, often, one link led to many others. At times there was a possibility of information overload. Students often remarked on the frequent distractions of the many links and their frequent tendency to lose track of the topic in question by links taking them away to other interesting topics.

All students found that the search engines and the large numbers of links in the various WWW pages often led them to very useful information. Many students commented on the fact that it was impossible to know if there was more or better information that had not been found, and the general impression of the group was that there was considerable untapped information that could still be found with appropriate energy and interest. Several students commented on the value of the WWW to provide access to information of a local flavour. The course textbook had a distinctly US flavour, and the students were pleased to be able to supplement this information with relevant information, examples and case study descriptions from sites within the Australian context. This facility of providing local information was seen as a very valuable outcome of the activity.

Problems with WWW access

Despite the students' generally strong and favourable impressions of the information provided by the WWW, there was a general feeling of disquiet among students concerning the difficulties faced in accessing the information. All students had tales of trouble concerning the reliability and capacity of the WWW to deliver its content. These comments came despite their privilege in accessing the WWW through the university server and a high speed Ethernet connection. Many students used their Internet accounts from home in completing requirements for the course. Problems cited as frequent events by most students using a variety of access modes included:

- difficulty accessing servers that appeared to down or overloaded;
- problems with pages requiring unexpected plug-ins and helpers;
- long download times caused by bottlenecks in external systems;
- frequent instability of university software and systems.

Throughout the course a number of students judged their lack of familiarity and experience with the WWW and appropriate search strategies as a major impediment to their success. It was interesting to note that by the end of the course, most students were still relative novices with developing appropriate search strings and keywords, although most had developed a preference for one or two particular search engines. When questioned, few could provide any particular information on their favourite search engine in terms of its indexing procedures or database format, factors that would have provided considerable help in searching more successfully.

WWW page postings

Use of a dynamic bulletin board was planned to be an integral part of the course with benefit derived from the action of finding and posting new and relevant pages, and through the extra WWW pages to which the bulletin board provided access. On both counts students' responses suggested that these ideas tended to be overly optimistic. In the first instance, students commented that it often took considerable time to find good pages to post. Students tended to spend large amounts of their time attempting to find WWW pages containing descriptions and details they could submit. Some commented that this action tended to impede their learning. They claimed often not to read and use the information they found when they were looking for such pages. In fact, finding an appropriate page often became more important than understanding the information it contained.

The need to post pages to a public bulletin board also presented some other unexpected outcomes. A number of the part-time students expressed concern at the fact that the full-time students tended to have more time to seek WWW information, and that the full-time students tended to find the more obvious sites more quickly. This left part-time students with the added problem of having to look further and to spend more of their valuable study time on these activities.

Collaborative learning

The purpose of the posting facility was to create a co-operative and collaborative learning environment where students benefited from the activities of their peers. The public bulletin board displayed the posted sites in the order in which they were posted. From the outset, it was apparent that the best sites were always being posted by the same small core of students. This was due to a number of factors. Naturally, some students were keener than others and were very well organized in their study habits. These students tended to start their preparation early and it was evident that those who commenced their WWW inquiry first had a much easier task locating relevant sites quickly.

Students were required to make some comments about the sites or pages with each posting. The personal comments were up to a paragraph or two in length and represented a student's summary or impression of the information presented at the site. Several students commented that they enjoyed reading others' comments before visiting the site to see how others interpreted the same information. There appeared to be a number of students who enjoyed and derived value from the multiple perspectives this activity provided. There were others, however, for whom the activity was unpleasant and unappreciated.

Learner independence and self-direction

There were a number of signs that the WWW-based activities were successful in fostering students' independence and self-direction. The strategies that some students developed to enable them to post relevant sites ahead of others have already been mentioned. In other instances, very positive feedback was gained from students concerning their perceptions of the value of the preparation ahead of the class sessions. A number of students remarked that they were encouraged to prepare adequately, because they enjoyed the class discussion and understood that the discussion needed informed comment. It was evident that the same form of preparation could have been performed using traditional information sources, but it was the scope and extent of the WWW information base that enabled the preparation for each student to differ and still be capable of contributing positively to the learning of others. Still others found the mandatory nature of the preparation discomforting and imposing.

Overall, the WWW activities tended to be less favoured by the students over more conventional activities, such as reading and discussion, mainly because they were fraught with problems caused by equipment failures, networking problems and general access. Students had considerable difficulty locating relevant information, found the WWW to be quite distracting at times and had difficulty coming to terms with the vast array of information that they had to deal with. On the other hand, the more structured learning tasks provided more instant access to relevant information and content, and were seen as more convenient and appealing. Interviews and discussions with the students revealed rather large differences in expectations and impressions between myself as the teacher and many learners.

While the environment appeared to be delivering a meaningful, engaging and challenging setting for students' inquiry and learning, a number of students found these attributes to be discomforting, inconvenient and unacceptable. It became apparent that it would have been very helpful to many learners had they been able to engage in some form of dialogue and negotiation, in order to craft learning environments more appropriate to their individual needs and preferences. There were particular differences of opinion found between part-time and full-time students and between the younger and mature aged students. It is likely that if the survey instruments used in the evaluation were more sensitive, even more differences might have been found among the genders, among students with different learning styles and among students with different levels of technology literacy.

Discussion

The results from this case study have provided some clear messages to assist in the further development of this teaching programme. The new educational technologies provided a range of engaging and interactive learning activities from which all students clearly benefited. The technologies helped to provide a collaborative and motivating learning environment, one that extended and challenged the students. From a teacher's perspective, use of the technology was a substantial success and the experience has provided strong encouragement to further explore new applications and uses. However, the outcomes also revealed that some learning activities require higher levels of cognitive engagement and processing than others, and that these activities will place more burdens and responsibilities onto learners.

The majority of students expressed a clear preference for learning activities with a high degree of structure and organization. The preferences for these types of learning stemmed primarily from the perception that such settings provided better learning outcomes. In this regard learning appeared to be seen primarily as exposure to knowledge and information rather than knowledge acquisition and meaning making. It was, therefore, not surprising to find students expressing a preference for the activities that required less effort and appeared to return more learning gains. The technology-based environment also placed demands on students for access to equipment and infrastructure and, in some instances, led to problems with the technologies that created barriers to their learning.

A clear message that flowed from the study was the need to consider the expectations of the learners in a changed learning environment. Plans to increase the scope and quality of learning in the course needed to include activities to lead learners down this path and to motivate and encourage their participation. Adult learners have firm views on how they learn best (Knowles, 1990). When new strategies are employed, learners need time to assimilate them. The results show that it cannot be assumed that all learners will be willing participants in changed learning environments. The different reasons and purposes for which adult learners come to universities, together with their perceptions on how best they learn, must be considered as courses are created and crafted. It can be said that an important part of teaching is to work with the students to create a match in expectations and mutual understanding.

Some will argue that universities should be free and able to structure and plan their courses as they see fit, and that learners must take what they are delivered. It is true that universities must set their courses and objectives to meet many requirements, including their own standards, the employers and those of the professional associations that act as gatekeepers for their professions. But it must also be remembered that other more direct clients are being served. It is neither fruitful nor useful if the various forms of teaching are not seen by the students to be in their best interests, and if teachers' expectations are not in accord with those of the students. In this regard, creating partnerships with learners in the teaching and learning process is one strategy that recognizes learners' needs.

Conclusions

In many instances, teachers implementing new technologies will hear few words of disquiet from learners. Learners usually accept quite willingly the actions of their teachers if they see them as contributing to the quality of their programmes. However, it is important to be aware that in some instances difficulties can occur, especially when expectations and perceptions of the teachers and students differ and also, when the requirements of technologies seem to provide barriers to students' learning. One strategy that enables common ground to be created and maintained between teachers and learners is to ensure that both parties view teaching and learning as a partnership. Meaningful partnerships enable students to have some choice in the form of learning environment in which they engage. Naturally the choices made by the students may impinge on the scope and extent of their learning, but this is where good teaching should come into play. Effective teachers are likely to encourage and motivate their students to move to the more effective forms of learning activity, despite the difficulty and inconvenience that may be incurred. Good teachers can help to inspire the forms of intellectual curiosity in their students, which will allow them to value learning. Again, this will occur more effectively when the relationship is a partnership with both parties accepting the rights and responsibilities of the other.

The new technologies are powerful tools in providing for learning environments where teachers and learners are partners, and where learners have scope and prospect for choice in the nature and form of their learning. Technology-supported learning environments offer many opportunities for both teachers and learners including:

- flexible modes of content presentation and delivery;
- situated and contextualized presentation of content and information;
- the provision of a myriad of information sources providing many wide and diverse perspectives on content and information;
- interactive and engaging learning settings;

- communicative elements to support the independent learner;
- collaboration, communication and co-operation between learners;
- place and time independence for learning.

The value of using new technologies in forming and sustaining learning partnerships with students is based on their capability in providing for many different types of learning activity, and their capacity to sustain the forms of communication needed to maintain the partnership. There is an emerging pattern in higher education for new technologies to be used in the delivery of student-centred courses and programmes. These moves must include active support for learning partnerships. Already the use of the communicative capabilities of the technology in both synchronous (eg chat) and asynchronous (eg e-mail and bulletin boards) modes provide means for this communication.

For some students, there is a perception that the best teaching takes place in a face-to-face mode through direct instruction. They see a direct link between face-to-face teaching and learning, and they are uncomfortable with moves to distinguish between the two. Student-centred learning can be uncomfortable for these students because it generates distance between themselves and their teacher. Technology can reduce this distance and remove many of the discomforts experienced by such learners. Teachers can now employ many creative ways through technology to stay in close contact with students despite the diminution of face-to-face contact. In this way, forms of teacher-directed learning can be maintained in a student-centred teaching environment.

Some students appear concerned that teachers' roles are diminished in student-centred learning environments due to their lack of involvement in the content delivery. Technology enables teachers to have an even bigger impact on content delivery through the construction and creation of the virtual learning spaces that technology-supported environments can create. In such settings, teachers can assume far more important roles as coaches and facilitators, and can have far more direct bearing and influence on what is learned. Once again, appropriate use of the communicative technologies can strengthen students' perceptions of the teachers' role and allay their fears.

Choice is one important outcome that technology-supported learning environments are capable of providing. It is clear that the more choices which adult learners are given, the more opportunities they will have to become immersed in learning that is appropriate to, and which meets, their various needs. The inclusion of choice creates settings where students can operate in personal zones of comfort yet, at the same time, can be challenged and encouraged to move beyond these to zones that extend their learning prospects (Vygotsky, 1978). It is important for teachers to see teaching and learning as a partnership between themselves and their students, and to bring students to view it this way too.

Teachers will always have firm views on what forms of learning are best and the forms they would prefer to employ. But likewise students have their views and perceptions on effective teaching and learning. An important part of the teaching process is for teachers to share their values with the students and at the same time to understand the students' values and perceptions. Part of the challenge for teachers is to provide flexible learning environments that cater for the needs and expectations of students and ensure that learners become partners in the learning setting. The new educational technologies provide exciting opportunities for developing the forms of learning environment that can do this.

Chapter 13

Understanding changes to university teaching

Terry Evans and Daryl Nation

Change, universities and teaching

Change is the name of the game in contemporary universities. At the top of the priority list for university managers, and the strategic planners who advise them, is the quest to address the challenges and prospects of *globalization*. As we recognized in our introductory chapter, many universities have responded strategically by embarking on reforms to their systems of teaching and learning, which are described, in an admixture of marketing hype and technical accuracy, as the *virtual university*. Students, a bare majority of whom remain full-time and attend classes on-campus, are reminded that the electronic university is about to emerge. Increasing numbers of beginning undergraduates arrive, 'notebook' in hand, fresh from a well-resourced secondary school that has made computer-based learning the basis of its programmes. University staff in many and various countries are reminded, some may say threatened, that they will soon be competing for students with the Cornells, Harvards and Oxbridges of the world who will offer their courses virtually and on a global basis (Cunningham *et al*, 1997: 37–105, 169–97).

In this chapter, we proceed from the basis laid down in previous discussions (Evans and Nation, 1989b; 1993a; 1996a), presenting a review of influential contributions to understanding contemporary changes to teaching and learning in higher education. Furthermore, we shall be discussing some outcomes of recent research on two Australian universities, which have espoused new educational technologies (Evans *et al*, 1996). We also draw together some of the themes and issues that our contributors have raised and provide our own analysis of *changing university teaching*. In our view, each of these terms needs to be critically examined for the theoretical and practical origins and implications that they obtain. *Changing*, and its derivations, is a term that is often associated with the fabric of the social conditions described as modernity and late-modernity by scholars such as Giddens (1991). For the past few generations in 'industrial' or 'knowledge societies' people have been implored to accept change, even to see it as the main 'challenge' of their social existence. Management educators and the like have developed courses on strategies for managing change in organizations. However, change requires moving from, or relinquishing, a particular condition or circumstance and adopting another. Within the process of change, there are various risks and harms to those making the change and those affected by the change, and there are perceived benefits to be gained once the change is made. The determination of the risks and benefits is usually in the hands of those who wield influence and power, and so typically changes are likely to benefit them, even if the rhetoric is in terms of a common good.

Arguably the biggest engine for change, worldwide, in the past 250 years has been industrial capitalism. In the Western European nations, which formed the bases of industrial capitalism, notions of change, development and progress have been dominant values. Through colonization by these European nations, these values were exported to the 'new world' of emerging independent nations, such as Argentina, Australia, Canada, New Zealand and, especially, the United States of America. However, these values have been continually contested as, for example, new scientific discoveries and industrial innovations are criticized and challenged for their potential or perceived harms. The Luddites (named after their leader, Ned Ludd) during 1811 to 1816 opposed the machinery (the new technology) which was being introduced into British fibre and cloth manufacturing. Their opposition, which included riots and damage to the new technology, was largely based on what they saw as the consequential disastrous effects on the employment of cloth and textile workers. The forces of law and order dealt with them severely and the rest, as they say, is history. It remains true today that an opponent of technological change is sometimes described as a Luddite and this is meant pejoratively. However, the Luddites were correct in their view that the effects on the cloth and textile workers would be harmful. The powerful interests of the day were able to press their case for technological change to enhance cloth and textile production, which it did. In contemporary circumstances, genetically modified crops and foods are being resisted and opposed by those who see the harms as either too great and/or insufficiently understood. The biotechnologists and food manufacturers are keen to develop and sell such products, and they argue for the benefits to food quality and consistency. As we argue later, change within university teaching is not without its Luddites and its 'manufacturing' interests. Our point here is to establish, at the outset, that change inevitably produces harms, risks and benefits to individuals and organizations. Also, the perception, and consequences, of such changes are viewed and experienced differently. Therefore, the different positions and powers of those involved affect their interests and capacities to force or resist change. This is no different in universities.

Such contestation is no different in terms of understanding the term, *university*.

At first one might consider that the notion of the university is quite unproblematic. However, as Peter Scott's work shows, the institution of the university has changed considerably since its inception in medieval times as a community of scholars through to the contemporary mass higher education institution (Scott, 1984; Scott, 1995). Rather than being a community of scholars, or 'university', such institutions are more communities of scholars, or 'multiversities' – to use Clark Kerr's term (Coaldrake and Stedman, 1998: 38–40; Nation, 1995a: 9–12). From somewhat different intellectual positions, Richard Barnett in the UK and Alan Bloom in the USA identify changes to university life or culture that now render them apathetic (or even antipathetic) to progressive or critical ideas and thinking (Barnett, 1997; Bloom, 1987; Campion, 1996). The notion of the university as a 'critical community of scholars' has changed into one of the university as an educational corporation. Indeed, as the budgets and staffing profiles of most universities today show, quite apart from their control or influence over the academic matters, the contemporary university is not a community (or communities) of academic staff at all. Rather, they are organizations with an equal, if not greater, proportion of non-academic staff to academic staff, and an equal or greater proportion of their budgets being expended on their non-academic elements. People who wish to understand (and change) contemporary universities need to grasp the nature, conditions and funding of their operations.

However, we must take the understanding of the contemporary university at least three steps further. One step is to understand the enormous amount of higher education that occurs outside of even the modern on-campus teaching 'multiversity'. As Sir John Daniel amply demonstrates, the really significant higher education landmarks globally are the enormous, distance teaching, 'mega-universities' (Daniel, 1996). Instead of having enrolments in the tens of thousands which are typical of the on-campus teaching universities, the mega-universities – such as the Indira Gandhi National Open University in India or the Chinese Radio and Television University – measure their enrolments in the hundreds of thousands. The second step is to recognize that there is a large number of 'dual-mode' institutions that have undertaken off-campus teaching as an essential or substantial part of their activities (Evans, 1999; Nation, 1995b: 30–44). These institutions are particularly located in the new world where they serve to help the development of the emerging nations (Bolton, 1986; Evans and Nation, 1993b). As Richard Johnson makes clear in the case of Australia, the politics of regional development and the history of distance teaching institutions are closely intertwined (Johnson, 1996). The third step is to appreciate the emergence and potential of 'brokering' and virtual universities, the former being organizations that usually draw on distance education courses from other institutions and/or commission new ones. They operate as agencies, which service, package and accredit courses and often are without any or a substantial scholarly community of their own. The others are the growing breeds of universities, which exist essentially in cyberspace; there is no campus or office block. Their courses are 'Web-based' and accessible via the Internet 'anywhere' on the globe. Of course, 'anywhere' needs qualification and/or clarification. Many people are too poor to afford the computer equipment, many people are illiterate or literate in local rather than 'international' languages (especially English), and/or their nations are too poor to afford the telecommunications infrastructure to provide ready access to the Internet.

There are probably some traditionalists who still regard institutions with the ivy covered cloisters as 'real universities', but most would acknowledge that the emerging group and the other on-campus institutions are also 'universities', even if they are different in nature and were once deemed 'colleges'. Some would also be quite comfortable including the dual-mode universities in their classification of university. Quite how many would think of the mega-universities as 'real universities' is difficult to tell, but their size and impact on the higher education sector are hard to ignore. The 'brokering' and 'virtual' universities are, perhaps, treated with the most disdain in terms of their status as universities. However, our contention is that universities are always changing and, in the current circumstances, even the august, ivy-clad, cloistered universities are exploiting the Web and creating their virtual campuses. In so doing, they are requiring of all their staff, especially their teachers, to change their *teaching*.

University teaching is the third and final term we wish to unravel before we continue further. Again 'teaching' is a taken-for-granted term that conceals unexpected complexities. As with most aspects of higher education, teaching itself has also been subjected to change (Nation, 1995a: 23–44). For our purposes, the most important period upon which to focus is probably since the 1960–1970s when the post-Second World War 'baby boomers' began to make their presence felt on educational policy makers and politicians. For example, Australia's higher education sector in 1963 consisted of seven universities. The next decade – which also experienced a considerable immigration boom – saw the sector expand to 17 universities and 27 colleges of advanced education (CAEs) (Marginson, 1997: 21). The new CAEs were expected to emphasize teaching and contributions to industry – rather than the research and teaching, which had become the central elements of the post-War universities in the developed world (Nation, 1995a: 12–21). In particular, CAE courses were focused on the commercial and industrial needs of the nation, in the same way as the 'polytechnic' colleges had been in the UK (Scott, 1984). Within the next two decades a shift occurred toward mass higher education with a consequential blurring of the distinction between the universities and CAEs; the latter becoming more involved in research and offered degrees and higher degrees, and the former offering more courses specifically geared to a range of newly emerging professions. During this same period, there were two global economic recessions and the consequential cost-cutting measures deployed were to reduce both public and private expenditure on higher education. Again, taking Australia as our example, there were moves to 'rationalize' higher education funding and operations during this period such that, by the end of the century, the distinction between CAEs and universities would be removed, and after a flurry of amalgamations and redesignations there were 37 universities.

One can well imagine that 'teaching' in a university during the 1960s was substantially different to teaching at the end of the 20th century. The influences of the CAEs, the financial reductions and the expansion into a mass higher education system have been substantial. The effects of new computer and communications technologies have also been profound. Even in the 1960s the range of activities which counted as 'teaching' would have been quite diverse. Apart from the lectures, tutorials and marking, there were also subjects, which called for practicals, fieldwork, performances, demonstrations and laboratory work, for example. The group sizes of lectures and tutorials increased markedly by the 1980s, and the trend has continued. The use of computer-based means of teaching has also occurred and flourished during the last period. The impact of distance education and its derivatives, open and flexible learning, is also a significant underlying feature that has important ramifications, as the computer and communications technologies are deployed by all universities to teach off-campus (Nation, 1995a: 24–40). It is now common for many (although not all!) senior staff in universities, who cut their teaching teeth in the 1960s and 1970s, to find the contemporary changes to teaching troubling and worthy of resistance. Likewise, the rising generation academics are pleased to have a university job, less troubled by the technologies, but worried by the pressure of numbers. As one might expect, their experiences and expectations are very different and require understanding by those who are engaged in *changing university teaching*.

Transmitters of change

In *Opening Education,* we offered an extensive discussion of the impact of globalization on education, and reviewed changes in policies and practices in open and distance education. This was done in the light of research and theory associated with the emergence of the 'information age', the 'knowledge society' and 'lifelong learning' (Evans and Nation, 1996a, 162–76). Recent changes in societies generally and in communications, education and the media particularly have strengthened our confidence in the analysis offered three years ago. Indeed, recent events and analyses confirm the view that an adequate understanding of these fields requires a medium to long view of the past, present and the future, active encouragement for interdisciplinary endeavours within 'the academies' and a firm connection to the social action 'outside' them (Cunningham *et al*, 1997).

Anthony Giddens (1998) continues to offer intellectual leadership as we come to terms with 'the global age'. His ideas invite critical debate rather than slavish adherence. In *The Third Way*, he maintains the theoretical substance derived from detailed critical and synthetic analysis transcending a range of disciplines while expressing it in the language of common sense. For Giddens (1998: 28–29), globalization is an ambiguous, 'unlovely' and contested term. It is also a fact of contemporary life:

> a complex range of processes driven by a mixture of political and economic influences. It is changing everyday life... at the same time as it is creating new transnational systems and forces. It is more than just a backdrop to contemporary policies:...[it] is transforming the institutions of the societies in which we live.
>
> (Giddens, 1998: 33)

In recognizing globalization, we accept that capitalism has won the contest for economic domination, at least for the foreseeable future. Capital has always been international. In the medieval era merchant entrepreneurs sought fortunes in unknown lands and seas, today, the emphasis is on the more intangible – but somehow more knowable – cyberspace. Rupert Murdoch secured a convenient change from Australian to United States citizenship (he still calls Australia 'home') to allow him to own a chunk of the North American media, in addition to his other international media interests. One senses, however, that he could just as deftly seek to obtain world citizenship, should the need and possibility of such citizenship arise.

What is truly global about this global world? Without doubt it is the communications infrastructure that allows for almost simultaneous transactions to occur in our business, domestic, political and social activities. If we are prepared to defy the daily calendar that has emerged through feudalism, thence to industrialism and to the 'post-modern era', we can enjoy reports of events 'as they happen'. In globalized business a corporate giant can always have one or two executives in the command post guiding those at the helm of their business ships through the trading day. The sun never sets on a successful global business.

The brain and heart of global capital are fed with oxygen processed by lungs that breathe the less than perfect air of the 'financial markets'. As the 'Asian crisis' of the late-1990s has demonstrated, financiers are prepared and able to depart from an investment at a few seconds notice. The International Monetary Fund (IMF) and other capitalist support systems struggle to compensate. Whether or not 'the markets will prevail' is an open question. As one of its key players, George Soros, is keenly aware:

> I'm afraid that the prevailing view, which is one of extending the market mechanism to all domains, has the potential of destroying society. Unless we review our concept of markets, our understanding of markets, they will collapse, because we are creating global markets, global financial markets, without understanding their true nature. We have this false theory that markets, left to their own devices, tend towards equilibrium. It's not, fortunately, believed in practice – I mean there are financial authorities who know that markets are not stable, and they try to maintain stability by exercising controls.
>
> (Giddens and Soros, 1998: 221)

Giddens and Soros are agreed that markets are not 'ecosystems', rather they are the creation of humans with reflexive capacities. They are the product of myriad human decisions. For Soros, markets also reflect the fallibility of many of the players involved and, in a disaster, the fallibility of key players and the collective consequences for us all (Giddens and Soros, 1998: 218–26). For Giddens, markets may be the best of the mechanisms for distributing income and expenditure within the economy, but they fall well short of the mark when dealing with distributions elsewhere in society, and with human interventions in the natural world. The Reaganites and Thatcherites may have partially destroyed the 'old welfare states' but a *Third Way* is required:

The new mixed economy looks instead for a synergy between public and private sectors, utilizing the dynamism of markets but with the public interest in mind. It involves a balance between regulation and deregulation, on a transnational as well as national and local levels; and a balance between the economic and non-economic in the life of the society.

(Giddens, 1998: 99–100)

Whether or not programmes such as *The Third Way* have any significant influence on corporations and public policy is yet to be determined. In his series of Reith Lectures, 'Runaway World', Giddens and the BBC attempted to put his ideas into practice. The lectures were broadcast in the conventional fashion on BBC Radio Four and the usual affiliated broadcasters worldwide (Giddens, 1999). Professor Giddens made a point of using the BBC Online Network's capabilities to the full. A special Homepage promoted the series in advance, featuring an 'interview' with Mr Giddens – in the format of a media release. The series open and closed at headquarters in London, but the intervening lectures occurred in Hong Kong, Delhi and Washington. Each lecture was delivered to a live audience and questions, from a stage-managed range of significant individuals, were fielded with aplomb. The Web site invited members of the radio and online audience/readership to submit questions by e-mail. The host at each lecture posed a select few of these, from suitably scattered locations. Following the main broadcast, the text of each lecture was available on the Web for reading and downloading. An audio and a video version were also available. The latter appeared to be a colourized version of an early live TV broadcast. It used a single camera, almost permanently offering a head and shoulders shot of the lecturer, apparently glued to the lectern, competently reading his well-crafted piece, obviously accustomed to such performances, and seemingly wearing the same fawn off-Saville Row suit and necktie at each venue. The audio track in the video version was degraded in comparison to the radio broadcast and the audio version on the Web site. Both, occasionally, had the lecturer affected by an electronic stutter.

The interrogation and debate was extended further on the Website, with a page headed 'Join the debate'. Giddens (1999) proffered:

> We want a global dialogue around the changes happening in the world. E-mail me. Tell me your views. I want to hear from you. Your views on globalization will help me to assess the impact of the Runaway World. Please take part and make it a truly global debate... E-mail your thoughts and opinions and see the debate grow on this site.

The questions and comments rolled in from around the world. Several weeks after the final broadcast of the series, contributions from countries occupied more than 50 pages of text on the Web site. There were 137 contributors, and 17 of these had offered multiple responses. Many were short, but most offered two or three paragraphs and a few went beyond a page. Many took Giddens at his word and expected replies. These were only offered within the lectures. To date, there is no sign of public replies by the lecturer himself. Yet, most of the questions and comments are very engaging and cry out for replies. Most are very positive in their critical comments and a few, constructively negative. Obviously, Giddens's ideas have struck in fertile soil.

None of the responses published engage with views expressed by fellow members of the audience: the focus is on the guru himself. Yet, in principle that could have been possible. Indeed, it should have been encouraged, as is often the case in the analogous debates occurring on 'quality' talkback radio. The committed teacher would feel obliged to reply. Professor Giddens has not had the inclination or encouragement to pursue this course, although his published work demonstrates that he does engage in public debate, and this is the case especially in his recent attempts to address a more popular audience. Indeed, those who are familiar with Giddens's work know that he is a writer who does his homework. As part of his research for his investigation of intimacy and the self, he immersed himself in the literature and activities of the 'self-help movement' (Giddens and Pierson, 1998: 121–22). One gets the impression that the published responses will be more than grist for his mental mill.

A small number of responses are of very direct interest from the perspective of a university teacher, as they come from people who have studied Giddens's ideas in the context of courses. Their responses reflect their understanding of broader aspects of his work, and they are clearly engaged by Giddens's use of these ideas in this context and appreciate the opportunity to address the master. Some respondents suggest that the ideas canvassed in the lectures were being discussed in sociology and other courses. The remarks of one US correspondent, Amy O'Connor, are particularly apposite in this regard:

> As a member of a class designed around these lectures, I would like to say that there is cause for a lot of pondering when I head home, and often during the week I think of something else to respond to from our discussion. My biggest disagreement with you is that globalization is not westernization or Americanization. I have only left this area twice for a distance of more than 400 miles... Even on a campus loaded with foreign students, I do not feel a cross-cultural connection at all. But many children in remote villages all around the world know plenty about my culture and lifestyle, and they have never travelled further from home than I.
>
> (Giddens, 1999)

Despite all these interesting and effective innovations the lectures, understandably, remain 'lectures'. The Web site offers very limited capacity for two-way communication. The lectures offer Giddens the opportunity to communicate his ideas to an audience, but only offer limited opportunities for debate and discussion. They are merely the beginnings of a thoroughly educational process. They will be better understood by members of the audience with well-developed capacities to process the ideas internally and in communication with others. To educators, like those engaging Amy O'Connor, they offer opportunities to engage others with their ideas by designing contexts within which they can be considered critically in conjunction with competing and comparable approaches. These revisions to lecturing also require educators to revise the techniques that are practised to retrieve and relate to these ideas. Quite literally, the capacities of the WWW allow for a 'seminar in cyberspace' which could include members from parts of the globe. Giddens himself, should personal time and resources permit, would find it much easier to accept an invitation to participate in such a seminar than he could by making personal visits to particular locations. How and why do some educators grasp these opportunities more substantially than others?

Prospects for educational change

For all these changes, many aspects of education have an air of permanence about them. Each generation that enters primary school, secondary school or university follows the well-worn paths of their predecessors. It is fashionable to talk about the globalization of economies and institutions as a result of the convergence brought about by the new communications technologies, but well before the bytes really bit into education, its key structures, institutions and practices had a global commonality about them. The outward appearance may have been different, but a 'school' operated very much like a 'school' whether it was in Brooklyn, Berlin, the Tiwi Islands or Teheran. Universities also had their common features so that a scholar on sabbatical would feel at home in a university in Manchester, Moscow, Christchurch or Caracas. Certainly, the relative wealth and the different histories, cultures and languages play their part in creating difference amongst the universities, but the commonalities remain fundamental. What we understand is that the global culture of education had its roots in the religious institutions of the Middle Ages. It then flowered in the colonial and trading interconnections that were laid during commercial and industrial development, thus creating the large global and international organizations, foundations and agencies that seek to encourage educational, social and economic development through their efforts and networks. For example, in the post-war period we have seen considerable activity by organizations such as UNESCO and the OECD, the Colombo Plan and Fulbright trust, and the various government and non-government agencies that have supported and influenced consultancies, scholarships and exchanges between nations.

A consequence of this global culture of education is that changing the values and practices of education is not merely an institutional exercise; it is necessary to take account of the broader implications and interpretations of change. The new communications and computer technologies have affected the work of education in what is almost a global way. While developing nations have generally not had the access to these facilities in the same way or at the same time as their developed world counterparts, with education being a global activity, they experience their own effects and consequences. These 'new educational technologies', as we prefer to refer to them, have their effects by their presence in some universities and by their absence from others. Those institutions which are 'early adopters' take the risks of dealing with the new and untried – what some like to refer to as being at the 'bleeding edge' of technology. In contrast, those institutions that fail to adopt the new technologies after the majority have taken them up, feel the chill of being out in the cold, and unable to participate in the new era. Arguably, this is particularly profound in the case of new educational technologies because of their potential to allow the wealthy and established universities to swamp the poor and fragile universities wherever they are in the globe.

The pressures towards *changing university teaching* are heightened in this age when these new technologies are being developed simultaneously with pressures from governments to cut costs and force the users to pay. Various political and commercial interests are coming to bear, imploring managers and others in education to make a paradigm shift; or, sometimes, it is implied that the paradigm has shifted and everyone needs to catch up. The term 'paradigm' is often interpreted rather loosely in everyday language, however, under the influence of Thomas Kuhn, the philosopher of science, it has taken on a particular, useful meaning (Kuhn, 1970). Paradigm in the Kuhnian sense meant an entire, all-embracing way of understanding and engaging in a field of science. Rather like a religion and its believers, to its adherents, there is no other way of understanding (theorizing), researching and conducting the science. When a discovery fundamentally threatens the paradigm it is either rejected as heresy, or if sufficiently powerful, it causes what Kuhn called a 'paradigm shift'.

In terms of education, we are left wondering about which effects of new educational technologies have caused a paradigm shift, or is even establishing the necessary pre-conditions for such. It seems that the global culture (or paradigm) of education to which we have referred has merely mutated to adapt, where necessary, to the new technologies. This is not to deny that things have changed as a result of the new educational technologies; rather it is to say that the changes have not threatened the prevailing ways in which education operates. The institutional and governmental arrangements have not been changed in any fundamental way: pedagogies have been modified rather than replaced; assessment has been revised rather than overthrown; the teacher is still in control when a mouse replaces the chalk. In some of our earlier work we offered a critique of the adoption of behaviourist-influenced mass-production models of distance education. We argued that such 'instructional industrialism' ran counter to educational practices which recognize that learners should be encouraged and supported to learn constructively through dialogic means (Evans and Nation, 1987; Evans and Nation, 1989a; Evans and Nation, 1989b). The use of new educational technologies has exacerbated, not alleviated, the tension. The computer's capacity to store large volumes of text, graphics and sound, and the communications networks' ability to provide access (globally) to their storage, provides a tempting combination for the instructional industrialist. This same combination can provide greater opportunities, choices and interaction for educators wishing to construct virtual learning environments that foster dialogue.

The advent of new educational technologies is less likely to constitute a paradigm change in university teaching than to cement the current paradigm into another interlocking real and virtual form. It emphasizes the point that the development of new educational technologies is not about plugging-in new equipment and being turned on to a new educational paradigm. Rather, educational technology, as we have argued elsewhere (for example, Evans and Nation, 1993a), is about the human and social application of tools for educational purposes. How people decide to use the new tools will affect whether there is a paradigm shift or not; the tools themselves are inanimate objects, only offering capacities for human endeavour.

Proponents of change

In her book, *Rethinking University Teaching: A framework for the effective use of educational technology*, Diana Laurillard (1993) set out to offer a programme for the effective use of the available media for teaching in contemporary universities. It remains the most comprehensive analysis in the field. The book is founded on a thorough review of research on students' learning through various media. It is addressed to individuals and organizations with an interest in exploring the strengths and weaknesses of various educational media, and hybrids of them, in individual subjects, whole courses and entire institutions.

Unlike many works dealing with teaching media and new educational technologies, addressed to university teachers, Laurillard's analysis includes classrooms as teaching media. Teaching is regarded as sets of mediated processes. Teaching materials, audio, audio visual, multimedia, print etc are not regarded as supplements or substitutes for forms of classroom teaching, but as integral aspects of any set of teaching processes. She has taken the incisive but sketchy observations made by researchers, such as David Hamilton (1990), much further (Evans and Nation, 1993: 198–203).

Following research on students' learning by Ference Marton and his associates, which has been the basis for influential works on university teaching, such as those by Paul Ramsden (1992), Laurillard believes that dialogue is at the centre of the processes of teaching and learning. These processes go well beyond interaction between students and teachers. She asserts 'there is no room for mere telling, nor practice without description, nor experimentation without reflection, nor for student action without feedback' (Laurillard, 1993: 85).

In introducing her analysis of the teaching media, Laurillard (1993: 97) addresses directly the issue of the primacy of face-to-face teaching in the minds of university teachers. By regarding 'teaching and learning... as inescapably and essentially a dialogue', she suggests, 'this may appear to rule out any contribution from teaching methods other than the one-to-one tutorial'. While the one-to-one tutorial may be possible in an élite system, such as the traditional Oxbridge, it is neither efficient nor effective as the basis for teaching in a mass system of higher education. Thus, universities have developed the traditional alternatives:

> to support learning as it is commonly understood to occur: through acquisition, so we offer lectures and reading; through practice, so we set exercises and problems; through discussion, so we conduct seminars and tutorials; through discovery, so we arrange field trips and practicals.
>
> (Laurillard, 1993: 97)

She reviews Ramsden's analysis of these traditional methods, from the perspective of their jointly held espousal of teaching methods, which foster active rather than passive learning, and notes his scepticism with regard to computers and other electronic media as effective bases for teaching (Evans and Nation, 1996b: 175).

Many of the proponents of electronic teaching media, Laurillard (1993: 98–99) contends, assume 'a transmission model for education'. In rejecting this view, but advocating a range of media inclusive of classrooms of various kinds, print and various electronic media, she develops a 'conversational framework' as a basis for designing teaching processes that use media effectively to engage students actively in learning processes. These technologies need to be employed to ensure that critical discussion is at the centre of the teaching and learning processes. Failure to do so will mean that 'universities will become training camps, unable to do more than expose their students to what there is to be known, and to rehearse them in the ability to reproduce it' (Laurillard, 1993: 178).

Since the publication of *Rethinking University Teaching*, Laurillard has been involved as a senior manager in reform of the teaching system of her own institution, the Open University, especially relating to the challenges and opportunities provided by electronic technologies. She has also continued to act as a consultant to Australian universities and recently co-wrote a discussion paper with Don Margetson as a basis for policy debate aimed at introducing 'flexible learning methodology' to Griffith University (Laurillard and Margetson, 1997).

The paper begins by recognizing that a contemporary university has to address the prospects of making flexible learning one of its central features as 'part of the radical changes affecting higher education'. That is globally, in terms of an argument in sympathy with the beginning of this chapter (Laurillard and Margetson, 1997: 1–2). They sound a familiar warning: 'if flexible learning is actually to increase flexibility (rather than merely becoming a code word for computer-mediated course "delivery")', one should not simply equate flexible learning with electronic technologies, or assume that because messages can be delivered quickly to enormous numbers of individuals that they are necessarily educative. Printed and other resource based forms of teaching and learning will remain fundamentally important and the nature of the pedagogy is the key determinant of educational value.

Continuing this theme, they home in on the vexed issues associated with 'collegiality' and the autonomy of individual staff in the teaching process which may be threatened by the need to mediate university teaching extensively inside and, especially, beyond classrooms. The substantial and sophisticated use of educational technologies requires teachers and those supporting them in the production of teaching materials to extend preparation time, to engage in teamwork and to use centralized infrastructure. However, the production and delivery of media are only a beginning to the educational process, and must be the basis for dialogue between students and teachers (Laurillard and Margetson, 1997: 2–6).

In a related research project, Peter Taylor, Lucy Lopez and Carol Quadrelli examined the use of print, communications and information technologies in teaching at Griffith University and Queensland University of Technology (QUT). At Griffith, the Faculty of Humanities had introduced 'resource-based teaching' in an arts degree. As a policy initiative the faculty had decided to mainstream the techniques it had explored for teaching part-time mature aged students, based on extensive printed teaching materials and limited face-to-face teaching, in its entire arts degree.

This involved reducing face-to-face classroom teaching for full-time students and employing the printed teaching materials with all students. Electronic technologies were considered, but never used extensively.

At QUT, the Faculty of Education created an 'open learning' programme for students in a Masters degree based on its distance education programme. Electronic technologies of various sorts were employed in many subjects. The School of Law embarked on the extensive use of computer-based technologies in many subjects, based substantially on a quest to improve teaching quality, the faculty's financial and moral support for innovative projects and the pursuit of finance and professional recognition available from national teaching grants (Taylor, Lopez and Quadrelli, 1996: 33–46, 85–111).

The project's conclusions accord with the principles articulated by Laurillard, Margetson and Ramsden. Contending that university teachers:

> can learn to use technology in educationally appropriate ways in order to achieve reform in the delivery of education; or we can use technology to lengthen one-way transmission – doing more of the same, but in broadcast mode.
>
> (Taylor, Lopez and Quadrelli, 1996: 111)

They present substantial evidence of both prospects. They emphasize the need to give attention to the provision of adequate infrastructure, and the skilled humans to support it, as well as supporting thoroughly collaborative efforts in developing the new pedagogies to employ these technologies for conversational purposes. Our own recent research, discussed below, supports these conclusions.

Before turning to the outcomes of this research, it is useful to re-visit themes we have pursued at length in other contexts. Theorists and practitioners, such as Laurillard, have embraced the need to ensure that attempts to mediate teaching and learning go beyond instructional industrialism. This is easier said than done. David Harris's (1987) examination of the OU's early developments has established a compelling case for the view that those who regard education as essentially 'telling' students what they should think are always alive, well and in the forefront of mediated approaches to teaching and learning. Of course, this has to be balanced with an appreciation that classrooms are mediated environments, and they too can all too frequently be contexts in which 'telling' is the name of the game. Must this always be the case?

Pursuing change in Australia

Recently, we have been engaged in a long-term research project in two Australian universities with a declared interest in incorporating new educational technologies in their teaching and learning. The project stemmed largely from previous research that we had undertaken into the ways in which educational organizations adapt their teaching approaches for new demands, contexts and 'clients'. In the current project, we completed a sequence of related case studies in two universities. We were particularly concerned to investigate the ways in which changes occurred, at the level of policy and practice (and the relationships between them), that focused principally on new computer and communications technologies (see Evans *et al*, 1996; Evans *et al*, 1997). Neither of the two universities had a history as 'dual-mode' institutions, although one has been involved in distance education on a small scale for many years, often in collaboration with other institutions; the other had a limited involvement many decades ago. Each university had an active 'teaching support unit' and well developed policies relating to the use of information technology in teaching.

The research was designed to explore the potential convergence between open and distance education and 'traditional' education (Evans and Nation, 1993a; 1993b; 1996). One line of investigation explores the extent to which ideas and practices from open and distance education were employed in the two universities under study. Another investigates the influence of the policies and activities of the Commonwealth government and, especially, the Committee for the Advancement of University Teaching (CAUT) and its successor, the Committee University Teaching and Staff Development (CUTSD). Another line studies the influence of the policies and practices of the 'teaching support units', in each institution and the changes which ensue or are resisted. The research involved the collection of policy, publicity and meeting documents, interviewing of staff and students, observations of teaching and other events, etc. We are currently at the stage of analysing the data and we draw on some overall findings here.

One key aspect of change to teaching in universities is that it is the result of a complex process that does not enable the identification of (a single) cause and effect. In each of the case studies we conducted there was evidence of a web of interlocking threads leading back into the life of the organization. Some threads led to the senior management, some to the government, some to key change agents in middle management, and some to 'grassroots' staff. None of these threads could be identified as pointing to students themselves, as agents of change, although sometimes the students, or their needs, problems or circumstances, were part of the fabric of change. In most cases, the institutional policies around new technology reflect the global push into new technologies in education and universities in particular. It is seen as inevitable that a 'competitive' university will need to keep pace with technological change, even if, as Katz muses of US university presidents, many would like to put the 'genie back in the bottle' (Katz and associates, 1999: xiii). Each institution had a significant number of policy documents or statements, which dealt with the use, deployment, funding and application of computer and information technologies in teaching. Although there were a few people who resisted these policies, more people were advocates of their implementation, and most were ignorant of, or indifferent to, their existence and implementation.

When endeavouring to identify the key agents who initiated particular policies it was often the case that this was a senior manager, sometimes connected to a relevant committee or organization within the university. However, it was often the case that this person had been strongly influenced in forming and prosecuting their views by relatively junior people in the organization. These people were often located within 'teaching support' or 'educational technology' units and saw their role as partly being about keeping the institution up-to-date in its practices. In this sense, they saw that their role was to facilitate change in these respects and that an important part of doing so was to 'bend the ear' of the senior management to obtain their explicit support. However, such moves can always be seen as congruent with broader government policy shifts, in this sense the change was never radical, although it was often much so for university staff in general.

Another form of grassroots initiator of change is an academic staff member whose inquiring mind and passion for teaching goes beyond their discipline, and into technology and pedagogy. Such persons were often active researchers and participants in university life generally, and yet managed to turn their skills to developing new ways of teaching using computer and information technologies. They would often work away at their 'pet' teaching project, in much the same way that a scholar might spend hours in the library, in the field or in the lab. The process was often analogous to the development of a research project with small trials and pilot projects before developing a submission or application for some funding, either to an agency within the organization supporting teaching and technological developments, or sometimes outside to agencies such as CAUT or CUTSD. If successful, the project would not only assume a larger scale, but often an increased status and significance within the department and university. The winning of a research grant is good academic currency, and so a grant for a teaching development confers a similar, if not equal, status.

It is also true to say that the pursuit of technology in teaching is accepted, if grudgingly by some, as a 'good thing'. The rhetoric of the necessity of technological change is so pervasive in some parts of universities, especially in the sciences and science-related fields, that it is uncritically accepted that the introduction of new technology is good in itself. This contributes to a similar spiralling upward of costs to that which occurs in medicine, even if the gross costs involved are proportionally smaller. Part of the reason is the cost of the new equipment, software and general infrastructure, not only in capital but also recurrent costs. However, another significant part is that in most respects these costs are additional and cumulative to the existing capital and recurrent costs of teaching. Rarely does a new development replace existing capital and recurrent costs for teaching, such as the removal of a lecture theatre and the ceasing of lectures. Rather, the new technology usually supplements and enhances the existing teaching. This is one reason why some university administrators occasionally wonder if it might be good to 'put the genie back in the bottle'.

Concluding comments

Computer and communications technologies will continue as significant influences in the social changes we now understand as *globalization*. Those pushing the 'edges of the envelope' advocate a *planetist future* (Ellyard, 1998). In some ways universities are driving this future and in others they tread the somewhat conservative path typical of educators through the centuries. There is immense evidence to support the view that the rhetoric and policy directions point towards the genuine emergence of *virtual universities*, at the very least, as aspects of individual institutions or entire systems of higher education. The requisite pedagogical theories – commonly branded as constructivism – have established themselves; at least, as respectable movements. The better versions of these approaches, such as that articulated by Laurillard, and based on plausible and sensible *reflexive* theories of human endeavour are becoming influential; as guiding lights, at least. The research evidence, however, suggests that in practise we have considerable distance to travel if our objective is to create and maintain reflexive forms of teaching and learning capable of engendering the critical examination and generation of knowledge.

There are many challenges facing policymakers, educators and students as 'traditional' universities 'virtualize' themselves through the new technologies, establishing new markets and responding to the forces of globalization. It is impossible to turn the clock back in these respects, just as it was impossible for the Luddites to prevent the Industrial Revolution. However, we would argue that there are many ways in which educators can harness these new circumstances to ends that produce educational reforms enabling graduates, citizens and workers to be more informed, indeed, more learned. From this perspective, communications and information technologies developed for business and military purposes are transformed, rather than merely adapted, through their adoption by universities. In a similar manner Giddens and the BBC have been attempting to practise such theories in public broadcasting. The fact that they fall well short of the mark drawn by educators, such as Laurillard, is very instructive.

Educators have 'not been backward in coming forward' at the rhetorical and experimental levels; and, the substantial resistance and enduring by university academics has to be assessed critically and never ignored. There is a 'dark side' of these educational reforms reflected in 'job cuts', shifts in capital and recurrent expenditure away from teachers' labour towards information technologies and new forms of labour to support them. Educators need to take these matters seriously, debate them critically, and then move forward positively to develop their practices using new technologies (and other means) in ways which have real educational potential and merit. In this way, educators will be at the leading edge and not the bleeding edge!

References

Aikenhead, G S (1997) Teachers, teaching strategies, and culture, in *Globalization of science education*, pre-conference proceedings for the International Conference on Science Education, pp 133–36, Korean Educational Development Institute, Seoul, Korea

Aikenhead, G S and Jegede, O J (1999) Cross-cultural science education: a cognitive explanation of a cultural phenomenon, *Journal of Research in Science Teaching*, **36** (3), pp 269–87

Alan, E (1995) The Electronic University Network, *GLOSAS News*, **1** (1), pp 45–49

Alexander, S and Hedberg, J (1994) Evaluating technology-based learning: which model?' in *Multimedia in Higher Education: Designing for change in teaching and learning*, ed K Beattie, C McNaught and S Wills, Elsevier, Amsterdam

Alexander, S and McKenzie, J (1998) *An Evaluation of Information Technology Projects in University Learning*, Australian Government Publishing Service, Canberra

Anderson, T, Varnhagen, S and Campbell, K (1998) Faculty adoption of teaching and learning technologies: contrasting earlier adopters and mainstream faculty, *Canadian Journal of Higher Education*, **28** (2/3), pp 71–98

Anderson, T D and Garrison, D R (1998) Learning in a networked world: new roles and responsibilities, in *Distance learners in higher education: Institutional responses for quality outcomes*, ed C Gibson, pp 97–112, Atwood Publishing, Madison, Wisconsin

Arnold, R (1995) Neue methoden betrieblicher bildungsarbeit, in *Handbuch der Berufsbildung*, ed R Arnold and A Lipsmeier, pp 294–307, Leske and Budrich, Opladen

Arnold, R (1996) Entgrenzung und Entstrukturierung der Hochschulen durch Fernstudium. A keynote speech presented at the Studium online Symposium, University of Kaiserslautern, 26 November

Bacsish, P (1998) Re-engineering the campus with Web and related technology for the virtual university, *Learning in a Global Information Society*, **14/15**, pp 9–13 and **16/17**, pp 9–11

Bardmann, T M and Franzpötter, R (1990) Unternehmenskultur ein Postmodernes Organizationskonzept, *Soziale Welt*, **4**, pp 424–40

Barnett, R (1997) *Higher Education: A critical business*, Society for Research into Higher Education/Open University Press, Buckingham

Baron, J and Hanisch, J (1997) Educating for a virtual world, paper presented at the 18th ICDE World Conference on *New Learning Environment: A global perspective*, conference abstracts, p 450, Pennsylvania State University, 2–6 June

Barthes, R (1977) *Image-Music-Text*, Fontana-Collins, London

Bates, A (1995) *Technology, Open Learning and Distance Education*, Routledge, London

Bates, A (1997a) The impact of technological change on open and distance learning, *Distance Education*, **18** (1), pp 93–109

Bates, A (1997b) Restructuring the university for technological change, presented at the Carnegie Foundation for the Advancement of Teaching, *What kind of university?* 18–20 June, 1997, London, http://bates.cstudies.ubc.ca/carnegie/carnegie.html

Beaudoin, M A (1998) New professoriate for the new millenium, *DEOS– The Distance Education Online Symposium*, Web site http://www.cdepouedu/ACSDE

Bennett, P (1997) The Dearing Report: Paving the way for a learning society, *Australian Universities Review*, **40** (2), pp 27–30

Benson, A and Selinger, M (1998) Exploring student teachers' perceptions of the science/mathematics relationship using electronic conferencing, *Teacher Development: An International journal of teachers' professional development* (in press)

Bernstein, B (1970) On the classification and framing of educational knowledge, in *Knowledge and Control: New directions for the sociology of education*, ed M Young, pp 47–69, Collier-Macmillan, London

Biggs, J and Telfer, R (1987) *The Process Of Learning*, Prentice Hall, Sydney

Bigum, C and Green, B (1993) Technologizing literacy: or interrupting the dream of reason, in *Literacy in contexts: Australian perspectives and issues*, ed P Gilbert and A G Luke, pp 4–28, Allen and Unwin, Sydney

Bigum, C and Kenway, J (1998) New information technologies and the ambiguous future of schooling: some possible scenarios, in *International Handbook of Educational Change*, ed A Hargreaves *et al*, pp 375–95, Kluwer Academic Publishers, Dordrecht

Bloom, A (1987) *The Closing of the American Mind*, Penguin, London

Bolton, G (1986) The opportunity of distance, *Distance Education*, **7** (1), pp 5–22

Boud, D, Cohen, R and Walker, D (1998) Understanding learning from experience, *The Teaching Professor*, **12** (3), p 7

Bourdieu, P (1988) *Homo Academicus*, tr P Collier, Polity Press, Cambridge

Bourdieu, P (1992) *Language and Symbolic Power*, Harvard University Press, Cambridge, MA

Brown, J and Duguid, P (1996) Universities in the digital age, *Change*, **28** (4), pp 10–19

Bruce, B C (1997) Critical issues. Literacy technologies: What stance should we take? *Journal of Literacy Research*, **29** (2), pp 269–309

Bruce, B and M? (1997) The disappearance of technology: towards an ecological model of literacy, in *Literacy for the 21st Century: Technologicial transformations in a post-typographic world*, ed M Reinking, L Labbo and R Kieffer, Erlbaum, Hillsdale, NJ

Bruner, J (1996) *The Culture of Education*, Harvard University Press, Cambridge, MA

Cairncross, F (1995) 'The death of distance'. A survey of telecommunications, *The Economist*, **336** (7934), S1–S28

Campion, M (1991) Critical essay on educational technology in distance education, in *Beyond the Text: Contemporary writing on distance education*, ed T Evans and B King, pp 183–203, Deakin University Press, Geelong

Campion, M (1996) Open learning, closing minds, in *Opening Education: Policies and practices from open and distance education*, ed T D Evans and D E Nation, pp 147–61, Routledge, London

Candy, P (1988) On the attainment of subject-matter autonomy, in *Developing Student Autonomy in Learning*, ed D Boud, pp 59–76, Kogan Page, London

Candy, P (1991) *Self-direction For Lifelong Learning: A comprehensive guide to theory and practice*, Jossey-Bass, San Francisco

Casper, G (1996) Eine welt ohne universitäten? Werner Heisenberg Vorlesung Bayerische Akademie der Wissenschaften und Carl Friedrich von Siemens Stiftung München, 3 Juli 1996, quoted from a broadcast transcript by the Tele-Akademie of the Südwestfunks, 26 January

Chick, J (1981) Communications in Distance Education, 5th Biennial Forum, Australian and South Pacific External Studies Association, Suva

Christensen, C M (1997) *The Innovator's Dilemma: When new technologies cause great firms to fail*, Harvard Business School Press, Boston

Clark, B R (1998) *Creating Entrepreneurial Universities: Organizational pathways of transformation*, Pergamon, New York

Clark, R E (1983) Reconsidering research on learning from media, *Review of Educational Research*, **42** (1), pp 21–32,

Coaldrake, P and Stedman, L (1998) *On the Brink: Australia's universities confronting their future*, University of Queensland Press, Brisbane

Collis, B (1997) Pedagogical reengineering: a pedagogical approach to course enrichment and redesign with the WWW, *Educational Technology Review*, **8**, pp 11–15

Commission for Higher Education (1990) *National Higher Education Plan*, Office of Higher Education, Port Moresby

Conference Board of Canada (1991) *Employability Skills Profile: The Critical Skills Required by the Canadian Workforce*, The Conference Board of Canada, Ottawa

Cuban, L (1986) *Teachers and Machines: The classroom use of technology since 1920*, Teachers College Press, New York

Cunningham, S *et al* (1997) *New Media and Borderless Education: A review of the convergence between global media networks and higher education provision*, Australian Government Publishing Service, Canberra

Currie, G, Gunther, J T and Spate, O (1964) *Report of the Commission of Enquiry on Higher Education in Papua New Guinea*, Department of Territories, Canberra

Curtis, S (1998a) *Project LEAD: Interim Progress Report to CUTSD*, University of Wollongong, Wollongong

Curtis, S (1998b) *Project LEAD: Information Management Team Feedback Report*, University of Wollongong, Wollongong

Daniel, J (1996) *Mega-universities and Knowledge Media Technology Strategies for Higher Education*, Routledge, London

Daniel, J (1998) Knowledge media for mega-universities: Scaling up new technology at the UK Open University, Keynote speech at the International Open and Distance Education Symposium at the Shanghai Television University, 16 April

Dearing Report, the (1997) *Higher Education in the Learning Society*, Report of the National Committee of Inquiry into Higher Education, HMSO, Norwich, UK

Dearing Report, the (1997) [online] http://www.dfee.gov.uk/highed/dearing.htm

Dede, C (1996) The evolution of distance education: emerging technologies and distributed learning, *The American Journal of Distance Education*, **10** (2), pp 4–36

Deleuze, G (1992) *Cinema 1: The movement-image*, The Athlone Press, London

DeLong, S E (1997) The shroud of lecturing, *First Monday* http://www.firstmonday.dk/issues/issue2_5/delong

Department of Employment, Education, Training and Youth Affairs (DEETYA) (1997) *Digital Rhetorics, Literacies and Technologies in Education: Current practices and future directions*, Queensland University of Technology, Brisbane

DEETYA (1998) *Learning for Life (final report): the review of higher education financing and policy*, Chair, R West, Australian Government Publishing Service, Canberra

Docherty, T (ed) (1993) *Postmodernism: A reader*, Wheatsheaf Harvester Press, Cambridge

Dohmen, G (1996) *Das lebenslange Lernen Leitlinien einer modernen Bildungspolitik*, Bundesministerium für Bildung, Wissenschaft, Forschung und Technologie, Bonn

Dohmen, G (1997) *Selbstgesteuertes lebenslanges Lernen: Leitlinien einer modernen Bildungspolitik*, Ministerium für Bildung, Wissenschaft, Forschung und Technologie, Bonn

Dreyfus, H and Rabinow, P (1982) *Michel Foucault: Beyond structuralism and hermeneutics*, Harvester Press, Brighton

Driver, R (1979) Cultural diversity and the teaching of science, in *Bilingual Multicultural Education and the Classroom Teacher: From theory to practice*, ed H Trueba and C Barnett-Mizahi, pp 23–31, Newberry, Rowley

Drucker, P A and Holden, C (1997) Untitled, *Science*, **275** (5307), p 1745

Eastcott, D and Farmer, R (1992) Planning Teaching for Active Learning, Module 3 of the *Effective teaching and learning in higher education project*, CVCP Universities Staff Development and Training Unit, Sheffield

Ehrhard, M (1997) Krise im Elfenbeinturm, transcript of a radio broadcast on 12 January, Tele-Akademie des Südwestfunks, Baden-Baden

Ehrmann, S C (1995) Asking the right questions: what does research tell us about technology and higher learning? *Change*, pp 20–27

Elliot, J (1991) *Action Research and Educational Change*, Open University Press, Milton Keynes

Ellyard, P (1998) *Ideas for the New Millennium*, Melbourne University Press, Carlton South

Entwistle, N J and Ramsden, P (1983) *Understanding Student Learning,* Croom Helm, London

Evans, T D and Nation, D E (1987) Which future for distance education? *International Council for Distance Education Bulletin*, **14**, pp 48–53

Evans, T D and Nation, D E (1989a) Critical reflections in distance education, in *Critical Reflections on Distance Education*, ed T D Evans and D E Nation, London, Falmer Press

Evans, T D and Nation, D E (ed) (1989b) *Critical Reflections on Distance Education*, Falmer Press, London

Evans, T D and Nation, D E (1989c) Dialogue in practice, research and theory in distance education, *Open Learning*, **4** (2), pp 37–43

Evans, T D and Nation, D E (1989d) Reflections on the project, in *Critical Reflections on Distance Education*, ed T D Evans and D E Nation, pp 9–20, Falmer Press, London

Evans, T D and Nation, D E (ed) (1993) *Reforming Open and Distance Education*, Kogan Page, London

Evans, T D and Nation, D E (1993a) Distance education, educational technology and open learning: converging futures and closer integration with conventional education, in *Distance Education Futures: The proceedings of the Australian and South Pacific External Studies Association biennial forum*, ed T Nunan, pp 15–35, University of South Australia, Adelaide

Evans, T D and Nation, D E (1993b) Educating teachers at a distance in Australia: some history, research results and recent trends, in *Distance Education for Teacher Training*, ed H Perraton, pp 261–86, Routledge, London

Evans, T D and Nation, D E (1993c) Introduction: reformations in open and distance education, in *Reforming Open and Distance Education*, ed T D Evans and D E Nation, pp 7–14, Kogan Page, London

Evans, T D and Nation, D E (1996a) Educational futures: globalization, educational technology and lifelong learning, in *Opening Education: Policies and practices from open and distance education*, ed T D Evans and D E Nation, pp 162–76, Routledge, London

Evans, T D and Nation, D E (1996b) Opening education: local lines, global connections, in *Opening Education: Policies and practices from open and distance education*, ed T D Evans and D E Nation, pp 1–6, Routledge, London

Evans, T D and Nation, D E (1996c) *Opening Education: Policies and practices from open and distance education*, Routledge, London

Evans, T D *et al* (1996) Educational reform and converging technologies in Australian higher education: preliminary findings from two case-studies, *Canadian Association of Distance Education*, Université de Moncton

Evans, T D *et al* (1997) The end of the line or a new future for open and distance education? Issues for practitioners, researchers, and theorists from a study of educational reform in post-secondary education, in *Open Flexible and Distance learning: Education and training for the 21st Century*, proceedings of the Open and Distance Learning Association of Australia Forum, University of Tasmania, Launceston, 29 September–2 October, ed J Osborne, D Roberts and J Walker, pp 151–55

Evans, T D (1999) From dual mode to flexible delivery: paradoxical transitions in Australian open and distance education, *Performance Improvement Quarterly*, **12** (2), pp 3–16

Fabro, K G and Garrison, G R (1998) Computer-conferencing and higher-order learning, *Indian Journal of Open Learning*, **7** (1), pp 41–53

Feldman, K A (1988) Effective college teaching from the students' and faculties' view: matched or mismatched priorities? *Research in Higher Education*, **28**, pp 291–344

Fiefia, N (1997) Getting started in the Republic of the Marshall Islands: a report of the Majuro Centre, *Te Kie: A forum for distance and continuing education at USP*, **2**, pp 10–20

Fox, R and Herrmann, A (1997) Designing study materials in new times: changing distance education? in *Research in Distance Education 4*, ed T Evans, V Jakupec, and D Thompson, pp 34–44, Deakin University Press, Geelong

Franklin, U (1990) *The Real World of Technology*, CBC Enterprises, Concord, Ontario

Freeman, M (1997) Flexibility in access, interactions and assessment: The case for Web-based teaching programs, *Australian Journal of Educational Technology*, **13** (1), 23–39

Freire, P (1982) Creating alternative research methods: learning to do it by doing it, in *Creating Knowledge: A monopoly*, ed B Hall, A Gillette and R Tandon, Khanpur, New Delhi

Friedrich, H F and Mandl, H (1997) Analyse und förderung selbstgesteuerten lernens, in *F Psychologie der Erwachsenenbildung (Enzyklopädie der Psychologie, Band 4 Erwachsenenbildung)*, ed W Weinert and H Mandl, pp 237–93, Hogrefe, Göttingen

Frost, S E Jr (1937) *Education's own stations: The history of broadcast licenses issued to educational institutions*, University of Chicago Press, Chicago

Gardner, H (1983) *Frames of mind: The theory of multiple intelligences*, Basic Books, New York

Garrison, D R (1985) Three generations of technological innovations in distance education, *Distance Education*, **6** (2), pp 235–41

Garrison, D R (1993) Quality and access in distance education, in *Theoretical Principles of Distance Education*, ed D Keegan, pp 22–38, Routledge, London

Geoghegan, W H (1994) *Whatever happened to instructional technology?* IBM Academic Consulting Paper presented at the 22nd Annual Conference of the International Business Schools Computing Association, Baltimore, Maryland, July. Available on line: http://ike.engr.washington.edu/news/whitep/whg/wpi.htm

Geoghegan, W H (1996) Instructional technology and the mainstream: risks of success, the Maytum distinguished lecture, SUNY College, Fredonia

Gibbs, Morgan, A and Taylor, E (1982) Why students don't learn, *Institutional Research Review*, **1**, pp 9–32

Giddens, A (1991) *The Consequences of Modernity*, Cambridge, Polity Press

Giddens, A (1994) *Beyond Left and Right: The future of radical politics*, Polity Press, Cambridge

Giddens, A (1998) *The Third Way: The renewal of social democracy*, Polity Press, Cambridge

Giddens, A (1999) *Runaway World*, Reith Lectures 1999, BBC Online Network, http://news.bbc.co.uk/hi/english/static/events/reith_99/default.html

Giddens, A and Pierson, C (1998) *Conversations with Anthony Giddens: Making sense of modernity*, Polity Press, Cambridge

Giddens, A and Soros, G (1998) Beyond chaos and dogma, in *Conversations with Anthony Giddens: Making sense of modernity*, A Giddens and C Pierson, pp 218–26, Polity Press, Cambridge

Gilbert, C (1998) *Report on the NCODE RBL Workshop*, July, internal report to National Council for Open and Distance Education

Giroux, H (1992) *Border Crossings: Cultural workers and the politics of education*, Routledge, New York

Glotz, P (1996) *Im Kern verrottet? Fünf vor zwölf an Deutschlands Universitäten*, Deutsche Verlags-Anstalt, Stuttgart

Goethe, J W (1994) Rede zur Eröffnung der Freitagsgesellschaft am 9 September 1791, in *Sämtliche Werke, Briefe, Tagebücher und Gespräche*, ed F Apel, pp 405–07, Deutscher Klassiker Verlag volume 17, Frankfurt am Main

Gottwald, F T and Sprinkart, P (1998) *Multi-Media Campus Die Zukunft der Bildung*, Metropolitan Verlag, Düsseldorf

Grabe, M and Grabe, C (1998) *Integrating Technology for Meaningful Learning*, Houghton Mifflin, Boston

Gris, G B (1974) *Report of the Committee of Enquiry into University Development*, University of Papua New Guinea, Waigani

Guba, E and Lincoln, Y (1981) *Effective Evaluation: Improving the usefulness of evaluation results through responsive and naturalistic approaches*, Jossey-Bass, London

Guy, R (1994) *Distance, Dialogue and Difference: A post-positivist approach to understanding distance education in Papua New Guinea*, Unpublished PhD thesis, Deakin University, Geelong

Guy, R (1995) Contesting borders: knowledge power and pedagogy in distance education in Papua New Guinea, in *Distance Education: Crossing frontiers*, ed F Nouwens, pp 79–82, Central Queensland University, Rockhampton

Guy, R, Haihuie, S and Pena, P (1996) Research, knowledge and the management of learning in distance education in Papua New Guinea, in *Research in Distance Education 4*, ed T Evans, V Jakupec and D Thompson, pp 173–85, Deakin University Press, Geelong

Habermas, J (1976) *Legitimation Crisis*, Heinemann, London

Habermas, J (1987) *The Theory of Communicative Action*, **2**, Polity Press, Cambridge

Hamilton, D (1990) *Learning about Education: The unfinished curriculum*, Open University Press, Buckingham

Hannafin, M and Land, S (1997) The foundations and assumptions of technology-enhanced student-centered learning environments, *Instructional Science*, **25**, pp 167–202

Harasim, L *et al* (1995) *Learning Networks: A field guide to teaching and learning online*, MIT Press, Cambridge, MA

Harding, J (1985) Values, cognitive style and the curriculum, in *Contributions to the Third GASAT Conference*, ASE, Hatfield, UK

Harris, D (1987) *Openness and Closure in Distance Education*, Falmer Press, Lewes

Harris, D (1992) *From Class Struggle to the Politics of Pleasure: The effects of gramiscianism on cultural studies*, Routledge, London

Harris, D (1998) [online] *Dave Harris Homepage*, URL http://ourworld.compuserve.com/homepages/Darris/

Heid, H (1995) Werte und Normen in der Berufsbildung, in *Handbuch der Berusbildung*, ed R Arnold and A Lipsmeier, pp 29–38, Lesk and Budrich, Opladen

Hendey, D (1994) *Distance Education: Implications for NZODA*, discussion paper, Appraisal, Evaluation and Analytical Unit, Development Cooperation Division, Ministry of Foreign Affairs and Trade, Wellington, New Zealand

Herrington, J and Oliver, R (1997) Avenues to understanding: A qualitative study into how students learn from multimedia, in *Educational Multimedia/Hypermedia and Telecommunications 1997*, ed T Muldner and T Reeves, pp 473–78, AACE, Charlottesville, VA

Herrmann, J (1997) Swimming against the tide: the case for keeping the human face of education, *Te Kie: A forum for distance and continuing education at USP*, **2**, pp 34–40

Hesse, F W and Giovis, C (1997) Struktur und Verlauf aktiver und passiver Partizipation beim netzbasierten Lernen in virtuellen Seminaren, in *Unterrichtswissenschaft*, **16** (1), pp 34–55

Hewson, M G (1988) The ecological context of knowledge: implications for learning science in developing countries, *Journal of Curriculum Studies*, **20**, pp 317–26

Hodson, D (1993) In search of a rationale for multicultural science education, *Science Education*, **77**, pp 685–711

Höhler, G (1989) Interne und externe Kommunikation – neue Anforderungen an die Legitimation unternehmerischen Handelns, Referat gehalten am Gottlieb Duttweiler Institut in Rüschlikon/Zürich am 19 May 1989

Holmberg, B (1989) *Growth and Structure of Distance Education*, Croom Helm, London

Howell-Richardson, C and Mellar, H (1996) A methodology for the analysis of patterns of participation within computer-mediated communication courses, *Instructional Sciences*, **24**, pp 47–69

Hoyer, H (1997) Inauguration address of the Rector of the Fernuniversität at the opening of the Informatikzentrums, on 29 November

Hoyer, H (1998) Reale Syteme im Virtuellen Labor, a research paper for the Chair of Control and Robotics, Fernuniversität-Gesamthochschule, Fachbereich Elektrotechnik, Hagen

Impart (1999) See http://www.impart.com.au/pathindex.html

IRRC (1997) *Swaziland*, <http://www.irrc.org/southern-africa/swaziland.html>

Iwamura, R (1994) [online] Letters from Japan: from girls who dress up like boys to trussed-up porn stars – some of the contemporary heroines on the Japanese screen, in *Continuum: The Australian Journal of Media and Culture*, **7** (2), URL http://www.cowan.edu.au/pa/continuum/

James, R and Beattie, K (1995) *Expanding Options: Delivery technologies and postgraduate coursework*, Department of Employment, Education, Training and Youth Affairs, Australian Government Publishing Service, Canberra

Jegede, O (1995) Collateral learning and the eco-cultural paradigm in science and mathematics education in Africa, *Studies in Science Education*, **25**, pp 97–137

Jegede, O (1996) Whose education, whose worldview, and whose framework?: an indigenous perspective on learning. A paper presented at the conference on *Pathways: Indigenous Education: Past, Present, Future*, University of Southern Queensland, Toowoomba

Jegede, O (1997) School science and the development of scientific culture: a review of contemporary science education in Africa, *International Journal of Science Education*, **19**, pp 1–20

Johnson, D, Johnson, R and Smith, K (1998) Co-operative learning returns to college: what evidence that it works? *Change*, **30** (4), pp 26–35

Johnson, R (1996) To wish and to will: reflections on policy formation and implementation, in *Opening Education: Policies and practices from distance education*, ed T D Evans and D E Nation, pp 90–101, Routledge, London

Johnson-Lenz, P and Johnson-Lenz, T (1991) Post-mechanistic groupware primitives: rhythms, boundaries and containers, *International Journal of machine Studies*, **34**, pp 395–417

Jonassen, D and Reeves, T (1996) Learning with technology: using computers as cognitive tools, in *Handbook of Research Educational on Educational Communications and Technology*, ed D Jonassen, pp 693–719, Macmillan, New York

Kade, J (1989) Universalisierung und Individualisierung der Erwachsenenbildung, in *Zeitschrift für Pädagogik*, **35** (6), pp 789–808

Kaplan, N (1995) [online] Politexts, Hypertexts, and Other Cultural Formations in the late Age of Print, *Computer-Mediated Communication Magazine*, **2** (3) URL http://sunsite.unc.edu/cmc/mag/1995/Katz, R N and associates (1999) *Dancing With the Devil: Information technology and the new competition in higher education*, Jossey-Bass, San Francisco

Katz, R N and associates (1999) *Dancing with the Devil: Information technology and the new competition in higher education*, Jossey-Bass, San Francisco

Kaye, A R (1992) Learning together apart, in *Collaborative Learning Through Computer Conferencing*, ed A R Kaye, pp 1–24, Springer, Berlin

Keegan, D (1994) *Very Large Distance Education Systems: The case of China,* ZIFF-Papiere 94, Fernuniversität-Gesamthochschule Zentrum für Fernstudienforschung, Hagen

Keegan, D (1995) Teaching and learning by satellite in European virtual classrooms, in *Open and Distance Learning Today*, ed F Lockwood, pp 108–18, Kogan Page, London

Kema, D and Guy, R (1991) Distance education in Papua New Guinea: access, equity and funding issues at the College of Distance Education and the University of Papua New Guinea, *Papua New Guinea Journal of Education*, **26** (2), pp 237–46

Kember, D (1995) *Open Learning Courses for Adults: A model of student progress*, Educational Technology Publications, New Jersey

Kember, D (1998) Action research: towards an alternative framework for educational development, *Distance Education*, **19** (1), pp 43–63

Kemmis, S and McTaggart, R (1988) *The Action Research Planner*, Deakin University, Geelong

Kennedy, D and McNaught, C (1997) Design elements for interactive multimedia, *Australian Journal of Educational Technology*, **13** (1), pp 1–22

Kiesler, S (1992) Talking, teaching and learning in network groups: lessons from research, in *Collaborative Learning through Computer Conferencing*, ed A R Kaye, pp 147–65, Springer, Berlin

Kirkpatrick, D L (1994) *Evaluating Training Programs: The four levels*, Berrett-Koehler, San Francisco

Kitchener, K and King, P (1981) Reflective judgement: concepts of justification and their relationship to age and education, *Journal of Applied Developmental Psychology*, **2**, pp 89–116

Kitchener, K and King, P (1990) The reflective judgement model, in *Fostering Critical Reflection in Adulthood*, ed J Mezirow and Associates, pp 159–76, Jossey-Bass, San Francisco

Klauder, W (1992) Die Arbeitswelt der Zukunft, in *Die Zukunft der Arbeit – die Arbeit der Zukunft,* ed S Ehses, pp 14–38, Symposium Oeconomicum, Münster

Kling, R (1996) Hopes and horrors: technological utopianism and anti-utopianism in narratives of computisation, in *Computerization and controversy: Value conflicts and social choices*, 2nd edn, ed R Kling, pp 40–58, Academic Press, San Diego

Knight, D (1996) *Learning and Cost-effectiveness of Instructional Technologies: A proposed research and evaluation agenda*, Centre for Innovation in Learning, Contact North, Sudbury, Ontario

Knowles, M (1990) *The Adult Learner: A neglected species*, Gulf Publishing, Houston

Kubler-Ross, E (1969) *On Death and Dying*, Macmillan Publishing, New York

Kuhn, T S (1970) *The Structure of Scientific Revolutions*, 2nd edn, University of Chicago Press, Chicago

Laffey, J, Tupper, T and Musser, D (1998) A computer-mediated support system for project-based learning, *Educational Technology Research and Development*, **46** (1), pp 73–86

Lange, B P and Hillebrandt, A (1996) Medienkompetenz – die neue Herausforderung der Informationsgesellschaft, *Spektrum der Wissenschaft*, August, pp 38–42

Lappia, A and Kirkland, J (1989) Audiocassette tapes in distance teaching: student evaluation, *Distance Education*, **10** (2), pp 277–84

Latour, B (1991) Technology is society made durable, in *A Sociology of Monsters: Chapters on power, technology, and domination*, ed J Law, pp 103–31, Routledge, New York

Laurillard, D (1993) *Rethinking University Teaching: A framework for the effective use of educational technology*, Routledge, London

Laurillard, D and Margetson, (1997) *Introducing a Flexible Learning Methodology: Discussion paper*, Occasional Paper 7, Griffith Institute of Higher Education, Nathan

Law, T (1998) Digital discourses, online classes, electronic documents: developing new university technocultures. Presented at *Learning Online'98: Building the virtual university*, 18–21 June, Roanoke, VA

Lefoe, G, Cordeoy, R M and Wills, S (1996) How well do we practice what we preach? An evaluation of teleteaching '96, in *Practising What we Preach, proceedings of Teleteaching '96*, ed S Wills, P Fritze and B Cavallari, Australian Computer Society, Melbourne

Lehner, H (1991) Autonomes Lernen und Fernlehre Methoden und Wirkungen, *Fernlehre und Fernlehrforschung*, ed B Holmberg and G E Ortner, pp 162–76, Lang, Frankfurt am Main

Levin, P (1998) Traditional university teaching fails to develop students' team-working skills, *The Times Higher Education Supplement*, 1318, p viii, 6 February

Linn, M C and Burbules, N (1993) Construction of knowledge and group learning, in *The Practice of Constructivism in Science Education*, ed K Tobin, pp 91–119, American Association for the Advancement of Science Press, Washington

Luke, C (1997) Adult Literacy Research Network, University of Queenland, Brisbane

Lyotard, J F (1986) *The Postmodern Condition: A report on knowledge*, Manchester University Press, Manchester

McGann, J (1995) [online] *The Rationale of HyperText* URL http://jefferson.village.virginia.edu/public/jjm2f/rationale.html

McTaggart, R (1991) Western institutional impediments to Australian Aboriginal education, *Journal of Curriculum Studies*, **23**, pp 297–325

Maddock, M N (1981) Science education: an anthropological viewpoint, *Studies in Science Education*, **8**, pp 1–26

Marginson, S (1997) *Educating Australia*, Cambridge University Press, Melbourne

Marton, F and Saljo, R (1976) On qualitative differences in learning: outcome and process, *British Journal of Educational Psychology*, **46**, pp 4–11

Matsebula, J S M (1988) *A History of Swaziland* (3rd edn), Longman, Cape Town

Matthew, D and Zeitlyn, D (1996) What are they doing? Dilemmas in analysing bibliographic searching: cultural and technical networks in academic life, *Sociological Research Online*, **1** (4), p 2

Meyer, J and Rowan, B (1988) The structure of educational organizations, in *Culture and Power in Educational Organizations*, ed A Westoby, pp 87–112, Open University Press, Milton Keynes

Mezirow, J (1985) Concept and action in adult education, *Adult Education Quarterly*, **35** (3), pp 142–51

Mezirow, J (1991) *Transformative Dimensions of Adult Learning*, Jossey-Bass, San Francisco

Mezirow, J (1998) On critical reflection, *Adult Education Quarterly*, **48** (3), pp 185–98

Mezirow, J and Associates (eds) (1990) *Fostering Critical Reflection in Adulthood*, Jossey-Bass, San Francisco

Mills, S (1997) *Turning Away from Technology*, Sierra Club Books, San Francisco

Minister's Forum on Adult Learning (1995) *The Future of Learning*, Edmonton, Alberta

Mittelstrass, J (1994) *Die unzeitgemäße Universität*, Suhrkamp, Frankfurt am Main

Moore, G A (1991) *Crossing the Chasm: Marketing and selling technology products to mainstream customers*, Harper Business, New York

Moore, M (1993a) The theory of transactional distance, in *Theoretical Principles of Distance Education*, ed D Keegan, pp 22–38, Routledge, New York

Moore, M (1993b) Three types of interaction, in *Distance Education: New perspectives*, ed K Harry, M John and D Keegan, pp 19–24, Routledge, London

Moore, M (1997) Editorial: lessons from history, *The American Journal of Distance Education*, **11** (1), pp 1–5

Moore, M and Kearsley, G (1996) *Distance Education: A System View*, Wadsworth, Belmont, California

Moran, L (1998) The F L A G Project on Internet Use: A Formative Evaluation. Internal report commissioned by the F L A G Group on Internet Use, University of Technology, Sydney, December

Morgan, A (1995) Student learning and students' experiences, in *Open and Distance Learning Today*, ed F Lockwood, pp 55–66, Routledge, London

Nation, D (1995a) Learning beyond classrooms, in *Becoming an Independent Learner*, ed D Nation, Monash University, Distance Education Centre, Churchill, pp 23–46

Nation, D (1995b) Understanding universities, in *Becoming an Independent Learner*, ed D Nation, Monash University, Distance Education Centre, Churchill, pp 7–21

NCODE (1998) National Council on Open and Distance Education,

Negroponte, N (1997) Keynote speech, International Council on Distance Education Conference, Pennsylvania State University, University Park, USA

Nicholson, P et al (1997) How should we teach teachers to change? Report from focus groups 1 & 2, in Supporting Change through Teacher Education, ed D Passey and B Samways, IFIP/Chapman and Hall, New York

Nipper, S (1989) Third generation distance learning and computer conferencing, in *Mindwave: Communication, computers and distance education*, ed R Mason and A Kaye, pp 73–83, Pergamon Press, Oxford

No Significant Difference Phenomena http://tenb.mta.ca/phenom/phenom.html

Noble, D (1998) Digital diploma mills: The automation of higher education, *Monthly Review*, **49** (9), pp 38–52, http://www.firstmonday.dk/index.html

Oberle, E M (1990) The National University Teleconference Network: A living laboratory for distance learning research, in *Contemporary Issues in American Distance Education*, ed M G Moore, pp 81–95, Pergamon, Oxford

Ogawa, M (1995) Science education in a multi-science perspective, *Science Education*, **79**, pp 583–93

Ogden, M (1992) *Higher Education, Telecommunications Networks and National Develoment in the Pacific Islands: A response with a focus on the future*, An International Symposium: The impact of higher education on social transformation in Asia and the Pacific, National Institute of Multimedia Education, Chiba, Japan

Oliver, R and McLoughlin, C (1997) Interactions in audiographics teaching and learning environments, *The American Journal of Distance Education*, **11** (1), pp 34–54

Oliver, R and Short, G (1996) The Western Australian Telecentres Network: a model for enhancing access to education and training in rural areas, *International Journal of Educational Telecommunications*, **2** (4), pp 311–28

Open University (1996) *ME832 Researching mathematics classrooms: Study guide*, The Open University, Milton Keynes

Open University (1982) *Popular Culture (U203)*, Open University Press, Milton Keynes

Otaala, B (1997) Educational research and quality of life in eastern and southern Africa. Keynote address delivered at *The Seventh BOLESWA Bi-Annual Symposium on Educational Research*, 28 July–1 August 1997, at the University of Swaziland, Kwaluseni, Swaziland. Published at <http://www.realnet.co.sz/boleswa/>

Papert, S (1991) Introduction, in *Constructionist Learning*, ed I Harel, The Media Laboratory, MIT, Cambridge, MA

Pask, G (1976) Styles and strategies of learning, *British Journal of Educational Psychology*, **46**, pp 128–48

Paul, R (1990) *Towards Open Management: Leadership and integrity in open learning and distance education*, Kogan Page, London

Paulsen, F (1965) *German Education: Past and present*, Fisher Unwin, London (original edition 1908)

Pearson, J and Mason, R (1992) *An Evaluation of the use of CoSy on B885 in 1992*, Centre for Information Technology in Education Report No.171, Milton Keynes, The Open University

Perkins, J and Newman, K (1996) Two archetypes in e-discourse: Lurkers and virtuosos, *International Journal of Educational Telecommunications*, **2** (2/3), pp 155–70

Peters, O (1997) *Didaktik des Fernstudiums*, Luchterhand, Neuwied, English version (1998) Learning and Teaching in Distance Education, Routledge, London

Peters, O (1993) Distance education in a post industrial society, in *Theoretical Principles of Distance Education*, ed D Keegan, pp 39–58, Routledge, London

Raidal, S (1997) Problem based learning for veterinary students using simple interactive WWW Pages, in *What Works and Why: Proceedings of the 14th Annual Conference of the Australian Society for Computers in Tertiary Education,* ed R Kevill, R Oliver and R Phillips, pp 476–80, Academic Computing Services, Perth

Ramsden, P (1992) *Learning to Teach in Higher Education*, Routledge, London

Ramsden, P *et al* (1995) *Recognising and Rewarding Good Teaching in Australian Higher Education*, Committee for the Advancement of University Teaching, Australian Government Publishing Service, Canberra

Renwick, W, Shale, D and King, St C (1991*) Distance Education at the University of the South Pacific*, Report of a review requested by the University and funded by the Commonwealth of Learning, August 1990, Vancouver

Ritzer, G (1994) *Sociological Beginnings: On the origins of key ideas in sociology*, McGraw-Hill, New York

Rogers, E (1995) *Diffusion of Innovations*, 4th edn, Simon and Shuster [or Free Press?], New York

Russell, T (1995) *The 'No significant phenomenon' as reported in 214 research reports, summaries and papers*, Office of Instructional Telecommunications, North Carolina State University, Raleigh, NC

Russell, A L (1995) Stages in learning new technology: naive adult e-mail users, *Computers and Education*, **25** (4), pp 173–78

Sage, S and Torp, L (1997) What does it take to become a teacher of problem-based learning?, *Journal of Staff Development*, **18**, pp 32–36

Scardamalia, M and Bereiter, C (1992) An architecture for collaborative knowledge building, in *Computer-based Learning Environments and Problem Solving*, ed E De Corte *et al*, pp 41–66, Springer, Berlin

Schlosser, C A and Anderson, M L (1994) *Distance Education: Review of the literature*, Research Institute for Studies in Education, Iowa State University, Iowa

Schon, D A (1987) *Educating the Reflective Practitioner*, Jossey-Bass, San Francisco

Scott, P (1984) *The Crisis of the University*, Croom Helm, Beckenham

Scott, P (1995) *The Meanings of Mass Higher Education*, Society for Research, Higher Education and Open University Press, Buckingham

Schrage, M (1995) *No More Teams! Mastering the dynamics of creative collaboration*, Currency Doubleday, New York

SEDA (1998) [online] URL http://www.seda.demon.co.uk/

Selinger, M (1996) Beginning teachers using IT: the Open University model, *Journal for Information Technology in Teacher Education*, **5** (3), pp 253–70

Selinger, M (1998) Forming a critical community through telematics, *Computers and Education*, **30** (1/2), pp 23–30

Senge, P (1990) *The Fifth Discipline: The art and practice of the learning organisation*, Doubleday, New York

Seyfferth, H (1998) Viel Glanz, kaum Gloria Ein Wettbewerb der Universitäten um die bessere Nutzung weltweiten Wissens, *Die Zeit*, **20**, 7 May

Sherman, T M *et al* (1987) The quest for excellence in university teaching, *Journal of Higher Education*, **48**, pp 66–84

Siegel, D (1996) *Creating Killer Websites*, Hayden Books, Indiana

Solomon, J (1987) Social influences on the construction of pupils' understanding of science, *Studies in Science Education*, **14**, pp 63–82

SOSIG (1999) [online] URL http://sosig.esrc.bris.ac.uk/

Spivak, G (1988) Can the subaltern speak?, in *Marxist Interpretations of Culture*, ed C Grossberg, pp 271–313, MacMillan Education, Basingstoke

Sproull, L and Kiesler, S (1991) *Connections: New ways of working in the networked organization*, MIT Press, Cambridge, MA

Sproull, L and Kiesler, S (1995) Computers, networks and work, *Scientific American*, **265** (3), pp 116–23

SSP2000 (1999) [online] URL http://www.soc.surrey.ac.uk/SSP2000/

Stake, R (1978) The case study method as social inquiry, *Educational Researcher*, **7**, pp 5–8

Szabo, M (1996) Professional Development, Faculty Renewal and Alternative Delivery Systems. Paper presented at World Conference on Multimedia & Hypermedia, Boston, June 1996. Available online at http://www.atl.ualberta.ca/articles/general/tie/home.cfm

Taylor, A (1990) A 'window' on student-centred learning, *British Journal of Educational Technology*, **21**, pp 229–30

Taylor, J C (1995) Distance education technologies: the fourth generation, *Australian Journal of Educational Technology*, **11**(2), pp 1–7

Taylor, J C (1998) The death of distance: the birth of the global higher education economy, invited paper presented at the International Council of Distance Education Standing Committee Of Presidents meeting, September, Coolum, Australia

Taylor, P *et al* (1997) Perspectives and possibilities: electronic interactivity and social constructivist teaching in a science, mathematics and technology teacher education program, *What Works and Why? The fourteenth annual conference of the Australian Society for Computers in Tertiary Education*, ed R Kevill, R Oliver and R Phillips, pp 599–605, Curtin University, Perth

Taylor, P G, Lopez, L and Quadrelli, C (1996) *Flexiblity, Technology and Academics' Practices: Tantalising tales and muddy maps*, Australian Government Publishing Service, Canberra

Tuza, E (1997) The future of Extension Centres: can and should we develop a measure of resource sharing?, *Te Kie: A forum for distance and continuing education at USP*, **2**, pp 21–25

Unger, C (1997) Der Fachbereich Informatik und die Virtuelle Universität, paper given at the Fernuniversität, 29 November, Fernuniversität-Gesamthochschule, Hagen

UniLearning (1999) See http://unilearning.net.au

UQ (1995) *Action Learning Report – Good Practice in Higher Education*, Quality Report, University of Queensland, St Lucia

Va'ai, M (1997) The Centre Director and Continuing Education, *Te Kie: a forum for distance and continuing education at USP*, **2**, pp 69–75

Van Trease, H (1990/1991) Distance education at the University of Papua New Guinea: issues and developments, *Papua New Guinea Journal of Education*, **26** (2) and **27** (1) (combined issue), pp 111–28

Vygotsky, L (1978) *Mind in Society*, Harvard University Press, Cambridge, MA

Waiko, J (1998) Vision for the higher education sector in Papua New Guinea, speech at the Higher Education Summit, Pacific Adventist University, Port Moresby

Walkerdine, V and the Girls and Mathematics Unit (1989) *Counting Girls Out*, Virago Press, London

Wedemeyer, C (1971) With whom will you dance? The new educational technology, in *The Changing World of Correspondence Study*, ed O Mackenzie and E L Christensen, pp 133–44, Pennsylvania State University, University Park

Weingartz, M (1991) Der Lernvertrag Ein effektiver Beitrag zum autonomen Lernen? in *Fernlehre und Fernlehrforschung*, ed B Holmberg and G E Ortner, pp 180–83, Lang, Frankfurt am Main

West, R (chair) (1998) *Learning for Life: Review of higher education financing and policy (Final Report)*, Department of Employment, Education, Training and Youth Affairs, Canberra

Wills, S (1997) (Chair) General and Academic Staff Development for Flexible Delivery, working party of the Educational Innovation Subcommittee of the University Education Committee, University of Wollongong, Wollongong. See http://cedir.uow.edu.au/CEDIR/flexible/staffdev.html

Wills, S and Yetton, P (1997) Strategy and information technology, in *Managing the Introduction of Technology in the Delivery and Administration of Higher Education*, Department of Employment, Education, Training and Youth Affairs, Evaluations and Investigations Program, AGPS: Canberra, p 20 See also http://cedir.uow.edu.au/programs/TAAD

Wills, S *et al* (1997) Teaching at a distance about teaching at a distance, in *Ascilite '97 What Works and Why*, 14th Annual Conference of ASCILITE, ed R Kevill, R Oliver, R Phillips, pp 628–35, Curtin University of Technology Printing Services, Perth

Winner, L (1977) *Autonomous Technology: Technics-out-of-control as a theme in political thought*, Massachusetts Institute of Technology, Boston

Woll, A (1988) Diskussionsbeitrag, in *Die Fernuniversität Wissenschaftliche Weiterbildung Aufgabe für Universitäten und Wirtschaft*, Fernuniversität-Gesamthochschule Hagen, pp 69–70 www.socresonline.org.uk/socresonline/1/4/2.html

Yetton, P *et al* (1997) *Managing the Introduction of Technology in the Delivery and Administration of Higher Education*, Department of Employment, Education, Training and Youth Affairs, Evaluations and Investigations Program, Australian Government Publishing Service, Canberra

Young, J (1998) Technorealists hope to enrich debate over policy issues in cyberspace, *The Chronicle of Higher Education*, 23 March http://chronicle.com/data/internet.dir/itdata/1998/03/t98032301.htm

Yuhudi, Zhao (1988) China, its distance higher education system, *Prospects*, **18**, (2), pp 218

Zuber-Skerrit, O (1993a) Improving learning and teaching through action research, in *Higher Education Research and Development*, **12** (1), pp 45–58

Zuber-Skerritt, O (1993b) The future of academic staff development in Australian universities, in *Education and Training Technology International*, **30** (4), pp 367–74

Index